UNIVERSITY OF
WOLVERHAMPTO

Harrison Learning Centre
City Campus
University of Wolverhampton
St Peter's Square
Wolverhampton WV1 1RH
Telephone: 0845 408 1631
Online Renewals:
www.wlv.ac.uk/lib/myaccount

Telephone Renewals: 01902 321333 or 0845 408 1631
Please RETURN this item on or before the last date shown above.
See tariff of fines displayed at the Counter. (L2)

A Written Constitution
for the
United Kingdom

Institute for
Public Policy Research

MANSELL

First published in 1991 in paperback under the title
The Constitution of the United Kingdom.

First published in hardback 1993 by
Mansell Publishing Limited. *A Cassell Imprint*
Villiers House, 41/47 Strand, London WC2N 5JE, England
387 Park Avenue South, New York, NY 10016–8810, USA

Reprinted in paperback 1995

British Library Cataloguing-in-Publication Data

Institute for Public Policy Research
    Written Constitution for the United Kingdom. – 2 Rev. ed.
    – (Constitutional Reform Series)
    I. Title   II. Series
    344.102

    ISBN 0–7201–2154–X (Hardback)
    ISBN 0–7201–2272–4 (Paperback)

Library of Congress Cataloging-in-Publication Data

A Written constitution for the United Kingdom/Institute for Public
    Policy Research.
        p.   cm. – (The Constitutional reform series)
    Rev. ed. of: The Constitution of the United Kingdom. 1991.
    ISBN 0–7201–2154–X (Hardback)
    ISBN 0–7201–2272–4 (Paperback)
    1. Great Britain – Constitutional law.   2. Great Britain –
Constitution.   I. Institute for Public Policy Research (London,
England)   II. Title: Constitution of the United Kingdom.
III. Series.
    KD3989.C657   1993
    342.42'02–dc20
    [344.1022]   92–39397
                                                                      CIP

Printed and bound in Great Britain by
Biddles Ltd, Guildford and King's Lynn

Contents

Preface

This Constitution was drafted in the conviction that an example of a written Constitution would advance the public argument more effectively than further general discussion of the problems which it raises and attempts to resolve. The work was undertaken between 1989 and 1991 and originally published by the Institute for Public Policy Research in September 1991. At the time it seemed possible, indeed likely, that the forthcoming general election might result in a hung Parliament and that constitutional issues would then be high on the political agenda. These hopes (or fears) have been disappointed, but the constitutional question has not gone away. Arguments about a Bill of Rights, the effectiveness of Parliament, the electoral system, devolution and local government continue. It may be worthwhile, therefore, to produce a more permanent edition of the Constitution, which even its sternest and most searching critics have been kind enough to commend at least as an aide to teaching. I am grateful to Dr Robert Blackburn for suggesting that it should appear in The Constitutional Reform Series, which he edits for Mansell.

The Project could not have been undertaken without the generous support of the Joseph Rowntree Charitable Trust, whose grant enabled us to hold countless meetings of the various drafting groups, to commission specific pieces of work and to employ a coordinator to keep the show on the road. We are grateful to the Trustees for their support and to the Assistant Secretary Heather Swailes for the helpful way in which she administered the grant.

Nor would the project have been possible without the willingness of many people to give freely of their time and knowledge, either as members of a working party, as contributors on particular subjects, or as advisers, consultants and critics:

ADVISORY GROUP

Professors Anthony Bradley, Terence Daintith, Jeffrey Jowell, Patrick McAuslan and Keith Patchett, and Anthony Lester QC.

WORKING PARTIES

Dr Robert Blackburn, Professor Gavin Drewry, Professor Ronald Dworkin, Ann Dummett, Patricia Hewitt, Sir William Goodhart QC, Nicola Lacey, John McEldowney, Dr Jeremy Mitchell, Nuala Mole, Dawn Oliver and Sarah Spencer.

CONTRIBUTORS TO DRAFT

Brice Dickson, Laurens Fransman, Josh Hillman, Beverley Lang, Dr Gerry Rubin and Professor Ian Willock.

ADVICE AND CONSULTATION

Geoffrey Bindman, Professor Kevin Boyle, Madeleine Colvin, Alistair Darling MP, Professor Keith Ewing, Tess Gill, Peter Gill, Professor Malcolm Grant, Professor John Kay, Professor Norman Lewis, Laurence Lustgarten, Professor David Marquand, Bob McCreadie, Ron Medlow, Richard Norton Taylor, Professor Claire Palley, William Plowden, Clive Ponting, Jim Ross, Anthony Scrivener QC, Stephen Smith, Ian Snaith, Dr Hugo Storey, Tony Travers, Sir Douglas Wass and Professor Sir David Williams.

A draft by many hands is apt to look like patchwork. That the final version has some consistency of style and substance is due to the heroic efforts of Keith Patchett who at a late stage took the draft in hand and imposed order upon it. We are greatly indebted to him. Likewise to Sarah Spencer whose skill, patience, good humour and persistence brought the project to completion.

Nobody involved agreed with everything in this Constitution and that includes myself. The responsibility for the final result is however my own and I am doubly grateful to all who contributed for their forbearance throughout this exercise in guided democracy.

James Cornford
August 1992

Introduction

I

This draft Constitution for the United Kingdom consists of 129 Articles and 6 Schedules, accompanied by a commentary which explains the derivation and purpose of each provision. The main features of the Constitution are as follows:

(1) The Constitution is the sole source of authority for all public action, executive, legislative or judicial. Henceforth authority must be sought not in common law principles such as parliamentary sovereignty or prerogative power, nor in constitutional conventions, such as ministerial responsibility, but in the written provisions of this Constitution (Article 1).

(2) The Constitution is placed in the context of the United Kingdom's international and European commitments (Article 1). Specific commitment to European Community law is provided under Article 50 and to international obligations under Article 51.

(3) The Constitution incorporates a Bill of Rights based on the European Convention on Human Rights and on the United Nations International Covenant on Civil and Political Rights, to both of which the United Kingdom is signatory, and provides the means for its enforcement (Articles 2 to 26). It also includes a declaratory statement of social and economic rights (Article 27) and public rights of access to official information and controls on the use of personal information by public authorities (Articles 28 and 29).

(4) British nationality is defined, together with the rules governing the acquisition and loss of British nationality, allegiance and dual nationality, and the civic rights of non nationals (Articles 30 to 33).

(5)   The position of the Queen as Head of State is confirmed but the residual prerogative powers of the Monarchy (e.g. over the appointment of the Prime Minister) are removed and the Monarchy becomes a wholly dignified part of the Constitution (Articles 34 to 39).

(6)   The prerogative powers exercised by the Executive are defined in the Constitution and subjected to parliamentary control: e.g. the making of treaties (Article 51), the declaration of war (Article 122), deployment of the Armed Forces (Article 123), national security (Article 126) and declarations of emergency (Article 128). Substantial areas of patronage are removed from the Executive by transferring powers of appointment from Ministers to the Public Services Commission (Article 115) and a Judicial Appointments Commission for the United Kingdom and Judicial Services Commissions for England and Wales, Scotland and Northern Ireland (Articles 102 and 103).

(7)   The Prime Minister is elected by the House of Commons and is subject to a personal vote of no confidence which does not involve the dissolution of the House. The Prime Minister appoints a deputy, Ministers and the Cabinet. Ministers are required to give a statement of their responsibilities to Parliament on taking office and are bound by a Code of Conduct (Articles 40 to 46).

(8)   The House of Commons is elected for a fixed term of four years, with the possibility of dissolution but with no extension of the term of Parliament (Article 60).

(9)   The House of Lords is replaced by an elected Second Chamber (Article 57), also elected for a four-year term, but at a two-year interval from the election for the House of Commons, and not subject to dissolution (Article 60 and Schedule 3).

(10)   Both Houses have a smaller membership than at present and both are to be elected by forms of proportional representation: the House of Commons by a variant of the Additional Member System and the Second Chamber by the Single Transferable Vote (Articles 83 to 86 and Schedule 3).

(11)   The House of Commons retains its present supremacy in relation to financial and general legislation, but the Second Chamber has equal powers concerning amendments to the

Constitution and to constitutional legislation: that is, statutes which give effect to or have a direct bearing on provisions of the Constitution, e.g. election law or arising from the Bill of Rights (Articles 65 to 70).

(12) Legislative power is shared between Parliament and elected Assemblies for Scotland, Wales, Northern Ireland and twelve English regions. Parliament retains exclusive rights over those matters normally retained for the central government in federal constitutions, while the Assemblies' powers are based on the Northern Ireland Constitution Act 1973 and the present executive responsibilities of the Scottish Office (Articles 52 to 54). Parliament retains concurrent powers to legislate on matters where legislation by an Assembly would be inadequate or would have adverse effects outside its boundaries (Article 55).

(13) The Assemblies are to be financed by an entitlement to the proceeds of the personal income tax, distributed according to an entrenched formula based on population, with power to vary the standard rate of tax at the margin. The income tax would continue to be a United Kingdom tax set by Parliament and administered by the Inland Revenue (Article 80 and Schedule 2).

(14) The Constitution requires that each Assembly shall establish elected local authorities but leaves the details of their formation and organisation to the Assemblies in order to recognise the different circumstances of the nations and regions and to encourage diversity. Local authorities are given by the Constitution the right to levy rates on domestic and commercial property (Article 82).

(15) A number of independent bodies are established to administer and monitor constitutional matters:

a. A **Human Rights Commission** to promote the public understanding of human rights, to investigate breaches of the Bill of Rights, to assist with individual complaints about the violation of rights, and to challenge legislation which is inconsistent with the Bill of Rights (Article 26).

b. A **Constitutional Commission** based in Parliament with the responsibility to monitor constitutional developments, to publish codes of conduct for elected officials, and through a separate committee to investigate the conduct of Ministers and other elected officials (Articles 76 and 77).

c. An **Electoral Commission** charged with responsibility for constituency boundaries at all levels from the European Parliament to local authorities: for keeping under review the workings of the electoral system including campaigning and election finance; for the investigation of complaints about the conduct of elections; and for the registration of political parties (Articles 88 to 91).

d. A **Judicial Appointments Commission** to make recommendations for the appointment to the Supreme Court (Article 102); and **Judicial Services Commissions** for England and Wales, Scotland and Northern Ireland, to make judicial appointments, and to investigate complaints of judicial misconduct; and **Judicial Councils** to advise the Minister of Justice on the administration of justice (Article 103 to 105).

e. A **Public Services Commission** to establish and monitor standards and codes of conduct for the public services and to make public appointments outside the regular civil service (Articles 115 and 116); and a **Public Services Complaints Commission** to investigate complaints into breaches of codes or regulations, malversation of a public service or improper conduct towards officials by Ministers or other elected executives (Article 117).

f. A **Commission for Public Administration** to investigate complaints of failures of administration or unfair administration, to investigate the conduct and practices of public authorities, to review the Constitution and workings of tribunals and inquiries, and to promote standards of good administration (Article 119).

(16) A written Constitution gives a much greater role to the judiciary and we have therefore given particular attention to the reorganisation of the administration of justice and the independence of the judiciary. There is to be a Supreme Court for the United Kingdom, appointed on the recommendation of a United Kingdom Judicial Appointments Commission, with original and exclusive jurisdiction in any proceeding concern-

ing the validity of parliamentary or Assembly legislation brought by the government of the United Kingdom or an Assembly Executive; and appellate jurisdiction in other constitutional matters. The office of Lord Chancellor will cease to exist and his functions in relation to the legal system will be taken over by a Minister of Justice (Articles 96 to 100). The Attorney-General becomes a non-political legal adviser to the government (Article 47).

These Articles and the many other provisions of the Constitution are more fully discussed in the commentary which follows the text of the Constitution itself. The second part of the Introduction gives a general account of some of the constitutional and political considerations which lie behind the detailed proposals we have made.

II

New Constitutions are generally born of crisis, political upheaval, the struggle for independence and the breakdown of regimes. Few appear to have arisen from peaceful and orderly reflection on the shortcomings of an existing and still functioning predecessor. With events in the former Soviet Union and South Africa before us, we do well to be sceptical about claims of a constitutional crisis in the United Kingdom and to keep a sense of proportion about our present discontents. Nevertheless they are real and there is no harm, and may be virtue, in trying to analyse present difficulties and to anticipate the problems to which they will give rise. Membership of the European Community has already raised constitutional issues of profound importance, to which we in the United Kingdom have made no ready or coherent response. The present government and its predecessors have launched far-reaching changes in the organisation of Whitehall and of local government with scant consideration for their constitutional implications. The major Opposition parties are committed to further changes, particularly with regard to Scotland, which would also have serious implications for current constitutional practice should they come to pass.

There has over the last twenty years been a growing chorus of complaint about aspects of British government which in any other system would be recognised as constitutional: that is, complaints of an electoral system which seriously distorts representation, excludes middle opinion, and threatens to perpetuate rule by the largest minority party; of a Parliament which is dominated by the Executive through its control of procedure and the disciplines of party, patronage and the press, and which therefore fails to scrutinise effectively the conduct of government or to play any constructive role in legislation; of a national administration which practises excessive secrecy and against whose actions there is inadequate redress; of a local government which is at once the dependant of and the scapegoat for central government and which enjoys little support either in Parliament or among the electorate; of security services which are protected from parliamentary scrutiny and which appear when the veil is briefly twitched aside to be barely under the control of Ministers; of a police force which has appeared increasingly in a political role, which has little accountability, which has absorbed more and more resources while crime rates rise, and whose reputation for probity has been sadly dented.

For each of these ills there is a specific remedy: electoral reform, more powers for select committees and a reformed Second Chamber, Freedom of Information, the restructuring of local government (again) and devolution, a Bill of Rights or incorporation of the European Convention on Human Rights, and other proposals for the statutory protection of privacy, the control of the security services, the strengthening of employment rights and of anti-discrimination measures brought together in Labour's *Charter of Rights*. What has emerged over the last three or four years is a growing interest across the political spectrum in bringing these separate complaints together. This reflects a common understanding of the underlying problem which is best expressed in Dunning's famous motion of 1780: 'the power of the Crown has increased, is increasing and ought to be diminished'. A more recent statement of the problem may be found in *The Scottish Claim of Right* (1988): 'The English Constitution provides for only one source of power: the Crown in Parliament. That one source is now mainly embodied in the Prime Minister, who has appropriated almost all the royal prerogatives . . . In fact, if not in theory, the Prime Minister is Head of State, Chief Executive and Chief Legislator, and while in office is not circumscribed by any clear or binding constitutional limitations. Against this there is in the United Kingdom not a single alternative source of secure constitutional power at any level.' Political power there certainly is. Even if it speaks indirectly through the Gothick Constitution of the Conservative Party, the electorate has the last word.

Entrenchment

But this is not *constitutional* power, and it is the belief that restraints on the Executive and on the centralisation of power must be given constitutional rather than political force that has become the common theme of reformers. The need for the entrenchment of rights both for individuals and for devolved governments implies a constitutional document. This has been for long the view of the Liberal Democrats and their predecessors, and has been given outline expression in their Federal Green Paper No. 13: *We the People . . . Towards a Written Constitution*. It is the theme of Charter 88, which has evoked such a remarkable response. It is at least implicit in the proceedings of the Scottish Convention. And it has been given an interesting dimension in recent work of the Institute for Economic Affairs as a protection against the encroachments of the European Community. There is one reforming voice not in harmony with this chorus, that of Mr Tony Benn, whose Commonwealth of Britain Bill attacks many of the same targets. But Mr Benn is a traditional radical, a robust defender of parliamentary supremacy and no friend to kings, lords, priests or judges.

Here we approach the heart of the matter: particular reforms may be important and interesting. But the essential question is whether the time has come not to change the historical constitution incrementally as has been done in the past, but to change the basis of the Constitution. That is, to change from a single fundamental principle, the supremacy of Parliament, which is founded in custom and usage as recognised by the courts, to a fundamental law which is prior to, independent of and the source of authority for the system of government. A codification of existing practice and convention might be convenient, but it would not be enough. It is the peculiarity of our Constitution not that it is not codified, but that the laws which make it up, whether statute, common or case law, have no special status. Parliament can make and unmake them as it chooses; a million British subjects can be deprived of their rights of abode by the same means as an alteration of the speed limit. Essential features of the Constitution have no basis in law at all.

All constitutions depend for their working on conventions and informal understandings; there is no machine which goes of itself. But in our case conventions govern essential constitutional issues: such as the Sovereign's use of her powers, the rules for the formation of governments and the dissolution of Parliament, the meaning of ministerial responsibility to Parliament, or the organisation of the civil service and the duties of civil servants. All these are governed by convention, and the beauty of conventions is that we do not know whether or how they will apply until they are put to the test. The one thing we can be certain of is the supremacy of Parliament, which can in theory do anything it likes: there is no part of the Constitution that cannot be changed by ordinary parliamentary procedures. Where else could a government confidently embark on a comprehensive review of local authorities, their finance, structure, functions and internal management, to be undertaken in a matter of weeks without any public discussion of the options? And this by a government which by the same process had just scored a spectacular own goal with the community charge.

The much vaunted flexibility of the Constitution suits nobody so much as an Executive which has inherited a reservoir of prerogative powers and enjoys a dominant position in relation to the legislature and all other public authorities. In the past these features of the Constitution, like the party system which exploits them, have been justified on the grounds that they help to provide firm and effective government. There is no doubt that single-party government has advantages of cohesion, speed of response and clear locus of responsibility. It is less clear that it performs any better than other systems in the promotion of effective and acceptable public policies. There may be some truth in the view that there would be less concern about the Constitution if the policies of successive British governments had been more successful. But there remains a constitutional case for reform: that the protection of individual rights, the decentralisation of power within the United Kingdom and the United Kingdom's role in the development of the European Community would all be more readily and more satisfactorily addressed within an explicitly constitutional framework.

Drafting concentrates the mind. It is for this reason that we have chosen to produce the text of a Constitution rather than another general discussion of the issues. The fact that we have gone to this trouble does not mean that we believe that the provisions of this Constitution are the only or even the ideal answer. Although the proposal for a written Constitution is in itself radical, much of the content is in the best (or worst) tradition of gradualism. The main features of the present Constitution are left more or less intact: in particular the Executive is drawn from the legislature, with all that entails for party government, the control of procedure, discipline and the purpose of elections. Some of the most disturbing effects of these proposals, from the political point of view, could be achieved by the introduction of proportional representation for elections by itself, or indeed without it by the chance of a hung Parliament. The supremacy of the Constitution, however, entails a problem of a different order: a much greater constitutional role for the judiciary.

The involvement of the judiciary in what are seen as essentially political issues is probably the strongest ground of objection across the political spectrum. The problem is that while not all political questions are constitutional, all constitutional questions are inherently political. To separate off some questions and declare them fit for judicial interpretation and decision is an act of political will: of abnegation for politicians and of distrust of politicians on the part of the rest of us. We can leave aside aspersions on the character, opinions, social background and intellectual formation of lawyers. Politicians are imperfect and the process of election which gives them legitimacy also exposes them to immediate pressures from which the judges are to some extent protected. We need rules to govern the exercise of power. It is in the interest of the less powerful that those rules should be clear and explicit, to lessen their manipulation by the more powerful. We need rules that we can accept as fair in general, though we object to their application in particulars. We need rules to protect ourselves and others against ourselves. And we need referees, even bad referees, to interpret and enforce the rules.

Nursery propositions, but none the worse for that: constitutional questions do not necessarily require intellectual subtlety so much as practical judgment. What are proper matters to be decided by judges depends in part on a view as to the likely outcome. We think that under present and foreseeable circumstances the present Constitution gives too much power to the Executive both in relation to individuals and in relation to its political opponents. Traditionally the exercise of this power has been tempered by the need to secure re-election and the existence of a constitutional Opposition ready to take over. Power has been and has had to be exercised with forbearance and this is a great and indisputable blessing. Nevertheless the advantage of incumbent governments over their opponents is substantial and increasing; and the replacement of one government by another is not a sufficient deterrent to the abuse of power by successive governments. We are therefore in favour of tightening the rules, endeavouring to provide greater protection to the rights and freedoms both of individuals and of other collectivities against the government, and therefore entrusting greater powers to the judges, warts and all.

The role of the judiciary is a vexed question both in the debate on the protection of individual rights and more generally when it is proposed to limit the powers of Parliament and substitute judicial for political decisions on matters of public policy. Those opposed to such limitations and substitution argue that, in a system of representative government, the views of the majority ought to prevail and that to entrench a statute which restricts Parliament's freedom to do what it thinks best in relation to freedom of speech or rights of property is to undermine the legitimacy of government itself. This argument has deep roots in British political thought; it is suspicious of entrenched rights and considers that the only way to determine their proper limits is by the political decision of the representatives of the people. Conversely, the argument contends that any restriction on what the majority wants is undemocratic.

We take a radically different view. Representative government cannot work fairly or at all without certain agreed prior conditions or 'rules of the game'. Everybody understands that a government which changes the entitlement to vote in elections is doing something different from fixing the rate of VAT. Although in the UK we do not currently distinguish between constitutional and ordinary law in our parliamentary procedures, the difference is real and fundamental.

Bill of Rights

In our view certain individual rights are also part of the rules of the democratic game. Freedom of expression is one such right. It protects the right to speak one's mind, to persuade others; and it protects the right of others to hear a differing view. It allows individuals to obtain official information and to comment on the record of the government of the day. There is not much point in holding elections if censorship prevents the electors from making a critical judgment of the government. Freedom of speech is therefore part of democracy's structure and not just an optional extra. The fact that in some countries constitutional rights are widely abused and subverted is not an argument against constitutional rights. It is a warning that they require to be guarded jealously even when they are given a special status in law.

Speech-related freedoms are not the only rights fundamental to a democracy. In a democratic society every individual is entitled to equal respect. Everyone should have an equal say in the election of the government and everyone should be protected from arbitrary arrest, expropriation of property without compensation, from cruel and unusual punishment and so forth. Failure to provide such protection may expose individuals to intimidation, harassment, discrimination, degradation or punishment that is inconsistent with the respect democracy requires government to accord each of its citizens.

Some of these rights and freedoms are protected now by statute and by the criminal law. In the past this protection has been judged by governments to be sufficient, and the sophisticated have comforted themselves with the thought that liberty lies in the interstices of the Constitution. We do not regard these protections as adequate now, if they ever were. The abuses of civil liberties in Britain and Northern Ireland are well documented elsewhere, and the United Kingdom's record at the European Court of Human Rights demonstrates that our domestic law and practice do not adequately conform with our international human rights obligations.

It is often argued that it is the legislature's role to protect individual rights and freedoms and that legislation enacting specific rights is preferable to a generally worded Bill of Rights. This argument is mistaken on a number of grounds. First, a Bill of Rights is intended to be open textured so that it can be applied, without amendment, to new issues and problems as they arise. These cannot always be foreseen and may therefore not be covered by earlier legislation, however detailed. Someone whose rights have been infringed should not have to wait until new legislation catches up with changing circumstances. Secondly, a Bill of Rights cannot be dismissed as simply a statement of good intent on the part of the government, because it is enforceable in the courts. As such it acts in a real way to strengthen the position of the individual *vis-à-vis* the State, government and public authorities.

Thirdly, there are occasions on which the legislature is unwilling to protect rights; for example, when panicked by an emergency or motivated by prejudice. Two apt examples are some anti-terrorist and immigration legislation. In such cases, enforcement of a Bill of Rights by the courts holds Parliament to a paramount commitment to protect basic freedoms, and protects minorities against the tyranny of the majority.

A further argument against adopting a Bill of Rights is that it would be no substitute for a comprehensive programme of legislative reform such as the introduction of a Freedom of Information Act, strengthening of statutory equality laws, reform of immigration legislation and the strengthening of statutory rights for suspects. We agree that a Bill of Rights would be no substitute for such a programme and do not propose it as an alternative. Both kinds of change are needed: they are not mutually exclusive.

It is also agreed that the working of the European Convention is, in some respects, unacceptable, allowing wide exceptions to certain rights and excluding others altogether. Our proposal, incorporating provisions from the International Covenant on Civic and Political Rights as well as the European Convention on Human Rights, seeks to overcome this difficulty. It would not only secure compliance with our international obligations but extend the protection which they provide, where necessary. Article 21 will ensure, for the avoidance of doubt, that the exception clauses are interpreted strictly in favour of individuals and minorities, allowing restriction of their rights only in circumstances which make it 'strictly necessary'. The burden of proof will be on the public authority to establish that this is the case. In respect of most of the Articles, exceptions are also limited to those circumstances which make restrictions 'necessary in a democratic society' for particular, limited reasons.

A government Discussion Paper of June 1976 ('Legislation on Human Rights – with Particular Reference to the European Convention. A Discussion Document') identified the following four special consequences of a Bill of Rights which its advocates claim as advantages:

a. its provisions, being drafted in general terms, would be open to reinterpretation by future generations in accordance with their needs;

b. its special status could mean that it provided an effective and quasi-permanent check on oppressive action by future governments and indeed Parliaments;

c. it could be held to ensure conformity with current international obligations which themselves are framed in general and quasi-permanent terms;

d. it would help to provide a more systematic concern with fundamental values, and more informed public discussion about them; and would bring about corresponding changes in current methods of making, applying and interpreting the law as a whole.

Fifteen years later, these advantages are more obvious.

The fourth of these arguments, which applies equally to the Constitution as a whole, has received the least attention in the debate, yet it could prove to be highly significant. Recent government restrictions on civil rights and liberties have not been marked by widespread public protest. The public in general is more aware of the importance of maintaining law and order, or national security, than of protecting the sometimes competing requirements of, say, freedom of speech, personal privacy and confidentiality. The Bill of Rights would provide us with a statement of principles, a set of basic values on which there would be a general consensus of support across the political spectrum (even though there would be disagreements about their implementation in practice). Learning about these principles would become part of the school curriculum and adult education, encouraging pupils and students to debate the importance of protecting human rights and the difficulties which arise when they conflict. Such a development would encourage a more informed public, more sensitive to the implications of restricting civil liberties and of extending them.

No one should suppose that the Bill of Rights will give an easy solution to every difficult issue concerning individual rights and the proper extent of collective interests. There will still be many important issues involving aspects of conscience, morality and religious belief that cannot be resolved in a way that will attract unanimous support. The Bill of Rights is no substitute for political decisions taken by the electorate and by Parliament, but it should help to ensure that those decisions do not violate fundamental human rights and freedoms.

Effective protection of human rights requires effective access to justice. The present legal aid scheme enables the very poor to face the risks of expensive litigation, but the great majority of people are unable to do so. In order to ensure that the Bill of Rights is effective we have created a United Kingdom Human Rights Commission to bring proceedings in its own name, assist individual complainants in cases involving alleged breaches of the Bill of Rights, and investigate practices and procedures which appear to be incompatible with it. In our view, the inclusion in the Constitution of measures to improve access to justice in the field of public law, including the creation of a Human Rights Commission, is a necessary condition for an effective Bill of Rights.

Although it would be important to avoid detracting from the Commission's primary law enforcement role, it would also be able to act in an advisory capacity to Parliament in relation to pending legislation and other matters. Much unnecessary litigation could be avoided if Parliament established its own Human Rights Committee to scrutinise proposed domestic (and European) legislation and to examine the effect of existing legislation and policies in the context of the UK's international human rights obligations and its own Bill of Rights. The government's attention could be drawn systematically to the implications of its policies and proposals for individual rights and the necessary adjustments made to avoid later litigation.

The growing importance of European institutions in Britain's political and legal system gives added weight to the case for constitutional protection. The UK is now the only member of the Council of Europe with no written Constitution or enforceable Bill of Rights, our partners in Europe providing remedies for their citizens which are not available to UK citizens through the British courts. Moreover, the Westminster Parliament has accepted, through the Treaty of Rome and Single European Act 1986, the supremacy of European Community law. The British courts have become increasingly accustomed to interpreting domestic law in the light of EC law and, where necessary, overriding the domestic legislation. It is hardly defensible for Parliament to qualify its own sovereignty in commercial and employment matters while refusing to do so in matters such as human rights.

We believe that it is necessary to adopt an alternative constitutional idea, namely that democracy is not the same thing as majority rule and that, to make democracy a reality, fundamental individual rights and the basic structure and rules of government should have legal protection that even a properly elected Parliament cannot change by ordinary legislation. Constitutional government requires that these ground rules be part of the fundamental law, and that judges, who are not elected and who are therefore removed from the pressures of partisan politics, should be responsible for interpreting and enforcing them as they are for all other parts of the legal system. These arguments as they apply to the Bill of Rights are set out in greater detail in *A British Bill of Rights* by A. Lester *et al.* (London: IPPR, 1990).

The judiciary

Opponents of a Bill of Rights often argue that British judges are not qualified by their training or experience to interpret and apply broadly phrased, open textured documents of this kind. According to this point of view, British judges would be likely to adopt restrictive interpretation of basic rights and freedoms, giving too much leeway to governments and public authorities by a loose interpretation of the exception clauses. On the other hand some, especially in Westminster and in Whitehall, fear that British judges would be too interventionist, usurping the role of government, or of the elected representatives of the people in Parliament, and limiting state power in favour of individual and minority rights.

It is undoubtedly true that British judges have interpreted the law in significant cases in a way which has restricted individual rights and freedoms. The record, however, has by no means been entirely negative. During the past quarter century, the British judiciary has strengthened a vital part of the British constitutional and legal system by developing principles and procedures in administrative law. The process of the judicial review of administrative action, for instance, undertaken by High Court judges, has been a significant success. Unaided by any legislation to codify the substantive principles of administrative law, the courts have used three main common law principles – legality, procedural propriety and rationality – to curb the misuses of power by public bodies and by private bodies exercising public power. They have done so in the case of many decisions of Conservative as well as of Labour Ministers. They have not been over-adventurous in this process but have remained careful to respect the separation of powers and the need to avoid usurping the role of the other branches of government.

In some areas, such as sex discrimination cases, our courts have acquired experience and shown great skill in interpreting and applying legislation dealing with human rights, and they have also shown themselves fully capable of interpreting and applying the relevant principles of Community law. Indeed, their record in this respect is much better than the record of some of the most senior courts elsewhere in the European Community.

The Law Lords, sitting as the Judicial Committee of the Privy Council, interpret and apply the Bills of Rights contained in the written Constitutions of independent Commonwealth countries. Again the record shows that, with some exceptions, the Privy Council has over the last fifteen years become generally more liberal in its interpretation of these Bills of Rights, which are modelled upon the European Convention: purposive and generous rather than literal and restrictive.

A recognition of the extent to which the British judiciary has adapted in recent years cannot, however, make us complacent about the approach which judges, and magistrates, might take. Being required to apply the Bill of Rights and uphold the Constitution would in itself influence their approach and encourage new ways of thinking. It is clearly unlikely that an incorporated Bill of Rights, for instance, would make the judges any less sensitive to fundamental rights and freedoms than they may now be. Nevertheless, there is well-founded concern that the narrow social and professional base from which the judiciary is drawn would be reflected in the decisions reached on some of the controversial issues likely to arise.

It is generally accepted that direct political considerations now play very little part in the selection of judges. This was not always the case in the past and it might not be in future when the courts have important constitutional powers. Appointments to the two highest levels of the Bench – the House of Lords and the Court of Appeal – are made by the Prime Minister, no doubt with the advice of the Lord Chancellor. All other judicial appointments are made by the Lord Chancellor, who is of course a politician and a member of the Cabinet. In our proposed system, the House of Lords is displaced by an elected Second Chamber and its Judicial Committee will be replaced by a Supreme Court with broadly similar functions. There will however be important changes: the Supreme Court will have power to declare Acts of Parliament unconstitutional. Any written Constitution needs to incorporate some special procedures for its own amendment: without that the Constitution has no special validity and merely becomes a codification of statutes. There are several reasons why a special procedure is needed. First, it gives the Constitution the status which it needs as a fundamental document which is incapable of being altered at the whim of a temporary majority. Second, it enables fundamental human rights to be entrenched and incapable of being overridden by ordinary legislation. And third, in a federal Constitution, power is shared between the central parliament and provincial parliaments. This means that the constitutional relationship between the State and its constituent nations and regions cannot be altered without the consent of both.

As soon as you have a Constitution which can only be altered by a special procedure, you get the possibility that the legislature may pass an Act which is inconsistent with the Constitution but cannot override it because it has not been passed by the special procedure. This leads to conflicts, and conflicts require adjudication: hence a Supreme or Constitutional Court. The Supreme Court in this Constitution will have the power to make ordinary Acts of Parliament unconstitutional and hence play a much more powerful role in the Constitution than the present House of Lords. As can be seen from the example of the USA, the power to appoint judges to courts with important constitutional powers can become a controversial political issue. If no changes were made to the present system of appointing judges, the temptation to depart from the recent tradition of impartiality in judicial appointments might become impossible to resist.

Judicial independence

We have thus been obliged to give particular attention to the problem of judicial independence: it is no good relying on the judges for protection if they are in the pocket of the Executive. The three essential features of judicial independence are:

(1) freedom from political influence in the appointment of judges;

(2) the protection of judges from undue political pressure while serving on the bench; and

(3) protection from improper removal from office.

We propose, first, that judges should be chosen by a Judicial Services Commission. This is made the more necessary by the replacement of the quasi judicial office of Lord Chancellor with the office of Minister of Justice, a more overtly political Minister who has no judicial function and will not have to be a qualified lawyer. There is nothing novel about the idea of a Judicial Services Commission. Many Commonwealth countries have one. Where the present proposals differ is that the membership is not predominantly judicial or legal.

The Judicial Services Commission is given the responsibility for initial appointments to the judiciary and for subsequent promotions, save at the highest level, where the critical appointments to the Supreme Court would be made in a manner similar to that for High Court judges. The names would be put forward by the Joint Appointments Commission, but the formal appointment would be made by the Head of State on the advice of the Prime Minister. The character of the Supreme Court will in the long run be determined by the pool of judges from which it is drawn. For that reason the Judicial Services Commission is specifically charged 'to adopt procedures . . . which will ensure . . . that adequate numbers of candidates of both sexes and from diverse racial, religious and social backgrounds are considered for appointments'. We do not pretend that this can have any immediate or dramatic effect on the character of the Bench, but in the longer run it ought to help.

The Constitution also provides protection for the independence of the judiciary by a better procedure and clear grounds for removal, and for protection against the judiciary by a new procedure for dealing with judicial misconduct under the Judicial Services Commission. We do not believe that the judiciary can be directly responsible for the finance and administration of the court system, as some have proposed, but do believe that judges must retain control over the listing of cases and their allocation to members of the Bench. In a controversial case the choice of the judge who is to hear it may be of crucial importance. Take, for example, the 'Spycatcher' case. The judiciary was deeply divided on the issues which it raised. It would have been possible to make a pretty accurate guess, in advance, as to the side of the fence on which many of the judges involved were likely to come down. In any such case, the power to allocate a case to a particular judge or judges may therefore effectively decide its outcome. A discretionary power of allocation must exist, and cases cannot be allocated by some mechanical formula. It would clearly conflict with judicial independence if the power of allocation were to be exercised by an official in the Ministry of Justice. The principle of judicial control of court business is therefore enshrined in the Constitution.

The Constitution thus does not contain a codification of existing practice in the administration of justice, but a series of important reforms which should, first, make it more efficient by creating a Ministry of Justice to end the present irrational and damaging division of responsibility for the courts between the Home Office and the Lord Chancellor's Department; second, increase the independence of the judiciary by transferring responsibility for appointment and promotion to an independent Judicial Services Commission; third, widen the background of the Bench and make it more responsive to the feelings of litigants by including a powerful lay element in the Judicial Services Commission and by creating a formal complaints procedure.

Local government

The second major reason for wanting a written Constitution rather than piecemeal reform is to deal with the centralisation of power.

If we can protect individuals by entrenching their rights, we should try to do the same for communities. We reject the vision of a super-market democracy, in which the citizen is the consumer free to choose among the identical goods in the local branch of the national government. Local government has to be more than a vehicle for delivering national policies. Not only do we want different policies in different places: democracy requires the active participation of many people in political decisions if it is to survive as anything more than a TV panel game. But we need to be imaginative in creating the opportunities for people to take part. We do not advocate compulsory immersion in politics. We all know that politics – party politics especially – is the passion of a few, the hobby of a few more and at best a spectator sport for the majority. Most people need to be involved in matters of direct personal concern, but often feel they are kept at arm's length and excluded by the professionals. Some experiments in participation have been better than others: involving a small number of parent governors in technical questions of school budgets and personnel management is much less important than actively involving all parents in the education of their children. There is no doubt that we can make local government more accessible. Local government is alive to the importance of its relations with the public and needs support and encouragement from national government, not the treatment to which it has been subjected in recent years.

It may, however, not be enough to restore good relations and reform the structure and finances of local government. The reason is this: central government has and will always have a pressing interest in what local government is doing. There will always be pressure for central government to intervene to protect the economy, to maintain common standards, to rescue a local minority and so forth. Constitutional entrenchment of the powers of local government will not alter that. Nor is it possible to draw tidy lines of demarcation between the responsibilities of central and local government: there will always be a degree of overlap, of fusion and indeed confusion. In federal government much public policy is implemented through partnership, a word once used in this country also to describe the relations between central and local government. The difference is that in a federal Constitution both central and local government have constitutional standing: local government has a base from which to negotiate. Here, local government is the creature of central government: it is whatever Parliament says it shall be, which is an invitation not only to continuous interference, but to occasional Whitehall engineering to reform local government structure, boundaries and functions to whatever the latest administration fashion or party advantage dictates. But there is of course no ideal or even best practical structure for local government. Experience in other countries suggests that local governments can adopt a variety of means to provide the services they want to give and that talk about x thousand population being necessary to provide such and such a service is the dogma of administrative convenience, not imaginative politics. What local government needs is a strong constitutional base and the sense of identity which comes from permanent boundaries.

Devolution

We have also to consider central government itself and ask whether it needs to do all that it tries to do. There are two reasons for this. First, because central government is overloaded: Parliament groans under a burden of business which it cannot manage properly: the result is a mass of ill-digested legislation, inadequate scrutiny of government activity and failure to grapple with new responsibilities at the European level. The second reason is the need to accommodate the legitimate aspirations of the nations that make up the United Kingdom, whilst preserving the benefits of the union which we have painfully created over the last five hundred years. This need not and should not produce a conflict of loyalties. The question is, what is the appropriate way to give political expression to these overlapping identities?

Anybody who has taken the trouble to follow the lively debates in Scotland will be aware that there is a growing conviction that Scottish identity requires a more visible political expression in the way Scotland is governed. We have faced this question before, and there was then strong opposition to the devolution proposals of the 1970s, and with good reason. They were incoherent and inherently unstable: a reluctant damage control operation with no constitutional backbone. We have a choice now between trying to treat Scotland as an exceptional case, a sort of autonomous region with special privileges which the Welsh and the Northern Irish will then demand as well; or using Scotland as a model for a general decentralisation of government across the United Kingdom, by which we create not only an elected Scottish Assembly to control the responsibilities of the Scottish office, but similar Assemblies for Wales, Northern Ireland and the regions of England. This would relieve Whitehall and

Westminster of much domestic business and provide a tier of government to discharge responsibilities for transport, planning and the environment and economic development more effectively than either central or local government, as our European partners have found. The German *Länder* are of course the standing example, but France, Italy and Spain are rapidly developing their regional institutions. A project of this scale needs to have formal constitutional expression, for the same reasons as local government. The balancing act between central, regional and local government requires each to have a firm base for negotiation and arrangements for revenue sharing, and will of course require an independent arbitrator in the form of a constitutional court.

We have followed this approach and have tried to develop a workable system. But we are bound to admit there are formidable practical and political objections to what we have proposed. We should therefore explain why we think the attempt is worth making.

The United Kingdom is awkward. It is not a nation state, but a state which embraces four identifiable 'national' units. One of these, England, dominates the union by reason of its size and population (four-fifths of the whole). One of the smaller nations, Wales, has been administered for four hundred years or so as part of England. Another, Scotland, has enjoyed a large and increasing degree of administrative devolution and retains independent national institutions. The fourth, Northern Ireland, until recently enjoyed a large degree of political devolution, which has been withdrawn because its continued presence within the United Kingdom is disputed. These differences of size, of institutional development and of political climate make it difficult to imagine a coherent constitutional settlement. Many may feel that if it works, don't fix it. Northern Ireland plainly doesn't work but is small and remote enough to be treated as a special case.

Scotland is another matter. Though dissent is expressed within constitutional bounds, Scotland presents an acute case of the general problem that large parts of the United Kingdom are ruled by a government for which most of the electors did not vote. The governing party in the United Kingdom holds only 11 out of 72 Scottish parliamentary seats and has recently had no more than 20 per cent support in opinion polls. The government's policies are deeply resented and there has been a strong revival of the demands for political devolution which failed to be carried in the 1970s, and substantial support in by-elections and in the opinion polls for the

Scottish National Party, whose policy is independence. The movement for devolution now commands support from a wider and more influential body of people, including the Scottish TUC, the majority of Scottish local authorities and the churches as well as the Labour and Liberal Democratic Parties. The Scottish Convention, in which these bodies have been represented, has been engaged in developing its own views on the future of Scottish political institutions, rather than waiting for some dispensation from London. As a result the Convention's demands go well beyond the 1978 Scotland Bill. The argument now concerns not simply what powers to devolve but how to entrench them.

The Scottish Labour Party, the largest party in Scotland, is also the major force in the Convention and is committed to major devolution. The British Labour Party has accepted this commitment as the price of the Union; without its Scottish members it has no prospect of commanding a majority in Parliament. Neither the Convention nor the Scottish Labour Party (nor the British Labour Party) has confronted the critical constitutional question: how is Scotland's continued representation at Westminster to be justified? – the 'West Lothian question'. It is not constitutionally coherent nor will it be politically acceptable to other UK parties for Scotland's seventy MPs to vote at Westminster on matters for which they have no responsibility.

One possible answer would be to reduce Scottish representation at Westminster in the way that was done for Northern Ireland before direct rule. This does not answer the constitutional question and would probably not work politically because of the greater number of Scottish MPs who would still be involved. The anomaly would be too large. Nor could it be overcome by the suggestion in the Liberal Democratic Constitution that Scottish members (or others) should not vote when matters devolved to Scotland but not to other parts of the UK were under discussion in Parliament. The withdrawal of significant numbers of MPs for particular business could change the party balance in Parliament in such a way as to make it impossible for the government to carry its business.

There would be political advantages in an old-style Northern Ireland solution, whatever the constitutional problems. The question is whether such a settlement would have much chance of stability. Once there is an elected Assembly to speak on Scotland's behalf, the terms of the union will be a matter of continuous reinterpretation and legitimate dispute.

These constitutional dilemmas are more acute for the Labour Party. It is already committed to a Scottish Assembly, without changing the basis of the present bargain, and that commitment has been given detailed expression. Donald Dewar's 1987 Scotland Bill and subsequent drafts produced for the Scottish Convention, which take the constitutional argument further, have been based on careful thought and much hard work. The latest versions set out what is a quasi-federal relationship between Scotland and the United Kingdom, including the fundamental notion that any statute establishing an Assembly should have a special status as a *constitutional* statute: that is, a statute which would require special parliamentary procedures to amend. Some Scottish constitutional lawyers have long argued that this is in fact the status of the Act of Union. No alteration in its terms should therefore be made by ordinary statute. If it is to be replaced, then it should be by an equally binding settlement, in which the conventions of the English Constitution do not prevail.

Labour also has plans for Assemblies for Wales and Northern Ireland and for some form of elected bodies for the English regions. These have not been worked through in the kind of detail of the Scottish proposals, but one may presume that the plans for Wales and Northern Ireland would be close to those for Scotland, allowing for major differences in administrative and political circumstances.

The proposals for the English regions bear a strong resemblance to those of the Minority Report of the Royal Commission on the Constitution, which advocated the creation of elected regional authorities to take over the regional responsibilities of central government. To those would be added a few strategic functions of local government, following the abolition of the county councils and the introduction of a new system of multi-purpose authorities based on the present district authorities and metropolitan boroughs. There are two sources of political pressure for this programme. One is based on a concern for regional economic development and the need to have more active and responsive authorities at a regional level to coordinate local, national and European economic initiatives. The second reflects concern in the conurbations, and especially London, about the absence of any strategic authority to deal with land use planning, transport, and other functions which cannot be effectively handled either by boroughs individually or through informal cooperation. The position in London is particularly serious, given political divisions among the boroughs and the powers of unsympathetic and uncoordinated central government departments over the city as a whole. A recent report to the London Regional Labour Party began to put together the case for a strategic metropolitan authority with many of the functions that regional authorities across the country might have. Other people, including some in the private sector, have been thinking on similar lines.

Is there a case for a grand design? It should be said at once that there are powerful arguments against doing anything more than is strictly and politically necessary. These apply with particular force to the proposals for England. Critics point to what they regard as the *ignis fatuus* of reorganisation: the notion that you can resolve or even address problems by institutional change. Local government is still reeling from the changes enforced on it over the last ten years. The last thing it needs is another upheaval. What is needed is a period of calm, of consolidation, a restoration of partnership between central and local government, based on agreed policies and adequate funding. It can be argued that there is nothing which a regional tier of government could do which could not equally well be done by such cooperation. Sort out local government taxation, and concentrate on those areas of policy, like education and housing, which require urgent attention. If you must make a bargain with the Scots, so be it. Otherwise constitutional change is a diversion, consuming time and political energy much better spent on the *real* business of government.

An alternative view is that, if the first step has to be taken, others will follow: and you might as well have a clear idea of where you are going and why. The constitutional changes proposed for Scotland are radical and in principle incompatible with current constitutional conventions. If they are enacted, with or without adjustments to the union bargain, they will prove unstable and unacceptable either to Scotland or to the rest of the United Kingdom, particularly England.

There is a general case for the decentralisation of government, quite apart from the need to give greater expression to national identity. Scotland, Wales and Northern Ireland, despite the latter's troubles, are better served by their departments than is England by Whitehall. Ministers and civil servants are closer to their constituencies, more familiar with and to the people with whom they have to deal in local government, in the health service, in education and in the public and private sectors of industry. There is a better chance of coordination within the departments themselves, even if it is not always achieved. It is easier to launch initiatives, to experiment, to reconcile interests, to persuade, to reach agreement. Even opponents are better understood. At the same time it is a commonplace that

Ministers in Whitehall are overwhelmed with detail, submerged by a flood of minor decisions, while Parliament struggles in vain to digest the mass of legislation driven through it.

We hear much less these days about overloaded government; but it is not clear that the new mood of confident assertiveness has actually produced a better performance. A general decentralization on the Scottish model would relieve central government of much domestic responsibility, particularly for the delivery of services, and allow it to concentrate on major economic policy, taxation, social security, trade, foreign policy, defence and all these matters as they relate to the European Community. Government and Parliament would have a much better chance of becoming effectively involved in the development of the Community if they could let go of some of their domestic preoccupations. They could tackle the fear of imposed uniformity from above if they were less intent on imposing uniformity below.

The details of the scheme we have proposed are set out in the text of the Constitution and discussed at length in the commentary. Apart from the obvious neglect of the special problems of Northern Ireland and the much less serious but equally intractable problem of the identity of the English regions, there are two features of the scheme which are likely to be controversial. The first is the way in which legislative power has been distributed between Parliament and the Assemblies. This is an attempt to put into effect the principle of subsidiarity: the Assemblies have rights to legislate on a broad range of domestic issues, but Parliament has concurrent powers to legislate where Assembly legislation would be inadequate or have external effects. Parliament in terms of the Constitution has exclusive legislative powers, but these in turn will effectively be shared with the European Community on the same basis. There are bound to be conflicts at both levels which, if they cannot be resolved politically, will have to be dealt with in the courts. The Assemblies will at least be able to fight their corner, as indeed the UK government will need to do against the continual and unnecessary encroachment of detailed regulation from above.

The second controversial proposal is that for revenue sharing as a source of finance for the Assemblies. This is an attempt to find a constitutional device to overcome the conundrum of regional and local government: how to find a tax base which provides a substantial proportion of local revenue and at the same time provide for the equalisation of resources between richer and poorer areas. Tax-raising powers are commonly held to be essential to any genuine political independence, but if regional and local governments are left to their own resources there will be great inequalities in standards of public services between different areas. If on the other hand central government provides a substantial proportion of local resources in the form of equalisation grants, it will inevitably become involved in prescribing the ways in which 'its money' is spent, and local autonomy or self-government will be undermined. This has proved the case even where redistribution has been carried through by elaborate formulae based on measurements of need. These do not remove the occasions for political judgment or the temptations to political manipulation. The suggestion here is to assign major tax revenues to the regions as of right with an entrenched formula for redistribution, while keeping the administration and control of the tax itself with central government.

The experience of most countries has been that the buoyant sources of revenue (income taxes, excises, corporation taxes) have been appropriated by central government. The assignation of indirect taxes to regional or local government (sales tax, excise, VAT) runs into difficulties with 'common market' constraints both within the UK and the European Community. In the longer term there are pressures to harmonise such taxes across the EC. This leaves income and property taxes as the most appropriate taxes for local and regional government.

There are, of course, serious problems in entrenching a financial formula in the Constitution and the political difficulties may outweigh the advantages. But some such solution is necessary if we are to reverse the current trend, where the government's new proposals for local taxation will provide less than 20 per cent of local authority revenue.

Parliament, patronage and the public service

The other main innovations in the Constitution require justification but less explanation. The approval of Parliament for important actions of the Executive, such as declarations of war and the making of treaties, now taken under the prerogative powers gives formal recognition to the underlying political reality and may at the same time render the Executive more immediately accountable. Changes in the methods of appointment will reduce the government's powers of patronage and help to ensure some consistency of standards and integrity in the burgeoning world of appointed office holders. This may in any event be decreased by putting many services under the control of the Assemblies. The new constitutional bodies, such as the Public Services Commission and the Election Commission, are also intended to insulate important features of the Constitution from direct political interference, at all levels in the system. They are in a sense the guarantors of fairness of the system. The significant changes to Parliament itself are limited but important.

The election of the Prime Minister again recognises the essential source of legitimacy, and may also avoid real difficulty and embarrassment for the Head of State. The House of Lords is a useful anachronism which does much good work but lacks the essential ingredient to act as an effective check on the Commons and the watchdog of the Constitution. In our proposals for elections, we have provided a different system for the new Second Chamber which would put more emphasis on the character of the individual candidate than on party. For the Commons we have adopted the system which seems closest to the present one, while providing a greater degree of proportionality in representation. We do not believe that the present system, which denies adequate representation to parties with substantial but geographically scattered support, is acceptable. And we think the adequate representation of minorities may be especially important in the elections to the Assemblies and local government. There is much more that could be said on all these issues, and some of it is said in the commentary on specific provisions of the Constitution.

We have taken the opportunity, where possible, to include provisions intended to strengthen equal opportunities. In the Bill of Rights, for instance, the equality Article taken from the International Covenant on Civil and Political Rights has been extended to cover discrimination on grounds of age, homosexuality or disability (Article 19). Three bodies responsible for making appointments – the Judicial Services Commission, the Public Services Commission and the authorities responsible for police appointments – are charged with a duty to ensure that adequate numbers of candidates of both sexes and from diverse racial, religious and social backgrounds are considered for appointment (Articles 104, 115 and 125). In relation to the appointment of the judiciary, the provision for part-time judges to be appointed in the superior courts will enable more women to take up such appointments; whilst Parliament itself should be made more accessible by the requirement that the hours and sittings of both Houses must 'have regard to the needs of all persons who are eligible to be members' (Article 63). Were a list system to be used for the appointment of Additional Members to the Commons, a further opportunity would arise for strengthening the representation of women and minority groups, although we are also aware of the disadvantages of using such a system.

The Constitution strengthens the hand of Parliament *vis-à-vis* the Executive but also that of the citizen *vis-à-vis* the State. Throughout, there are provisions which would enhance our control over our own lives and give us the means to call to account those whose decisions affect our interests: access to official information and control over the use to which personal information is put (Articles 28 and 29); an electoral system in which each individual's vote is reflected in the outcome (Chapter 8); a Bill of Rights and Human Rights Commission to assist individuals whose rights are infringed (Chapter 2); a duty on public authorities to give reasons for decisions; and a right to complain to the Commission for Public Administration of any failure of administration or unfair administration by public authorities (Articles 118 and 119) are but some examples.

A written Constitution should come into force by special means, such as a constitutional convention followed by a referendum, rather than by Act of Parliament. This is a first attempt at the main text of a Constitution: we have not embarked on the necessary but secondary apparatus of interpretation, transition and adoption. This is not because we regard them as straightforward, rather the reverse. They present knotty problems, constitutional, political and technical. They are however consequential problems that follow on agreement as to whether we want a written Constitution at all.

PART I

The Constitution

Preamble

We the People of the United Kingdom

affirm
that the United Kingdom shall be founded upon principles which acknowledge human rights and fundamental freedoms, the dignity of the human person and the equal and inalienable rights with which all human beings are endowed;

respect
the principles of social justice; and

therefore believe
that the material resources of the community must be so managed that there shall be adequate means of livelihood for all; that no one shall be exploited or forced by economic necessity to work in inhumane or degrading conditions; that there shall be opportunity for advancement on the basis of merit, ability and integrity; that equal protection shall be given to all children regardless of their family circumstances; and that provision for education and for health shall be made for all on a basis of equality;

further believe
that the informed consent and active participation of the people are fundamental to a democratic system of government, which must be based on free elections by universal adult suffrage and whose institutions must provide for the expression of national, regional and local loyalties and enhance the opportunities for self-government in all institutions, public and private;

recognise
that freedom can only flourish when founded upon a respect for the rule of law both by individuals and by government;

require

government policies, consonant with membership of the European Community and the furtherance of the objectives of the Community, which protect and safeguard the freedom and territorial integrity of the United Kingdom; which eliminate economic and social discrimination among the citizens of the United Kingdom whether based on race, colour, creed or gender; which protect the rights of the individual to life, liberty and the pursuit of happiness; which prohibit the exploitation of man by man or by the state; which ensure a just system of social security and welfare; which protect the environment; which promote peace, security and cooperation among the nations, based upon an equitable international economic order and a respect for international law and treaty obligations in dealings among nations;

desire

that their society shall reflect and promote the above principles, beliefs and needs and that their constitution should therefore make provision for the achievement of the same in the United Kingdom; and

declare

therefore that the following provisions shall have effect as the Constitution of the United Kingdom —

CHAPTER 1
The Constitution

> ## 1. CONSTITUTION AS FOUNDATION OF POWER IN UNITED KINGDOM

1.1   This Constitution is the sole foundation for the exercise of executive, legislative and judicial power in the United Kingdom.

1.2   This Constitution recognises and gives effect to the obligations assumed by the United Kingdom as a member of the Community of Nations and of the European Community.

1.3   All Acts of Parliament, and all other laws, shall be interpreted and applied subject to this Constitution, and, so far as is practicable, in such a way as to conform to it.

1.4   Any law (including a rule of the common law), and any convention or other constitutional practice or usage in force immediately before the coming into force of this Constitution, that is inconsistent with this Constitution ceases to have effect to the extent of the inconsistency.

CHAPTER 2
Rights and Freedoms

PART 1: FUNDAMENTAL RIGHTS AND FREEDOMS

Division 1: The Bill of Rights

2. RIGHT TO LIFE

2.1   Everyone's right to life shall be protected by law.

2.2   No one shall be deprived of life intentionally.

2.3   Deprivation of life shall not be regarded as inflicted in contravention of this Article when it results from the use of force which is no more than absolutely necessary —

    .1   in defence of any person from unlawful violence; or

    .2   in action lawfully taken for the purpose of quelling a riot or insurrection.

2.4   No one shall be condemned to death or executed.

3. FREEDOM FROM TORTURE

3.   No one shall be subjected to torture or to cruel, inhuman or degrading treatment or punishment.

4. FREEDOM FROM SLAVERY AND FORCED LABOUR

4.1   No one shall be held in slavery or servitude.

4.2   No one shall be required to perform forced or compulsory labour.

4.3 For the purpose of this Article, the expression 'forced or compulsory labour' does not include —

.1 any work required to be done in the ordinary course of detention according to Article 5 or during conditional release from such detention;

.2 any service of a military character or, in case of conscientious objectors, service exacted instead of compulsory military service;

.3 any service exacted in case of an emergency or calamity threatening the life or well being of the community;

.4 any work or service which forms part of normal civic obligations.

5. RIGHT TO LIBERTY AND SECURITY

5.1 .1 Everyone has the right to liberty and security of person.

.2 No one shall be deprived of their liberty except, on reasonable grounds and in accordance with fair procedures established by law, in the following cases —

.1 the lawful detention of a person after conviction by a competent court;

.2 the lawful arrest or detention of a person for non-compliance with the lawful order of a court or in order to secure the fulfilment of any obligation prescribed by law;

.3 the lawful arrest or detention of a person effected for the purpose of bringing them before the competent legal authority on reasonable suspicion of having committed an offence or when it is reasonably considered necessary to prevent their committing an offence or fleeing after having done so;

.4 the lawful detention of persons for the prevention of the spreading of infectious diseases constituting a serious threat to public health, or of persons suffering from mental disorder where necessary for the prevention of harm to themselves or others;

.5 the lawful arrest or detention of a person to prevent their effecting an unauthorised entry into the United Kingdom or of a person against whom action is being taken with a view to deportation or extradition.

5.2 Anyone who is arrested shall, at the time of arrest, be informed in a language which they understand of the reasons for their arrest and shall be promptly informed of any charges against them.

5.3 .1 It shall not be the general rule that persons awaiting trial shall be detained in custody.

.2 Anyone arrested or detained on a criminal charge shall be brought promptly before a judge or other officer authorised by law to exercise judicial power and is entitled to trial within a reasonable time or to release pending trial.

.3 Release may be subject to guarantees to appear for trial or at any other stage of the judicial proceedings.

5.4 Anyone who is deprived of liberty by arrest or detention is entitled to take proceedings before a court in order that the court may decide without delay on the lawfulness of the detention and may order their release if the detention is not lawful.

5.5 Anyone who has been the victim of unlawful arrest or detention has an enforceable right to compensation.

5.6 All persons deprived of their liberty shall be treated with humanity and with respect for the inherent dignity of the human person.

5.7 Accused persons in detention shall, save in exceptional circumstances, be segregated from convicted persons and shall be subject to separate treatment appropriate to their status as people who have not been convicted.

5.8 .1 Accused juvenile persons in detention shall be separated from adults and brought as speedily as possible for adjudication.

.2 Juvenile convicted persons shall be separated from adults and accorded treatment appropriate to their age and legal status.

5.9 No one shall be imprisoned merely on the ground of inability to fulfil a contractual obligation.

6. RIGHT TO FAIR AND PUBLIC HEARING

6.1   .1 In the determination of their civil rights and obligations or of any criminal charges against them, everyone is entitled to a fair and public hearing within a reasonable time by an independent and impartial tribunal established by law.

    .2 Judgment shall be pronounced publicly but the press and public may be excluded from all or any part of the trial to the extent strictly necessary in the opinion of the court:

      .1 in the interests of public order or national security in a democratic society;

      .2 where the interests of juveniles or the protection of the private life of the parties so require; or

      .3 where publicity would prejudice the interests of justice.

6.2   Everyone charged with a criminal offence is presumed innocent until proved guilty according to law.

6.3   Everyone charged with a criminal offence has the following minimum rights:

    .1 to be informed promptly in a language which they understand and in detail of the nature and cause of the accusation against them;

    .2 to have adequate time and facilities for the preparation of their defence;

    .3 to defend themselves in person or through legal assistance of their own choosing or, if they have not sufficient means to pay for legal assistance, to be given it free when the interests of justice so require;

    .4 to examine or have examined witnesses against them and to obtain the attendance and examination of witnesses on their behalf under the same conditions as witnesses against them;

    .5 to have the free assistance of an interpreter if they cannot understand or speak the language used in court;

    .6 not to be compelled to testify against themselves or to confess guilt.

6.4　When a person has, by a final decision, been convicted of a criminal offence and has suffered punishment as a result of such conviction, and it is subsequently shown that there has been a miscarriage of justice, that person shall be compensated according to law.

6.5　Everyone convicted of a crime has the right to have their conviction and sentence reviewed by a higher tribunal according to law.

6.6　No one is liable to be tried or punished again for an offence for which they have already been finally convicted or acquitted in accordance with the law and penal procedure.

7. RETROSPECTIVE OFFENCES PROHIBITED

7.1　.1 No one shall be held guilty of any criminal offence on account of any act or omission which did not constitute a criminal offence under national or international law at the time when it was committed.

　　　.2 Nor shall a heavier penalty be imposed than the one that was applicable at the time the criminal offence was committed.

7.2　This Article does not prejudice the trial and punishment of any person for any act which constitutes the crime of genocide or a crime against humanity.

8. RESPECT FOR PRIVATE AND FAMILY LIFE

8.1　Everyone has the right to respect for their private and family life, their home and their correspondence.

8.2　There shall be no interference with the exercise of this right except such as is in accordance with the law and is necessary in a democratic society —

　　　.1 in the interests of national security or public safety; or

　　　.2 for the prevention of disorder or crime; or

.3 for the protection of health or morals; or

.4 for the protection of the rights and freedoms of others.

9. FREEDOM OF THOUGHT

9.1   .1 Everyone has the right to freedom of thought, conscience and religion.

     .2 This right includes freedom to change one's religion or belief, and freedom, either alone or in community with others and in public or private, to manifest one's religion or belief in worship, teaching, practice and observance.

9.2   Freedom to manifest one's religion or belief is subject only to such limitations as are prescribed by law and are necessary in a democratic society —

     .1 in the interests of public safety; or

     .2 for the preservation of public order; or

     .3 for the protection of health or morals, or

     .4 for the protection of the rights and freedoms of others.

9.3   .1 No law shall be made establishing any religion or imposing any religious observance.

     .2 No religious test shall be required as a qualification for any office of public trust under any government in the United Kingdom.

10. RIGHT TO EDUCATION

10.1   No person shall be denied the right to education.

10.2   In the exercise of their functions in relation to education and teaching, public authorities shall respect the right of parents to ensure such education and teaching in conformity with their own religious and philosophical convictions, so far as is compatible with the provision of efficient instruction and training and the avoidance of unreasonable public expenditure.

11. FREEDOM OF EXPRESSION

11.1 Everyone has the right to hold opinions without interference.

11.2 .1 Everyone has the right to freedom of expression.

.2 This right includes freedom to seek, receive and impart information and ideas of all kinds regardless of frontiers, either orally, in writing or in print, in the form of art, or through any other media of their choice.

11.3 The exercise of this right carries with it special duties and responsibilities. It may therefore be subject to certain restrictions, but only such as are provided by law and are necessary in a democratic society —

.1 for respect of the rights or reputations of others; or

.2 for the protection of national security or of public order or of public health or morals.

11.4 A requirement by law that radio or television broadcasting, or cinema enterprises, must be licensed is not inconsistent with this Article.

12. FREEDOM OF ASSEMBLY AND ASSOCIATION

12.1 Everyone has the right to freedom of peaceful assembly and to freedom of association with others, including the right to form and to join trade unions.

12.2 No restriction shall be placed on the exercise of these rights other than such as are prescribed by law and are necessary in a democratic society —

.1 in the interests of national security, public safety or the preservation of public order; or

.2 for the protection of public health or morals; or

.3 for the protection of the rights and freedoms of others.

12.3 This Article does not prevent the imposition of restrictions prescribed by law and necessary in a democratic society on the exercise of this right by members of the Armed Forces or of the police or by persons charged with the administration of the state.

13. RIGHTS IN RESPECT OF MARRIAGE

13.1 Everyone of marriageable age has the right both to marry and to found a family.

13.2 No marriage shall be entered into without the free and full consent of the intending spouses.

13.3 .1 Spouses have equality of rights and responsibilities as to marriage, during marriage, and at its dissolution.

.2 In the case of dissolution, provision shall be made for the necessary protection of any children.

13.4 Every child has the right to such measures of protection as are required by their status as a minor, on the part of their family, society and public authorities.

14. RIGHT TO ENJOYMENT OF POSSESSIONS

14.1 .1 Every natural or legal person is entitled to the peaceful enjoyment of their possessions.

.2 No one shall be deprived of their possessions except in the public interest and subject to the conditions provided for by law and to prompt, adequate and effective compensation.

14.2 This Article does not in any way impair the right to enforce such laws as may be necessary to control the use of property in accordance with the general interest or to secure the payment of taxes or other contributions or penalties.

15. RIGHT TO PARTICIPATE IN PUBLIC LIFE AND SERVICE

15. Every adult citizen has the right and the opportunity, without unreasonable restrictions —

.1 to take part in the conduct of public affairs directly or through freely chosen representatives;

.2 to vote and to stand for election at genuine periodic elections, which shall be by universal and equal suffrage and shall be held by secret ballot, guaranteeing the free expression of the will of the people;

.3 to participate, on general terms of equality, in public service.

16. FREEDOM OF MOVEMENT

16.1 Everyone lawfully within the United Kingdom has the right of liberty of movement and freedom to choose their residence within the United Kingdom.

16.2 Everyone is free to leave the United Kingdom, and everyone holding British nationality is entitled to a passport.

16.3 No restrictions shall be placed on the exercise of the rights set out in this Article other than such as are in accordance with law and are necessary in a democratic society —

.1 in the interests of national security, public safety or the preservation of public order; or

.2 for the prevention of crime or under an order imposed by a court on conviction of crime; or

.3 for the protection of health; or

.4 for the protection of the rights and freedoms of others.

16.4 The rights set out in paragraph .1 may also be subject, in particular areas, to restrictions imposed in accordance with law and justified by the public interest in a democratic society.

17. FREEDOM FROM EXPULSION FROM UNITED KINGDOM

17.1 No British national shall be expelled from the United Kingdom or deprived of the right to enter the United Kingdom.

17.2 .1 Other persons may be expelled from the United Kingdom only in pursuance of a decision reached in accordance with law.

.2 Any such persons who have been lawfully admitted to the

United Kingdom shall be allowed, prior to expulsion, —

.1 to submit reasons against expulsion; and

.2 to have their cases reviewed by, and be represented for the purpose before, the competent authority or a person or persons especially designated by the competent authority.

17.3 This Article does not prevent the extradition of persons, through established legal procedures, for the purpose of standing trial for a criminal offence or serving a sentence lawfully imposed on them in another jurisdiction.

18. RIGHT OF ASYLUM

18.1 Every person has the right to seek and be granted asylum in the United Kingdom in accordance with the law of the United Kingdom and international conventions, if they are being pursued for political offences.

18.2 In no case may an alien be deported or returned to a country, regardless of whether or not it is their country of origin, if in that country their right to life or personal freedom is in danger of being violated because of their race, nationality, religion, social status, or political opinions.

19. EQUALITY

19.1 Everyone has the right to recognition as a person before the law.

19.2 All persons are entitled without any discrimination to the equal protection of the law.

19.3 The equal protection of the law and the enjoyment of the rights and freedoms set out in this Bill of Rights shall be secured without discrimination on any ground such as sex, race, colour, language, religion, political or other opinion, national or social origin, association with a national minority, property, birth, homosexuality, disability, age, or other status.

Division 2: Application and interpretation

---

20. APPLICATION OF BILL OF RIGHTS

---

20. The Bill of Rights applies to any act or omission by or on behalf of any person or body in the performance of any public function, including an omission by Government to take appropriate steps to secure compliance with any provision of the Bill of Rights.

---

21. SCOPE OF EXCEPTIONS

---

21. Where the protection of any right or freedom by the Bill of Rights is subject to any restriction or qualification, that restriction or qualification —

  .1 has no wider effect than is strictly necessary in the circumstances; and

  .2 shall not be applied for any purpose other than that for which it has been prescribed.

---

22. INTERPRETATION

22.1 The Bill of Rights —

  .1 is intended to give effect in the United Kingdom to the International Covenant on Civil and Political Rights and the European Convention for the Protection of Human Rights and Fundamental Freedoms; and

  .2 shall be interpreted and applied accordingly, but without prejudice to any rights and freedoms protected by the Bill of Rights which are more extensive than those protected by the International Covenant or the European Convention.

22.2 Judicial notice shall be taken of —

  .1 the International Covenant on Civil and Political Rights and the European Convention on Human Rights;

.2 reports and expressions of views by the United Nations Human Rights Committee;

.3 reports of the European Commission of Human Rights; and

.4 judgments and advisory opinions of the European Court of Human Rights.

22.3 Any question as to the meaning or effect of the International Covenant or the European Convention shall be treated as a question of law and, in the case of the European Convention, shall be for determination as such in accordance with the principles laid down by, and any relevant decision of, the European Court of Human Rights.

23. RIGHTS UNDER OTHER AGREEMENTS

23. Nothing in this Chapter shall be interpreted as limiting or derogating from any of the human rights or fundamental freedoms which may be enjoyed under any other agreement to which the United Kingdom is a party.

24. ABUSE OF FREEDOMS

24. Nothing in the Bill of Rights shall be interpreted as implying for any group or person a right to engage in any activity or perform any act aimed at the destruction of any of the rights and freedoms set out therein.

Division 3: Remedies

25. Remedies

25. Without prejudice to any right to apply for judicial review, any person whose rights or freedoms protected by the Bill of Rights have been infringed or are threatened with infringement may

bring civil proceedings for damages, an injunction or any other relief authorised by Rules of Court.

---

26. HUMAN RIGHTS COMMISSION

26.1 There is established by this Constitution a Human Rights Commission —

.1 the composition of which shall be determined by Act of Parliament; and

.2 the members of which shall be appointed by the Minister of Justice on the recommendation of the Public Services Commission.

26.2 The Commission has the duty to encourage an understanding and acceptance of, and compliance with, the fundamental rights and freedoms guaranteed by the Bill of Rights.

26.3 The Commission —

.1 may investigate any act or practice which may be inconsistent with the Bill of Rights, whether on its own initiative or following a complaint; and

.2 has the appropriate powers to secure the attendance of witnesses and the production of documents.

26.4 The Commission has the power —

.1 to assist individual complainants in legal proceedings in relation to the Bill of Rights;

.2 to institute such legal proceedings, whether or not it has received a complaint.

26.5 The Commission may challenge the validity of any provision of an Act of Parliament or of an Assembly that, in its view, is inconsistent with or in contravention of the Bill of Rights, by initiating legal proceedings in the High Court, the Court of Session or the High Court for Northern Ireland, as the case requires.

26.6 The Commission may intervene in any proceedings that involve human rights issues, where it considers it appropriate, and with the leave of the court hearing the proceedings.

26.7 The Commission may examine legislation and proposed legislation for the purpose of ascertaining whether it is inconsistent with any of the provisions of the Bill of Rights and shall report any such inconsistency to Parliament.

26.8 The Commission shall report to Parliament on the action which, in its opinion, needs to be taken in order that there is compliance with the Bill of Rights or any relevant international instrument.

26.9 The Commission may prepare and publicise guidelines for the avoidance of acts or practices inconsistent with the Bill of Rights.

26.10 The Commission shall submit an annual report to Parliament.

PART 2: SOCIAL AND ECONOMIC RIGHTS

27. SOCIAL AND ECONOMIC RIGHTS

27.1 In making provision for the social and economic welfare of the people of the United Kingdom, Parliament and the Assemblies shall be guided by the principles contained in the International Covenants and Charters to which the United Kingdom is signatory, and in particular by —

.1 the right of workers to earn their living in an occupation freely entered upon;

.2 the right of everyone to an adequate standard of living, including adequate food, clothing and housing;

.3 the right of everyone to social security;

.4 the right of everyone to the enjoyment of the highest attainable standard of physical and mental health;

.5 the right of everyone to education;

.6 the right of workers to resort to collective action in the event of a conflict of interests, including the right to strike;

.7 the right of every worker to enjoy satisfactory health and safety conditions in their working environment.

27.2 Parliament and the Assemblies of Scotland and Northern Ireland shall—

.1 secure that the working of the legal system promotes justice on the basis of equality of access; and

.2 in particular, provide by law for legal aid and services to ensure that no one is prevented from securing justice by reason of economic or other disabilities.

27.3 The provisions of this Article are not enforceable in any court.

PART 3: FREEDOM OF INFORMATION

---
28. ACCESS TO OFFICIAL INFORMATION

28.1 There is a right of access by the public to the information held by any public authority performing functions with respect to the government of the United Kingdom, a nation or a region, or to local government.

28.2 This right is subject only to such limitations as are prescribed by law and are necessary in a democratic society—

.1 for the protection of national security;

.2 in the interests of law enforcement or the prevention and detection of crime;

.3 for the protection of personal privacy, legal privilege or commercial processes or transactions;

.4 to enable a public service to perform its constitutional functions or a public authority, when acting in the capacity of regulator, contractor or employer, to perform its functions.

28.3 Act of Parliament shall—

.1 prescribe the procedures to enable the right of access to official information to be readily exercised and enforced; and

.2 make provision for the appointment, powers and procedures of a Parliamentary Commissioner for Information.

28.4 The Commissioner —

.1 shall investigate refusals of access to official information and complaints of delay or obstruction in the granting of such access; and

.2 may require public authorities to give access to official information or to compensate for unwarranted delays in giving such access.

---

29. USE OF INFORMATION BY PUBLIC AUTHORITIES

29.1 Any person required by law to provide information to a public authority shall be informed of the purposes for which that information is required.

29.2 Any information so provided shall be used for those purposes only.

29.3 No such information shall be communicated to any other public authority unless —

.1 that communication is authorised by law; and

.2 at the time the information was required, the person from whom it was required was informed that it might be communicated to the other public authority and of the purposes for which it might be used by that other public authority.

29.4 Paragraph .3.2 does not apply where the communication of the information is sought for the purposes of investigating fraud or crime.

CHAPTER 3
Nationality

30. BRITISH NATIONALITY

30.1 There is established by this Constitution a new British nationality, the holders of which are known as British nationals.

30.2 Every person is a British national who, immediately before the coming into force of this Constitution, held the status of any of the following —

.1 British citizen;

.2 British Dependent Territories citizen;

.3 British Overseas citizen;

.4 British subject;

.5 British National (Overseas);

.6 British Protected Person.

30.3 Every person who is a British national by reason of paragraph .2 shall be treated as holding that nationality by descent, unless, immediately before the coming into force of this Constitution, the person held a status of —

.1 a British citizen otherwise than by descent; or

.2 a British Dependent Territories citizen otherwise than by descent.

31. ACQUISITION AND LOSS OF BRITISH NATIONALITY

31.1 .1 A person who is born in the United Kingdom, one of the other British Islands or a dependent territory after the coming into force of this Constitution acquires British nationality by birth.

.2 Such a person does not acquire British nationality if, at the time of the birth, —

.1 the mother or father possesses the immunity from suit and process accorded to an envoy of a foreign sovereign, and neither is a British national; or

.2 the mother or father is a national of a country at war with the United Kingdom and the birth occurs in a place occupied by that country.

31.2 A person who is born in any other place after the coming into force of this Constitution acquires British nationality by descent if, at the time of the birth, the mother or father is a British national otherwise than by descent.

31.3 Act of Parliament shall provide for, and regulate, acquisition (in particular, acquisition by adoption, descent, registration and naturalisation), loss and withdrawal of British nationality.

31.4 .1 British nationality shall not be withdrawn arbitrarily or so as to render the holder stateless, and shall be lost only in the circumstances prescribed by Act of Parliament.

.2 Act of Parliament shall provide for the right of any person from whom British nationality is withdrawn to apply for judicial review.

32. ALLEGIANCE AND DUAL NATIONALITY

32.1 Every person holding British nationality owes a duty of allegiance to this Constitution.

32.2 Nothing in this Chapter prevents a person who holds British nationality from holding the nationality or citizenship of another country.

32.3 Every person holding British nationality has the right of abode in any part of the United Kingdom.

33. CIVIC RIGHTS OF NON-NATIONALS

33. Act of Parliament —

.1 shall determine the extent to which persons under the jurisdiction of the United Kingdom who do not hold British nationality are entitled to the civic rights, and are subject to the civic duties, attached to British nationality; and

.2 may provide for the continued entitlement of citizens of the Republic of Ireland and of Commonwealth countries to rights to which they were entitled immediately before the coming into force of this Constitution.

CHAPTER 4

The Head of State

---

34. THE HEAD OF STATE

34.1 .1 There is established by this Constitution the office of Head of State of the United Kingdom, which is held by Her Majesty Queen Elizabeth II and her Heirs and Successors.

    .2 The Heirs and Successors are as determined by the Act of Settlement 1700, except that, in relation to persons born after the coming into force of this Constitution, the succession shall be in order of primogeniture without regard to gender or religion. *first born child*

    .3 Nothing in this Constitution prevents Her Majesty or any Heir or Successor from abdicating the office of Head of State in favour of the Heir to the Throne. *give up / renounce throne*

34.2 .1 If—

      .1 on Accession, the Head of State is under the age of 18 years; or

      .2 at any time the Head of State is incapable of performing the functions of the Head of State,

    those functions shall be performed in the name of and on behalf of the Head of State by a Regent, who shall be appointed as Act of Parliament shall prescribe, until the Head of State attains that age or ceases to be incapacitated.

    .2 Act of Parliament shall provide with respect to the performance of the functions of the Head of State in the case of absence from the United Kingdom, or the temporary incapacity, of the Head of State.

34.3 The Head of State is personally entitled to—

    .1 immunity from suit and legal process in any civil cause

in respect of all things done or omitted to be done by the Head of State in a private capacity and;

.2 immunity from criminal proceedings in respect of all things done or omitted to be done by the Head of State either in an official capacity or in a private capacity.

34.4 .1 Act of Parliament shall provide with respect to the annual sum for the income, maintenance and upkeep of the Head of State and of such members of the family of the Head of State as the Cabinet, after consultation with the Head of State, considers appropriate (referred to in this Constitution as the 'Civil List').

.2 The Head of State is entitled to immunity from taxation in respect of the Civil List.

34.5 The Head of State may, after considering such advice as may be given by the Prime Minister, appoint or dismiss such officers and other members of the Head of State's household as the Head of State considers necessary.

35. FUNCTIONS OF THE HEAD OF STATE

35.1 .1 After the coming into force of this Constitution, the functions of the Head of State, other than those of a ceremonial or formal nature, are derived only from this Constitution or Act of Parliament.

.2 In performance of any function under this Constitution or an Act of Parliament, the Head of State may act only as required or permitted by this Constitution or the Act of Parliament.

35.2 .1 In the performance of any function under this Constitution or Act of Parliament, the Head of State shall act in accordance with the advice of the Prime Minister, except where the Head of State is required thereunder to act —

.1 on the advice or recommendation of any person (when the Head of State shall act in accordance with that advice or recommendation); or

.2 after consultation with any person (when the Head of State shall act only after such consultation); or

.3 in the discretion of the Head of State (when the Head of State shall exercise an independent judgment); or

.4 in a way directed by this Constitution.

.2 If the Head of State so requests, the Prime Minister shall reconsider the advice given by him or her.

35.3 Where the Head of State is required by this Constitution or an Act of Parliament to act on the advice or recommendation of, or after consultation with, another person, no court shall consider —

.1 whether or by whom the advice or recommendation was given or whether and with whom the consultation took place; or

.2 the nature of the advice, recommendation or consultation; or

.3 whether the Head of State acted in accordance with the advice or recommendation.

---

36. DUTIES OF THE HEAD OF STATE

36.1 The Head of State shall —

.1 on the report of the Speaker of the House of Commons, appoint as the Prime Minister the person elected to that office by the House of Commons;

.2 accept the resignation of the Prime Minister when tendered by the Prime Minister;

.3 appoint to, and remove from, the office of Minister the persons whose names are submitted by the Prime Minister;

.4 signify Assent to all Bills which, in accordance with this Constitution and the law and custom of Parliament, have passed through their stages in Parliament and are presented to the Head of State for Assent;

.5 appoint such military officers, members of a public service and other persons whose appointments are, under this Constitution or an Act of Parliament, required to be made by the Head of State;

.6 confer such honours, awards, decorations and distinctions upon such persons as are recommended by the Prime Minister;

.7 prorogue and dissolve Parliament.

36.2 The Head of State is the supreme commander of all the Armed Forces of the United Kingdom but shall exercise powers in relation thereto only in accordance with this Constitution or Act of Parliament.

37. PERSONAL POWERS OF THE HEAD OF STATE

37.1 The Head of State may —

.1 give advice and make comments upon affairs of state and the governance of the United Kingdom to the Prime Minister and to other Ministers;

.2 confer honours, awards, decorations and distinctions that are within the personal gift of the Head of State;

.3 make public statements in right of the office of Head of the Commonwealth.

37.2 .1 The Head of State shall exercise the powers in this Article in the discretion of the Head of State and shall not be obliged to seek or comply with any advice before so doing.

.2 In exercising a power under this Article, the Head of State shall not manifest a preference, directly or indirectly, for any political party.

37.3 No court shall consider, in relation to the exercise by the Head of State of any power under this Article, —

.1 whether and to whom the Head of State offered advice or whether and by whom advice was given to the Head of State;

.2 whether the Head of State has manifested any preference for a political party.

38. THE POWER OF MERCY

38.   The Head of State, acting on the advice of the Minister of Justice, may —

.1 grant a pardon, either free or subject to lawful conditions, to a person convicted of an offence; or

.2 grant a delay, either indefinite or for a specified period, from the enforcement of any sentence or order imposed on a person for an offence; or

.3 substitute a less severe form of punishment for any punishment imposed on a person for an offence; or

.4 remit the whole or part of any punishment imposed on a person for an offence or of any penalty, fine or forfeiture otherwise due to the Government on account of an offence.

39. THE PRIVY COUNCIL

39.1 .1 There is established by this Constitution a Privy Council, the members of which consist of —

.1 the Heir to the Throne;

.2 persons who hold or have held any of the following offices —

.1 Speaker of either House of Parliament;

.2 Prime Minister;

.3 member of the Cabinet;

.4 Leader of the Opposition;

.3 such other persons as may be appointed, for life, to be members by the Head of State on the advice of the Prime Minister.

39.2 .1 Orders in Council under this Constitution or Act of Parliament shall be made by the Head of State acting in accordance with the advice of the Privy Council.

.2 The Privy Council shall perform such other functions as Act of Parliament may prescribe.

CHAPTER 5
The Executive

Division 1: The Government of the United Kingdom

40. THE EXECUTIVE POWER FOR THE UNITED KINGDOM

40.1 The executive power for the United Kingdom is vested in, and, subject to this Constitution, shall be exercised by, the Government of the United Kingdom.

40.2 There is established by this Constitution a Government for the United Kingdom, which shall comprise —

.1 the Prime Minister; and

.2 the members of Parliament appointed as the Ministers of the Government.

40.3 The Government has all the rights, powers and capacities of a person of full age and capacity, in addition to the rights, powers and capacities conferred by this Constitution and by or under Act of Parliament.

40.4 The Government may act through the Cabinet, the appropriate Minister or any member of the public service for the United Kingdom duly authorised by the Cabinet or a Minister.

41. THE PRIME MINISTER

41.1 .1 There is established by this Constitution the office of Prime Minister.

.2 The Prime Minister shall be elected by the House of Commons from among its members.

41.2 The Prime Minister ceases to hold office—

.1 if he or she ceases to be a member of the House of Commons for any reason other than the expiry or dissolution of the House; or

.2 on the receipt by the Head of State of a letter of resignation from the Prime Minister; or

.3 when a new election to the office is completed; or

.4 if a motion of no confidence in the Prime Minister is passed by a majority of all the members of the House of Commons, or a motion for the confidence of the House of Commons in the Prime Minister defaults.

42. DEPUTY PRIME MINISTER

42.1 The Prime Minister shall appoint a Deputy Prime Minister from among the members of the Cabinet who are members of the House of Commons.

42.2 The Deputy Prime Minister shall perform the functions of the Prime Minister when the Prime Minister is for any reason unable to perform them or the office of Prime Minister is vacant.

43. MINISTERS

43.1 .1 There are established under this Constitution such number of offices of Minister as the Prime Minister from time to time determines.

.2 Appointments to these offices shall be made, from among members of Parliament, by the Head of State on the advice of the Prime Minister.

.3 The Ministers shall include—

.1 a Chancellor of the Exchequer (having responsibility for finance);

.2 a Minister of Justice (having responsibility for courts and legal services);

.3 a Minister having responsibility for international relations,

who shall be appointed from among members of the House of Commons.

43.2 A Minister shall be responsible for the conduct of such business of government and for the administration of, or within, such department of government as the Prime Minister assigns to the Minister.

43.3 A Minister ceases to hold office —

.1 if he or she ceases to be a member of a House of Parliament for any reason other than the expiry or dissolution of the House; or

.2 if removed from office by the Head of State, acting on the advice of the Prime Minister; or

.3 on the receipt by the Prime Minister of a letter of resignation from the Minister; or

.4 when a new election to the office of Prime Minister is completed.

---

44. THE CABINET

44.1 There is established by this Constitution a Cabinet which consists of —

.1 the Prime Minister;

.2 the Chancellor of the Exchequer; and

.3 the Minister of Justice; and

.4 the Minister responsible for international relations; and

.5 such other Ministers as the Prime Minister appoints.

44.2 The Cabinet —

.1 has the general direction and control of the government of the United Kingdom; and

.2 is collectively responsible to Parliament for the performance by the Government of its functions.

44.3 .1 The Cabinet may appoint such committees as it considers necessary, or are required, to assist the Cabinet in the discharge of its responsibilities.

.2 The purpose, membership, terms of reference and duration of the committees shall be reported to Parliament by the Prime Minister.

45. MINISTERIAL RESPONSIBILITY

45.1 The Prime Minister shall keep Parliament and the Head of State fully informed about all matters pertaining to the conduct of government.

45.2 A Minister shall—

.1 exercise general direction and control over all matters within the area of responsibility assigned to that Minister; and

.2 render a full and regular account to Parliament and its committees concerning those matters.

45.3 .1 As soon as practicable after appointment, a Minister shall—

.1 lay before Parliament a full description of the responsibilities assigned to the Minister; and

.2 indicate, with reasons, any matter concerning which the Minister may be unwilling to give a full account to Parliament.

.2 A Minister shall inform Parliament of any significant change in those responsibilities or with respect to any matter for which the Minister may be unwilling to give such an account.

46. CODE OF MINISTERIAL CONDUCT

46.1 The Prime Minister shall lay before Parliament a Code of Conduct for Ministers.

46.2 The Code, and any amendments to the Code, shall take effect when approved by resolutions of both Houses of Parliament, and is binding on all Ministers.

46.3 The Integrity Committee of the Constitutional Commission may investigate any alleged breach of the Code of Conduct by a Minister in accordance with Article 77.

Division 2: Legal officers

---
47. ATTORNEY-GENERAL

47.1 There is established by this Constitution the office of Attorney-General.

47.2 The Attorney-General shall be appointed by the Prime Minister from among persons who —

.1 are not members of Parliament; and

.2 have rights of audience, or are entitled to conduct litigation, in the superior courts of any part of the United Kingdom.

47.3 Act of Parliament shall provide for the conditions of service in respect of the office, but the Attorney-General ceases to hold office —

.1 if he or she ceases to have a qualification for appointment to the office; or

.2 if removed from office by the Prime Minister; or

.3 on the receipt by the Prime Minister of a letter of resignation from the Attorney-General; or

.4 when a new election to the office of Prime Minister is completed.

47.4 The Attorney-General —

.1 is the principal legal adviser to the Government; and

.2 has responsibility, on behalf of the Government, with respect to the conduct of litigation to which the Government is a party.

47.5 The Attorney-General shall attend, but shall not vote at, meetings of the Cabinet.

---

48. DIRECTOR OF PUBLIC PROSECUTIONS

48.1 .1 There is established by this Constitution, within the Ministry of Justice, the office of Director of Public Prosecutions.

.2 Act of the Assembly for Scotland shall establish and make provision with respect to an office for Scotland with equivalent powers.

.3 Act of the Assembly for Northern Ireland shall establish and make provision with respect to an office of Director of Public Prosecutions for Northern Ireland with equivalent powers.

48.2 The Director of Public Prosecutions shall be appointed by the Minister of Justice, acting in accordance with the recommendation of the Judicial Services Commission for England and Wales, from persons having rights of audience in the superior courts of the United Kingdom.

48.3 The holders of the offices established by or under this Article have the same tenure as a judge under Article 108, and the provisions of Parts 3 and 4 of Chapter 9 with respect to complaints relating to judges and the removal of judges apply as if those office-holders were judges.

48.4 The Director of Public Prosecutions has the power, where the Director considers it in the public interest —

.1 to institute and undertake criminal proceedings before any United Kingdom court or any court in England or Wales (other than a court trying offences by members of the Armed Forces);

.2 to consent or refuse consent to the institution of any such proceedings for which the consent of the Director is required by law;

.3 to take over and continue any such criminal proceedings instituted by another person or authority;

.4 to discontinue, at any stage before a decision is announced, any such criminal proceedings (other than an appeal by the person convicted), whether instituted or undertaken by the Director or by another person or authority.

48.5 .1 The powers in paragraphs .4.2 to .4.4 are vested in the Director of Public Prosecutions to the exclusion of any other person or authority.

.2 The powers of the Director under paragraph .4 are not subject to the direction or control of any other person or authority, but before exercising the power of consent under paragraph .4.2, the Director shall consult the Attorney-General.

48.6 The powers of the Director of Public Prosecutions under paragraph .4 may be exercised by the Director personally or through other persons, who shall act in accordance with any general or specific instructions of the Director.

49. DIRECTOR OF CIVIL PROCEEDINGS

49.1 .1 There is established by this Constitution, within the Ministry of Justice, the office of Director of Civil Proceedings.

.2 Act of the Assemblies for Scotland and Northern Ireland shall establish and make provision with respect to an office for Scotland and for Northern Ireland with equivalent powers.

49.2 The Director of Civil Proceedings shall be appointed by the Minister of Justice, acting in accordance with the recommendation of the Judicial Services Commission for England and Wales, from persons having rights of audience in the superior courts of the United Kingdom.

49.3 The holders of the offices established by or under this Article have the same tenure as a judge under Article 108, and the provisions of Parts 3 and 4 of Chapter 9 with respect to complaints relating to judges and the removal of judges apply as if those office-holders were judges.

49.4 The Director of Civil Proceedings has the power, where the Director considers it in the public interest, —

.1 to institute and, with the leave of the court, to intervene in, civil proceedings before any United Kingdom court or any court in England or Wales, and in particular, any proceedings —

.1 in connection with any contravention of the Bill of Rights or other provisions of this Constitution; or

.2 as a result of which the compliance of the United Kingdom with obligations under the law of the European Community or under treaty may come in issue;

.3 for judicial review;

which, in the opinion of the Director, give rise to issues of public importance;

.2 to consent or refuse consent to the institution of any proceedings for which the consent of the Director is required by law.

49.5 .1 The power in paragraph .4 is vested in the Director of Civil Proceedings to the exclusion of any other person or authority.

.2 The powers of the Director under paragraph .4 are not subject to the direction or control of any other person or authority, but before exercising the power of consent under paragraph .4.2, the Director shall consult the Attorney-General.

49.6 The powers of the Director of Civil Proceedings under paragraph .4 may be exercised by the Director personally or through other persons, who shall act in accordance with any general or specific instructions of the Director.

Division 3: International relations

---
50. EUROPEAN COMMUNITY LAW
---

50.   The law of the European Community has effect in the United Kingdom as provided by sections 1 to 3 of the European Communities Act 1972 (as amended by the European Communities (Amendment) Act 1986), and those sections have effect as part of this Constitution.

---
51. INTERNATIONAL RELATIONS

51.1   The Government —

    .1 shall conduct the international relations of the United Kingdom; and

    .2 subject to this Constitution and Acts of Parliament, has all necessary powers for that purpose, including the powers to maintain diplomatic representatives abroad and to receive in the United Kingdom diplomatic representatives from other states.

51.2   No treaty concluded by the Government of the United Kingdom shall be binding upon the United Kingdom, unless —

    .1 the treaty is laid before Parliament; and

    .2 within 3 months after it has been so laid, each House of Parliament, by resolution, authorises the Government to give consent for the United Kingdom to be bound as a party to the treaty.

51.3   A treaty to which the Government has given consent under the authority of such resolutions has effect, on coming into force, as part of the domestic law of the United Kingdom to the extent that it is capable of having such effect.

51.4   For the purpose of this Article, the expression 'treaty' means an agreement in writing, governed by international law, between the United Kingdom and another state or an organisation of which only states are members.

CHAPTER 6

The Legislatures

PART 1: THE LEGISLATIVE POWER

52. THE LEGISLATIVE POWER

52.1 The legislative power in the United Kingdom is vested in Parliament and the Assemblies.

52.2 The division of competence between Parliament and the Assemblies is as determined by this Constitution.

52.3 .1 Nothing in this Constitution prevents an Act of Parliament or of an Assembly conferring legislative functions upon another authority.

.2 No Bill may be passed by Parliament or by an Assembly which transfers permanently, or divests Parliament or the Assembly of, legislative power.

53. EXCLUSIVE LEGISLATION POWERS OF PARLIAMENT

53.1 Parliament has exclusive powers to make laws with respect to —

.1 the seat of government of the United Kingdom and all places acquired by the Government of the United Kingdom for public purposes;

.2 matters relating to any department, authority or agency which, by this Constitution, is under the Government of the United Kingdom;

.3 other matters declared by this Constitution to be within the exclusive power of Parliament, which include —

.1 the Constitution, including the Head of State, Parliament, elections and the courts of the United Kingdom and of England and Wales;

.2 membership of the European Community, the British Islands outside the United Kingdom and the dependent territories, Commonwealth and international relations;

.3 the Armed Forces, civil defence and national security;

.4 citizenship, nationality and immigration;

.5 taxation and social security;

.6 coinage, legal tender, interest rates and credit, banking and insurance;

.7 postal services and telecommunications;

.8 matters affecting the freedom of trade and commerce within the United Kingdom and trade outside the United Kingdom.

53.2 Parliament has exclusive power to legislate where legislation is required to give effect, as part of the domestic law of the United Kingdom, to —

1. treaties; or

2. European Community obligations.

53.3 Parliament may, by Act of Parliament, delegate to an Assembly the power to legislate on any matter that is within the exclusive legislative powers of Parliament.

---

54. LEGISLATIVE POWERS OF ASSEMBLIES

54.1 The Assemblies have powers to make laws, in relation to their nation or region, with respect to the following matters —

.1 agriculture and fisheries;

.2 arts and leisure;

.3 education;

.4 energy;

.5 the environment;

.6 health;

.7 housing;

.8 local government;

.9 regional policy and development;

.10 social welfare;

.11 trade and industry;

.12 transport.

54.2 The Assemblies for Scotland and Northern Ireland, in addition, have powers to make laws, in relation to their nation, with respect to the following matters—

.1 the courts and legal services;

.2 tribunals and inquiries;

.3 civil law;

.4 crime;

.5 police and prisons.

54.3 A law made by an Assembly may amend or repeal a provision of law made by or under an Act of Parliament before the coming into force of this Constitution.

54.4 It is not within the powers of an Assembly to make any provision of law which—

.1 extends to any part of the United Kingdom beyond the national or regional boundaries of that Assembly, except in the case of the Assemblies of Wales and the regions of England, in so far as is necessary to enable legal proceedings to be brought to enforce the provision;

.2 has the effect of amending this Constitution;

.3 is inconsistent with any provision of European Community law.

55. CONCURRENT LEGISLATIVE POWERS

55.1 Parliament may make laws with respect to any matter that is within the legislative powers of the Assemblies under Article 54, if —

   .1 that matter cannot be adequately regulated by an individual Assembly; or

   .2 the regulation of a matter by an Assembly would prejudice the interests or interfere with the rights of citizens of other parts of the United Kingdom.

55.2 Unless Act of Parliament otherwise expressly provides, a matter with respect to which Parliament has made a law under this Article shall be within the executive powers of national, regional or local authorities.

56. CONFLICTS OF LEGISLATION

56. Subject to Article 54.3, if an Act of an Assembly is inconsistent with an Act of Parliament —

   .1 the Act of Parliament prevails; and

   .2 the Act of the Assembly, to the extent of the inconsistency, is void.

PART 2: PARLIAMENT

Division 1: Composition of Parliament

57. PARLIAMENT

57.1 There is established by this Constitution a Parliament for the United Kingdom, which consists of the Head of State, the House of Commons and the Second Chamber.

57.2 Parliament —

.1 subject to this Constitution, may make laws for the peace, order and good government of the United Kingdom; and

.2 shall hold the Government of the United Kingdom to account.

---

58. MEMBERSHIP

58.1 The elections for members of Parliament shall —

.1 be conducted in accordance with this Constitution and the electoral law made under Article 83;

.2 be held at the times prescribed in Part 3 of Schedule 3; and

.3 be supervised by the Electoral Commission.

58.2 The House of Commons shall be composed of not more than 525, and not fewer than 475, members, as determined by Act of Parliament.

58.3 The Second Chamber shall be composed of not more than 265, and not fewer than 225, members, as determined by Act of Parliament.

58.4 No member of a House of Parliament may stand for election to, or sit as a member of, the other House.

58.5 The number of members of a House of Parliament who hold ministerial office shall not exceed one-tenth of the membership of that House.

58.6 The right of members of the Houses of Parliament to vote in Parliament shall be exercised in person.

---

59. QUALIFICATIONS AND DISQUALIFICATIONS FOR MEMBERSHIP

59.1 A person is qualified for election as a member of either House of Parliament if that person is entitled under Article 83.2 to vote in elections for Parliament.

59.2 No person is qualified for election as a member of either House of Parliament, if that person—

.1 is not a British national;

.2 holds or is acting in any office in the public service under the Government or is a full-time member of the judiciary, the regular Armed Forces or the police;

.3 is an undischarged bankrupt;

.4 is detained under the provisions of any law on the ground of suffering from mental illness;

.5 is serving a sentence of imprisonment for more than one year, or an indefinite sentence, following conviction for a criminal offence;

.6 holds or is acting in any office the function of which involves any responsibility for, or in connection with, the conduct of any election for Parliament or the compilation or revision of any electoral register;

.7 is disqualified for membership of Parliament under any law by reason of having been convicted of any offence connected with an election for Parliament.

59.3 The seat of a member of a House of Parliament becomes vacant—

.1 upon the next expiry or dissolution of that House after the election of the member; or

.2 on the receipt by the Speaker of that House of a letter of resignation from the member; or

.3 if the member is expelled by resolution of that House for misconduct or for persistent neglect of Parliamentary duties;

.4 if any other circumstances arise which would cause the member, if he or she were not a member, to be disqualified from election as a member of that House.

60. EXPIRY AND DISSOLUTION OF HOUSES OF PARLIAMENT

60.1　The term of each House of Parliament is 4 years, which expires 21 days before the date upon which the election for that House is required by Part 3 of Schedule 3.

60.2　If, within 20 parliamentary days following the passing of a motion of no confidence in the Prime Minister, the House of Commons fails to elect a Prime Minister, the Head of State shall dissolve the House of Commons forthwith, by Proclamation.

60.3　If a motion of no confidence in the Government is passed by the House of Commons, or a motion for the confidence of the House of Commons in the Government defaults, the Head of State shall dissolve the House of Commons within the 7 days following, by Proclamation.

60.4　The term of the House of Commons summoned after the general election immediately following a dissolution is the remainder of the term of the previous House of Commons.

60.5　.1 On the same day that the term of a House ends, whether by expiry or dissolution, the Head of State shall summon a new House, by Proclamation.

.2 The meeting of the new House shall be held within one month of the general election at such time as the Proclamation shall appoint.

60.6　For the purposes of this Constitution, the expression 'parliamentary days' means days on which either House of Parliament meets, and includes days comprised in any period of not more than 4 days when both Houses are adjourned.

Division 2: Powers and procedure

61. POWERS AND PRIVILEGES OF PARLIAMENT

61.1　.1 Each House of Parliament, and its members, have the rights, powers, privileges and jurisdiction vested in the corresponding House, or its members, immediately prior to the coming into force of this Constitution, except to the extent that they are altered by, or are inconsistent with, this Constitution or Act of Parliament passed after this Constitution comes into force.

.2 The rights and privileges of members apply notwithstanding the Bill of Rights, contained in Chapter 2.

61.2 The freedom of speech and debates or proceedings in Parliament shall not to be impeached or questioned in any court or place out of Parliament.

61.3 Each House of Parliament may regulate its own procedure, and for that purpose may make standing orders.

61.4 Each House of Parliament has the power to send for persons, papers and records, and this power may be delegated by the House to its committees.

---

62. THE SPEAKERS

62.1 At its first meeting after the summoning of a new House of Parliament and before proceeding to the despatch of any other business, that House shall elect one of its members, other than a Minister, to be the Speaker of that House.

62.2 If the office of Speaker in either House falls vacant at any time before the expiry of the House, that House shall, as soon as practicable, elect another such member of the House to the office.

62.3 Standing orders of each House shall—

.1 provide for deputies to the Speaker; and

.2 regulate proceedings connected with the election of the Speaker and deputies.

.3 provide for the appointment of a Counsel to the Speaker who shall provide such legal advice as the Speaker, a deputy to the Speaker or the House may require.

62.4 A certificate that is endorsed on any Bill by the Speaker of the House of Commons or the Speaker of the Second Chamber, and in particular on a Money Bill under Article 67, a public Bill under Article 68, a Bill for the amendment of the Constitution under Article 69, or a Constitutional Bill under Article 70, is conclusive and its validity shall not be considered by any court, other than the Supreme Court.

63. SALARIES AND FACILITIES

63.1 Members of the Houses of Parliament shall receive salaries and pensions and facilities appropriate to the full time performance of their responsibilities.

63.2 Standing orders of both Houses shall ensure that the time and hours of their sittings have regard to the needs of all persons who are eligible to be members.

64. DECLARATIONS OF INTEREST

64.1 In any debate or proceeding of either House or of any of its committees or in transactions or communications which a member may have with other members of Parliament or with Ministers or with members of a public service, the member shall disclose any relevant pecuniary interest or benefit of whatever nature, whether direct or indirect, that he or she may have had, may have, or may be expecting to have.

64.2 .1 Each House of Parliament shall maintain a Register of Members' Interests, which shall be available for public inspection.

.2 There shall be established a joint Select Committee of both Houses to examine, and make recommendations to Parliament on, matters connected with the Register.

Division 3: Legislative powers

---
65. INTRODUCTION OF BILLS

65.1 .1 A Bill for a Public General Act (referred to in this Constitution as a 'public Bill'), other than a Money Bill, may be introduced in either House by any member.

.2 Subject to this Constitution, a public Bill becomes law when it is passed by the affirmative vote of a majority of the members of both Houses of Parliament, sitting separately, and the Assent of the Head of State is signified.

65.2 The presentation, and procedure for enactment, of Bills for Local and Personal Acts shall be regulated by standing orders of both Houses.

65.3 Except on the recommendation or with the consent of the Cabinet, signified by a Minister, neither House of Parliament shall—

.1 proceed with any Bill (including any amendment to a Bill) which, in the opinion of the person presiding, makes provision for any of the following purposes—

.1 for imposing, increasing, reducing or abolishing any tax;

.2 for imposing or increasing any charge on the Consolidated Fund, or other public fund or the public revenue, of the United Kingdom, or for altering any such charge otherwise than by reducing it; or

.3 for compounding or remitting any debt due to the Government;

.2 proceed upon any motion (including any amendment to a motion) the effect of which, in the opinion of the person presiding, would be to make provision for any of those purposes; or

.3 receive any petition which, in the opinion of the person presiding, requests that provision be made for any of those purposes.

65.4 The validity of the proceedings leading to the enactment of an Act of Parliament shall not be considered by any court.

65.5 The words of enactment for public Bills shall be as set out in Schedule 6.

66. SUBORDINATE LEGISLATION

66.1 A Standing Committee shall be established by each House of Parliament which shall examine and, where in the opinion of the Committee it is necessary, report to the House with respect to —

.1 an enabling provision in any public Bill presented to the House which delegates legislative power; and

.2 any subordinate legislation laid before the House which, in the opinion of the Committee —

.1 imposes or prescribes a charge on the public revenues of the United Kingdom; or

.2 requires payment to be made for any licence or consent or other service from a public body; or

.3 is made under an enactment excluding it from challenge in the courts; or

.4 purports to have retrospective effect where the enactment under which it is made does not so provide; or

.5 has been unjustifiably delayed in publication or in being laid before Parliament; or

.6 has not been duly notified to the Speaker where it comes into effect before being laid before Parliament; or

.7 gives rise to doubts whether it is *intra vires* or appears to make an unusual or unexpected use of the powers conferred by the enactment under which it is made; or

.8 requires elucidation as to its form or purport or is defective in drafting.

66.2 Nothing in this Constitution shall be construed as affecting the power of either House of Parliament to annul subordinate legislation that is subject to annulment by resolution of either House, or to disapprove subordinate legislation that is subject to approval by resolution of either House.

---

67. RESTRICTIONS ON POWERS OF SECOND CHAMBER AS TO MONEY BILLS

67.1 If a Money Bill, that has been passed by the House of Commons and sent to the Second Chamber at least 30 parliamentary days before the end of the session, is not passed by the Second Chamber, without amendment, within 30 parliamentary days after it is sent, the Bill shall —

.1 unless the House of Commons otherwise directs, be presented to the Head of State for Assent; and

.2 become an Act of Parliament on Assent being signified,

notwithstanding that the Second Chamber has not consented to the Bill.

67.2 .1 For the purposes of this Constitution, the expression 'Money Bill' means a public Bill which, in the opinion of the Speaker of the House of Commons, contains only provisions dealing with all or any of the following matters —

.1 the imposition, repeal, remission, alteration, or regulation of taxation;

.2 the imposition, for the payment of debt or other financial purposes, of charges on the Consolidated Fund, the National Loans Fund or on money appropriated by Parliament, or the variation or repeal of any such charges;

.3 supply;

.4 the appropriation, receipt, custody, issue or audit of accounts of public money;

.5 the raising or guarantee of any loan or the repayment thereof;

.6 matters incidental to those matters or any of them.

.2 For the purposes of this Article, the expressions 'taxation', 'public money' and 'loan' do not include, respectively, taxation, money or loan raised by an Assembly or local authority.

67.3 There shall be endorsed on a Money Bill presented to the Head of State for Assent the certificate of the Speaker of the House of Commons, signed by the Speaker, that the Bill is a Money Bill.

---

68. RESTRICTIONS ON POWERS OF SECOND CHAMBER AS TO CERTAIN BILLS

68.1 This Article—

.1 applies to any public Bill which has been passed by the House of Commons, after considering the Bill as passed by the Second Chamber, and which is sent back to the Second Chamber;

.2 does not apply to a Money Bill, a Bill for the amendment of the Constitution or a Constitutional Bill.

68.2 If a Bill to which this Article applies is rejected by the Second Chamber, then, subject to this Article, the Bill shall—

.1 if the House of Commons so resolves, be presented to the Head of State for Assent; and

.2 become an Act of Parliament on Assent being signified,

notwithstanding that the Second Chamber has not consented to the Bill.

68.3 A resolution under this Article shall not be moved in the House of Commons until a period of delay of 12 calendar months has elapsed—

.1 from the day on which the Bill was rejected by the Second Chamber; or

.2 if the Bill was so rejected more than 120 parliamentary days after being sent to that House, from the last of those days.

68.4 .1 A resolution under this Article may be passed, and the Assent of the Head of State may be signified accordingly, notwithstanding any prorogation or the expiry or dissolution of either House during the period of delay.

.2 In that case, the resolution shall not take effect unless passed within 30 parliamentary days after the end of the period of delay or the first meeting of the new House, as the case may be.

68.5 For the purposes of this Article, a Bill is rejected by the Second Chamber in the following circumstances (and not otherwise) —

.1 if a motion for the rejection of the Bill is carried, or a motion at any stage that the Bill be read or be passed is rejected or amended, by the Second Chamber;

.2 if the Bill is passed by the Second Chamber with substantive provisions that are not identical with those in the Bill sent back to it by the House of Commons;

.3 if, after 120 parliamentary days beginning on the day on which the Bill was sent back to the Second Chamber and in the session in which it was so sent —

.1 a motion relevant to the progress of the Bill in the Second Chamber and expressed to be made pursuant to this Article, is proposed by the member in charge of the Bill and is rejected by the Second Chamber; or

.2 the House of Commons resolves, on a motion of which at least 10 parliamentary days' notice has been given, that the Bill be treated for the purposes of this Article as rejected by the Second Chamber.

68.6 The date on which a Bill is rejected by the Second Chamber shall be endorsed on the Bill by the Clerk of the Parliaments or, if the Bill is then in the possession of the House of Commons, by the Clerk of that House.

68.7 On the expiration of the period of delay, the Bill shall, unless it is then in the possession of the House of Commons, be returned to that House.

68.8 A Bill shall not be presented to the Head of State for Assent under this Article, unless there is endorsed upon it the certificate of the Speaker of the House of Commons, signed by him, that this Article has been complied with.

Division 4: Constitutional amendments and legislation

69. AMENDMENT TO THE CONSTITUTION

69.1   .1 Parliament may, by Act of Parliament, amend any of the following provisions of this Constitution —

.1 this Article;

.2 Chapters 1, 2 and 3;

.3 Articles 34 to 36 in Chapter 4;

.4 Articles 40, 41, 44, 47 to 49 and 50 in Chapter 5;

.5 Articles 52 to 57 and 70 in Chapter 6;

.6 Articles 78 and 79 and Schedules 1 and 2;

.7 Articles 83 to 86, 88 and 89 in Chapter 8 and Part 1 of Schedule 3;

.8 Chapter 9 and Schedule 4 and Chapters 5, 10, 11 and 12.

.2 The Bill for the Act is passed if, at its final reading, it is supported by the votes of —

.1 not less than two-thirds of all the members of the House of Commons; and

.2 not less than two-thirds of all the members of the Second Chamber.

69.2   .1 Parliament may, by Act of Parliament, amend any of the provisions of this Constitution not mentioned in paragraph .1.

.2 The Bill for the Act is passed if, at its final reading, it is supported by the votes of —

.1 not less than two-thirds of the members of the House of Commons present and voting, where that two-thirds is not less than half of all the members of the House of Commons; and

.2 not less than two-thirds of the members of the Second Chamber present and voting, where that two-thirds is not less than half of all the members of the Second Chamber.

69.3 A Bill for the amendment of any provisions of Articles 53 to 55 or of Chapter 7, which has been passed in accordance with paragraph .1 or .2, as the case may be, shall not be presented to the Head of State for Assent unless it has been ratified by at least two-thirds of the Assemblies, by the affirmative votes of a majority of the members present and voting in each such Assembly.

69.4 .1 A Bill for the amendment of this Constitution—

.1 which provides that any part of the United Kingdom should cease to be so; and

.2 which has been passed in accordance with paragraph .1,

shall not be presented to the Head of State for Assent unless it has been approved by a majority of the registered voters in that part of the United Kingdom voting in a referendum held solely for that purpose.

.2 Act of Parliament shall provide for the holding of referenda for that purpose.

.3 The conduct of the referendum shall be under the supervision of the Electoral Commission.

69.5 A Bill for the amendment of this Constitution shall not be presented to the Head of State for Assent unless there is endorsed upon it, as the case may require—

.1 a certificate of the Speaker of the House of Commons, signed by the Speaker, that paragraph .1.2.1 or .2.2.1, .3 or .4 has been complied with; and

.2 a certificate of the Speaker of the Second Chamber, signed by the Speaker, that paragraph .1.2.2 or .2.2.2 has been complied with.

69.6 For the purpose of this Constitution, the expression 'amendment', in relation to this Constitution or any Article or provision of any Article, includes—

.1 revocation, with or without re-enactment, or the making of different provision in lieu;

.2 modification, whether by omitting, or altering, or inserting additional provision, or otherwise; and

.3 suspension of operation for any period or the termination of any such suspension.

69.7 Nothing in this Article affects the terms of Article I of the Anglo-Irish Agreement 1985, or section 1 and Schedule 1 of the Northern Ireland Constitution Act 1973 for such time as these measures are in force.

70. CONSTITUTIONAL BILLS

70.1 A Constitutional Bill shall not be presented to the Head of State for Assent unless it is passed, at its final reading in both the House of Commons and the Second Chamber, by a majority of all the members of the House.

70.2 If a Constitutional Bill, which has been passed by one House of Parliament, is not passed by the other House, the Bill shall be returned to the House by which it was passed, endorsed with the certificate of the Speaker of the other House, signed by the Speaker, that the Bill is a Constitutional Bill.

70.3 For the purposes of this Constitution, the expression 'Constitutional Bill' means a public Bill which, in the opinion of the Speaker of the Second Chamber, whilst not containing an amendment to the Constitution,

.1 is required by or under this Constitution to be enacted; or

.2 gives detailed effect to any Article of the Constitution; or

.3 affects any Article of the Bill of Rights, contained in Chapter 2; or

.4 affects the functions of the Head of State or the composition, powers or jurisdiction of the House of Commons, the Second Chamber, the Assemblies, the Supreme Court or the judiciary;

and the expression 'Constitutional legislation' shall be construed accordingly.

Division 5: Public finance

71. PUBLIC FUNDS

71.1 There are established by this Constitution a Consolidated Fund and a National Loans Fund for the United Kingdom.

71.2 All revenues or other sums raised or received for the purposes of the government of the United Kingdom shall be paid into the Consolidated Fund, except revenues or other sums raised or received which, under this Constitution or another law, are payable into the National Loans Fund or another public fund established for a specific purpose.

71.3 No sums shall be withdrawn from the Consolidated Fund except —

.1 to meet expenditure that is charged upon the Consolidated Fund by this Constitution or another law; or

.2 where the issue of the sums has been authorised by an Appropriation Act or under this Constitution.

71.4 .1 All public funds, other than the Consolidated Fund and the National Loans Fund, shall be established and authorised by Act of Parliament.

.2 No sums shall be withdrawn from the National Loans Fund or any public fund so established, unless the issue of those sums has been authorised by or under an Act of Parliament.

71.5 .1 The public debt of the United Kingdom shall be a charge upon the Consolidated Fund, the National Loans Fund and such other public funds as may be established in accordance with paragraph .4.

.2 The expression 'public debt' includes interest on that debt, the repayment of that debt, charges in respect of public funds, and all expenditure, costs, and charges in connection with the management of that debt.

72. CONTINGENCIES FUND

72.1 Act of Parliament may—

.1 provide for the establishment of a Contingencies Fund; and

.2 authorise the Chancellor of the Exchequer to make advances from that Fund to meet any urgent and unforeseen need for expenditure for which no other provision exists.

72.2 Where an advance is made from the Contingencies Fund, a supplementary estimate shall be presented and a supplementary Appropriation Bill shall be introduced as soon as possible for the purpose of replacing the amount so advanced.

72.3 The Treasury shall authorise the necessary arrangements for the accounting of all moneys authorised to be paid out of the Contingencies Fund.

73. APPROPRIATION

73.1 .1 The Chancellor of the Exchequer shall cause to be prepared and laid before the House of Commons in each financial year estimates of the revenues and expenditure of the United Kingdom for the next following financial year.

.2 The estimates of expenditure shall show separately—

.1 the total sums required to meet expenditure charged on the Consolidated Fund; and

.2 the sums required to meet other expenditure.

73.2 .1 When the estimates of expenditure have been approved by the House of Commons, a public Bill, known as an Appropriation Bill, shall be introduced into the House of Commons, which shall provide for the issue from the Consolidated Fund of the sums (other than sums charged on the Consolidated Fund) necessary to meet that expenditure and for the appropriation of those sums for the purposes specified therein.

.2 Estimates of expenditure charged upon the Consolidated Fund shall not be voted upon by the House of Commons.

73.3 If, in respect of any financial year, it is found that —

.1 the sum appropriated by the Appropriation Act for any purpose is insufficient; or

.2 a need has arisen for expenditure for a purpose for which no amount has been appropriated by the Act; or

.3 sums have been expended for any purpose in excess of the amount appropriated for the purpose by the Appropriation Act,

a supplementary estimate showing the sums required or spent shall be laid before the House of Commons, and a supplementary Appropriation Bill shall be introduced into the House.

73.4 If the Appropriation Act for any financial year has not come into force, or is not likely to come into force by the beginning of that financial year, the House of Commons may, by a vote on account, authorise the withdrawal from the Consolidated Fund of such sums as are considered necessary to carry on the government of the United Kingdom until the expiry of 4 months after the beginning of that financial year or the coming into force of the Act, whichever is the earlier.

73.5 The Treasury shall make appropriate arrangements, including virement, for the authorisation of supply to ensure that all money shall be appropriated by Act of Parliament in accordance with this Constitution.

---

74. BUDGET

74.1 In each financial year, the Chancellor of the Exchequer shall prepare a comprehensive budget for the United Kingdom, which shall include proposals with respect to the raising of revenue for following financial year.

74.2 The Chancellor of the Exchequer shall present the budget, when approved by the Cabinet, to the House of Commons.

74.3 Nothing in this Article prevents the Chancellor of the

Exchequer during a financial year from presenting supplementary budgets, when so approved, to the House of Commons for the purpose of raising additional revenue for that year.

74.4 No revenue may be raised except under the authority of an Act of Parliament.

---

75. COMPTROLLER AND AUDITOR GENERAL

75.1 There is established by this Constitution the office of Comptroller and Auditor General.

75.2 Act of Parliament shall provide for the appointment, tenure of office and conditions of service of the Comptroller and Auditor General, who shall—

.1 be an officer of the House of Commons; and

.2 perform the functions set out in this Article and as Act of Parliament may prescribe.

75.3 .1 The Comptroller and Auditor General shall—

.1 audit the public accounts of the United Kingdom and of all officers and authorities of the Government, and of the courts for United Kingdom and for England and Wales; and

.2 report to Parliament thereon.

.2 For that purpose, the Comptroller and Auditor General has access to all books, records, reports and other documents relating to those accounts.

Division 6: Constitutional Commission

---

76. CONSTITUTIONAL COMMISSION

76.1 .1 There is established by this Constitution a Constitutional Commission, which consists of not more than 16 members.

.2 The members shall be appointed, in equal numbers from among their members, by the House of Commons and the Second Chamber, as soon as practicable after the House first meets following a general election.

.3 The Commission may co-opt members who are not members of Parliament, but the co-opted members shall not exceed one third of the total membership of the Commission.

.4 No Minister shall be a member of the Commission.

76.2 The Chairman of the Commission shall be elected by the members from among their own number.

76.3 The Commission —

.1 shall keep under review —

.1 the working of the Constitution and the Constitutional legislation; and

.2 the reports of the investigations of its Integrity Committee;

and shall report its findings annually to Parliament, together with any recommendations for the amendment of the Constitution or such legislation; and

.2 shall prepare Codes of Conduct and other guidelines concerning the standards of conduct with which persons may reasonably be expected to comply when holding a public office to which they have been appointed or elected by virtue of being persons elected to either House of Parliament, to an Assembly or to a local authority.

---

77. INTEGRITY COMMITTEE

77.1 .1 The Constitutional Commission shall establish from among its members who are members of Parliament a committee to be known as the Integrity Committee.

.2 The Chairman of the Constitutional Commission shall be the Chairman of the Integrity Committee.

77.2 The Integrity Committee —

.1 may investigate the propriety of the conduct as a Minister of any person who is or has at any time been a Minister, whether of its own initiative or on a reference by either House of Parliament or by a committee of either House;

.2 for that purpose, has all the powers of a tribunal of inquiry appointed under the Tribunals of Inquiry (Evidence) Act 1921;

.3 shall lay before the House of Parliament of which the person under investigation is or was a member at the time of the conduct investigated, and shall publish, the report of its findings.

77.3 The House of Parliament before which a report is laid under paragraph .2.3 shall consider that report within 60 days after it has been laid.

CHAPTER 7
National and Regional Government

---

78. ASSEMBLIES

78.1 .1 There is established by this Constitution an Assembly for Scotland, for Wales, for Northern Ireland and for each of the regions of England, having the areas set out in Schedule 1.

.2 Each Assembly—

.1 may, subject to this Constitution and in particular Part 1 of Chapter 6, make laws for the peace, order and good government of its nation or region; and

.2 shall hold its Executive to account.

.3 Act of Assembly may provide with respect to the names by which the Assembly and the members of the Assembly may be known.

78.2 The elections for members of the Assemblies shall—

.1 be conducted in accordance with the electoral law enacted by Parliament under Article 83;

.2 be held at the times prescribed in Part 3 of Schedule 3; and

.3 be supervised by the Electoral Commission.

78.3 Act of Parliament shall provide—

.1 with respect to the numbers of the members of the Assemblies;

.2 subject to Article 83.2, with respect to the qualifications and disqualifications for the members.

78.4 The term of an Assembly is 4 years, which expires 21 days before the date upon which the elections for Assemblies are required by Part 3 of Schedule 3.

78.5 The procedure of each Assembly shall, subject to any Act of the Assembly, be regulated by standing orders of the Assembly, which shall include provision for —

  .1 the appointing of a date for the first meeting of the Assembly after each election;

  .2 the election of a presiding officer from among the members of the Assembly and for the tenure of that office;

  .3 the nomination, mode of election and removal of the Chief Executive;

  .4 the requirements to be met by the Executive in the presentation of policies and legislative proposals;

  .5 the information to be made available by the Executive to the Assembly;

  .6 securing disclosure by members of pecuniary interests, any consequent restriction of participation in the debates of the Assembly, and the consequences of failure to disclose pecuniary interests.

78.6 An Assembly may do anything which is calculated to facilitate or is conducive or incidental to the discharge of any of its functions.

78.7 .1 Laws made by an Assembly are called Acts of the Assembly.

  .2 A Bill for an Act becomes an Act of the Assembly when it is —

    .1 passed by the affirmative vote of a majority of the members of the Assembly voting; and

    .2 so certified by the presiding officer of the Assembly and the Clerk to the Assembly.

  .3 The validity of the proceedings leading to the enactment of an Act of an Assembly shall not be considered by any court.

79. EXECUTIVES

79.1　There is established by this Constitution an Executive for Scotland, for Wales, for Northern Ireland and for each of the regions in England.

79.2　.1 Each Executive consists of —

.1 a Chief Executive, who shall be elected by the appropriate Assembly from among its members, in accordance with its standing orders; and

.2 such members of the Assembly as are appointed by the Chief Executive to be members of the Executive.

.2 The Chief Executive may appoint members of the Assembly to be assistants to the members of the Executive.

.3 Act of Parliament shall provide with respect to the number of the members of an Assembly who may be appointed to be members of the Executive or assistants to such members.

.4 Act of Assembly shall provide with respect to the titles by which the Chief Executive and the members of the Executive may be known.

79.3　.1 In Scotland and Northern Ireland, notwithstanding paragraph .2, the Chief Executive may appoint a person who is not a member of the Assembly as a member of the Executive to perform functions corresponding to those performed before the coming into force of this Constitution by a Law Officer of the Crown.

.2 A member of the Executive appointed under this paragraph may participate in the proceedings of the Assembly but shall not vote.

79.4　The Executive shall exercise the executive powers of the Government with respect to —

.1 all matters which fall within the legislative competence of the appropriate Assembly as provided by this Constitution; and

.2 such other matters as Act of Parliament may prescribe.

79.5 A member of an Executive is responsible for the conduct of such business of the Executive as the Chief Executive assigns to the member.

79.6 A member of an Executive, or an assistant to a member, ceases to hold office —

.1 if the member or assistant ceases to be a member of the Assembly for any reason other than the expiry of the Assembly; or

.2 if removed from office by the Chief Executive; or

.3 on the receipt by the Chief Executive of a letter of resignation from the member or assistant; or

.4 when a new election to the office of Chief Executive is completed; or

.5 if a motion of no confidence in the Executive is passed by a majority of all the members of the Assembly.

80. FINANCE AND REVENUE SHARING

80.1 .1 There is established by this Constitution a Consolidated Fund and a Loans Fund for each nation and region.

.2 Sums may be transferred in a nation or region from one to the other of these Funds on the authority of the Executive, signified by the member of the Executive having responsibility for finance.

80.2 There shall be paid into the Consolidated Fund for a nation or region —

.1 the share of the personal income tax raised in the United Kingdom that is allocated to that nation or region in accordance with Schedule 2; and

.2 such other receipts of its Executive that are not paid into the Loans Fund and have not been disposed of and accounted for under an order under paragraph .4.

80.3 Sums forming part of a Consolidated Fund may be appropriated by an Executive only for purposes related to those matters in which, under Article 79.4, the Executive may exercise executive powers or to meet expenses incurred under Article 78.6.

80.4 Sums forming part of the Loans Fund, and sums forming part of the receipts of the Executive, may be appropriated by order of the Executive, which shall provide with respect to their disposal and accounting.

80.5 No order appropriating any sum shall be made by the Executive unless a draft of the order appropriating that sum has been laid before the Assembly and has been approved by a resolution of the Assembly.

81. BORROWING

81.1 .1 The Executive may borrow such sums as appear to the Executive to be necessary to meet expenditure approved by the Assembly.

.2 No such sums may be borrowed unless the borrowing has been approved by a resolution of the Assembly.

.3 The total sums that may be borrowed in any financial year under this Article shall not exceed one-third of the annual expenditure approved by the Assembly for that financial year.

81.2 No borrowing may be undertaken by the Executive if, in consequence, the total sums borrowed for the time being under this Article would exceed 3 times the annual revenue of the Assembly at the time.

81.3 The Executive may borrow such sums as appear to the Executive to be required —

.1 to meet a temporary excess of sums paid out of the Consolidated Fund or the Loans Fund over the sums paid into the Fund; or

.2 to provide a working balance in either Fund.

81.4 Sums borrowed by the Executive shall be paid into the Loans Fund or Consolidated Fund.

81.5 Any sums required for the repayment of, or the payment of interest on, sums borrowed under this Article that are not paid out of the Loans Fund shall be a charge upon the Consolidated Fund.

82. LOCAL GOVERNMENT

82.1 Act of Assembly shall provide for the establishment of elected local authorities in each nation and region.

82.2 The boundaries for each local authority shall be determined by the parent Assembly, with the approval of the Electoral Commission.

82.3 The elections to local authorities shall—

.1 be conducted in accordance with the electoral law enacted by Parliament under Article 83;

.2 be held at the times prescribed in Part 3 of Schedule 3; and

.3 be supervised by the Electoral Commission.

82.4 A local authority—

.1 shall perform such functions as Act of the parent Assembly shall determine; and

.2 has general competence to undertake whatever measures it sees fit for the benefit of all those within its area, including the making of bye-laws;

but in performing such functions or undertaking such measures, the local authority shall not act in conflict or inconsistently with any legislation enacted by or under the authority of Parliament or by the parent Assembly.

82.5 Each local authority is entitled—

.1 to levy rates upon domestic and business properties within its jurisdiction; or

.2 raise any other form of local tax authorised by Act of Parliament,

in accordance with Act of the parent Assembly.

CHAPTER 8
Elections

83. ELECTORAL LAW AND QUALIFICATIONS

83.1 Elections for Parliament, the European Parliament, the Assemblies and the other elected bodies established by or under this Constitution shall be general, direct, equal and free and by secret ballot under conditions which ensure the free expression of the people of the United Kingdom.

83.2 A British national who has attained the age of 18 years is entitled to vote in elections for, and stand for election to, Parliament, the European Parliament, the Assemblies and the other elected bodies established by this Constitution, subject to such disqualifications as Act of Parliament shall prescribe.

83.3 Act of Parliament shall

.1 determine the extent to which the franchise shall be extended to other classes of persons; and

.2 provide for the electoral law which shall govern the franchise, the qualification and nomination of candidates, election expenditure and other matters concerning the conduct of elections to Parliament, the European Parliament, the Assemblies and local authorities.

84. ELECTIONS TO HOUSE OF COMMONS

84.1 The constituencies for the House of Commons shall be determined in accordance with Part 1 of Schedule 3.

84.2 At each general election one member shall be returned for each constituency in accordance with Part 2 of Schedule 3.

84.3 Following each general election, additional members equal in number to the number of constituencies shall be declared by the returning officer in accordance with Part 2 of Schedule 3.

85. ELECTIONS TO SECOND CHAMBER

85.1 The constituencies for the Second Chamber shall be determined in accordance with Part 1 of Schedule 3.

85.2 At each general election there shall be returned for each constituency such number of members (being not less than 5 and not more than 9) as is determined for that constituency in accordance with Part 2 of Schedule 3.

85.3 Members shall be elected by a system of single transferable voting in accordance with Part 2 of Schedule 3.

86. BY-ELECTIONS

86.1 Upon a vacancy arising in the membership of either House of Parliament in respect of a seat held by an elected member, an election for a new member shall be held as soon as is practicable in the constituency concerned.

86.2 No election shall be held under this Article if the vacancy occurs within the 3 months immediately preceding the date upon which the term of Parliament will expire.

87. ELECTIONS TO EUROPEAN PARLIAMENT, ASSEMBLIES AND LOCAL AUTHORITIES

87. Act of Parliament made under Article 83 shall provide, in like terms to Articles 84 to 86 and Schedule 3, with necessary modifications, with respect to the constituencies, return of members and by-elections in connection with elections to the European Parliament, the Assemblies and local authorities.

88. ELECTORAL COMMISSION

88.1 There is established by this Constitution an Electoral Commission for the United Kingdom.

88.2 The Electoral Commission consists of —

.1 the Speaker of the House of Commons (who shall chair the Commission);

.2 the Speaker of the Second Chamber; and

.3 not fewer than 5 and not more than 9 Ordinary Commissioners (one of whom shall be elected by the Commission to be Deputy Chairman).

88.3 Ordinary Commissioners shall be appointed by the Head of State acting on the advice of the Public Services Commission.

88.4 No person may be appointed an Ordinary Commissioner who is a member of, or a candidate for election to, either House of Parliament, the European Parliament, an Assembly or a local authority.

88.5 An Ordinary Commissioner ceases to hold office —

.1 at the expiry of 5 years from the date of appointment (which may be renewed); or

.2 upon the Commissioner attaining the age of 65 years; or

.3 on the receipt by the Chief Commissioner of the Public Services Commission of a letter of resignation from the Ordinary Commissioner; or

.4 if the Commissioner is removed from office, upon grounds of misconduct or incapacity, by the Head of State on the advice of the Public Services Commission; or

.5 if the Commissioner becomes a candidate for election to either House of Parliament, the European Parliament, an Assembly or a local authority.

88.6 Ordinary Commissioners shall receive salaries, and office and administrative facilities, appropriate to the full time performance of their responsibilities.

89. FUNCTIONS OF ELECTORAL COMMISSION

89.1 The Commission has the duty —

.1 to keep under continuous review —

.1 the number of constituencies into which the United Kingdom is to be divided for the purposes of elections to the Houses of Parliament, the European Parliament, the Assemblies, and local authorities;

.2 the boundaries of such constituencies;

.3 the practice and working of political campaigning affecting elections in the United Kingdom, including matters of finance, broadcasting and advertising,

and to submit reports thereon, with its recommendations, to Parliament at such intervals as Parliament shall determine;

.2 to appoint a returning officer for each nation and region;

.3 to consider any matter affecting the conduct of elections in the United Kingdom (including any matter affecting the franchise or candidatures) that —

.1 is referred to it by the Prime Minister or the Speaker of the House of Commons; or

.2 the Commission on its own initiative determines,

and to submit a report thereon, with any recommendations, to Parliament;

.4 to receive, investigate and report to Parliament upon complaints in connection with the conduct of any election in the United Kingdom.

89.2 The Commission has the power —

.1 to assist individual complainants in legal proceedings in relation to electoral malpractice;

.2 to institute such legal proceedings on its own initiative, whether or not it has received a complaint.

89.3 The Commission has the appropriate powers to require any person to provide information or documents which, in its opinion, appear likely to assist the Commission in the performance of its functions.

90. FUNCTIONS AS TO POLITICAL PARTIES

90.1 The Commission shall maintain a register of political parties.

90.2 .1 The Commission shall, from time to time, prepare regulations for the registration of political parties, which shall include provisions requiring—

.1 a political party applying for registration to provide a copy of its constitution and of its accounts;

.2 every registered political party to submit annually a copy of its accounts to the Commission.

.2 Such regulations shall have effect when approved by resolutions of both Houses of Parliament.

90.3 The Commission shall submit an annual report to Parliament with respect to—

.1 the income, expenditure and financial status of all registered political parties; and

.2 such matters in connection with the registration of political parties as the Commission determines.

91. REGISTRATION OF POLITICAL PARTIES

91.1 Every political party is entitled to register with the Electoral Commission, in accordance with the regulations made under Article 90.

91.2 A registered political party is eligible for public financial support and entitled to access to political broadcasting to the extent that Act of Parliament provides.

91.3 Act of Parliament may, notwithstanding Article 11, place such restrictions as are reasonable in a democratic society on election expenditure by candidates, political parties, whether registered or not, and other bodies.

CHAPTER 9
The Judiciary

PART 1: THE JUDICIAL POWER

92. THE JUDICIAL POWER

92.1 Judicial power within the United Kingdom is vested in the courts in accordance with this Constitution.

92.2 The courts are independent and subject only to this Constitution and the law.

92.3 No court or tribunal shall be established to exercise judicial functions of a public nature in any part of the United Kingdom except as provided or authorised by this Constitution.

93. ESTABLISHMENT OF COURTS

93.1 .1 There is established by this Constitution a Supreme Court for the United Kingdom, having the membership and jurisdiction set out in Part 2.

.2 Further United Kingdom courts may be established under that Part.

93.2 There are established by or under this Constitution —

.1 for England and Wales, the courts having the membership and jurisdiction set out in Part 1 of Schedule 4;

.2 for Scotland, the courts having the membership and jurisdiction set out in Part 2 of Schedule 4;

.3 for Northern Ireland, the courts having the membership and jurisdiction set out in Part 3 of Schedule 4.

93.3 .1 The courts established under this Chapter have the jurisdiction which was exercised by the courts of England and Wales, Scotland and Northern Ireland immediately before the coming into force of this Constitution.

.2 That jurisdiction shall, subject to this Part and Schedule 4, be allocated between the courts by Act of Parliament.

93.4 Act of Parliament shall provide concerning the respective territorial and extra-territorial jurisdiction of the courts in the different parts of the United Kingdom.

---

94. LIMITATIONS ON INVALIDATING OF LEGISLATION

94.1 .1 No intermediate or inferior court may hold that any Act of Parliament or of an Assembly is wholly or partly void.

.2 If any question as to the validity of an Act of Parliament or of an Assembly arises in the course of proceedings in an intermediate or inferior court, the court shall refer the question to a superior court, unless it is satisfied that there is no substance in the question.

94.2 An appeal from any decision of a superior court holding an Act of Parliament wholly or partly void shall be taken directly to the Supreme Court.

94.3 This Article does not apply to subordinate legislation.

---

95. FULL FAITH AND CREDIT

95.1 Full faith and credit shall be given throughout the United Kingdom to —

.1 the laws, acts and records of the Assemblies; and

.2 the judicial proceedings of the courts of England and Wales, Scotland and Northern Ireland.

95.2 Act of Parliament shall provide concerning the enforcement in one part of the United Kingdom of the judgments and orders of courts in another part of the United Kingdom or outside the United Kingdom.

PART 2: THE SUPREME COURT AND OTHER UNITED KINGDOM COURTS

96. THE SUPREME COURT

96.1 The Supreme Court of the United Kingdom consists of the President and 10 other justices or such greater number as may be prescribed by Act of Parliament.

96.2 The justices of the Supreme Court shall be selected from persons —

.1 who have served as judges of a superior court within the United Kingdom; or

.2 who, in the opinion of the United Kingdom Judicial Appointments Commission, have shown outstanding distinction in the practice or teaching of law in the United Kingdom.

96.3 The justices of the Supreme Court shall include (except for the duration of any vacancy) —

.1 at least 5 persons who have served as judges of a superior court in England and Wales;

.2 at least 2 persons who have served as judges of a superior court in Scotland;

.3 at least 1 person who has served as a judge of a superior court in Northern Ireland.

96.4 The President and the other justices of the Supreme Court shall be appointed by the Head of State on the advice of the Prime Minister who shall select one of two names submitted by the United Kingdom Judicial Appointments Commission (subject to the right to invite the Commission to reconsider the submission).

96.5 During any vacancy in the office of President or during the temporary incapacity of the President the functions of the President shall be discharged by the senior justice of the Supreme Court willing to act.

---

97. COMPOSITION

97.1 .1 The Supreme Court may, if the President so directs, sit as a single body to hear an appeal which appears to the President to be of exceptional importance.

.2 It shall otherwise sit in divisions containing not fewer than 3 members.

97.2 .1 Where in the opinion of the President it is reasonably necessary to do so to ensure the proper dispatch of the business of the Supreme Court, the President may invite —

.1 a former justice of the Supreme Court who has ceased to hold office under Article 108.1.1 or .1.2 or under Article 108.1.4 if no longer holding an inconsistent office;

.2 with the approval of the United Kingdom Judicial Appointments Commission, any person eligible for appointment as a justice of the Supreme Court;

to sit as a member of a division of the Supreme Court for the purposes of any particular proceedings.

.2 But a majority of the members of any division of the Supreme Court shall consist of persons currently holding office as justices of the Supreme Court or acting under Article 108.6.

---

98. JURISDICTION

98.1 The Supreme Court has original and exclusive jurisdiction —

.1 in any proceedings brought by the Government of the United Kingdom seeking a ruling that any Assembly Act is wholly or partly invalid under this Constitution;

.2 in any proceedings brought by the Executive of an Assembly seeking a ruling that any Act of Parliament is wholly or partly invalid under this Constitution.

98.2 The Supreme Court has appellate jurisdiction in the following matters —

.1 the interpretation and effect of this Constitution;

.2 any dispute (other than under paragraph .1) in which nations or regions are opposing parties, or in which the United Kingdom and a nation or region are opposing parties;

.3 any proceedings alleging a contravention of the Bill of Rights, contained in Chapter 2;

.4 the validity, interpretation and effect of Acts of Parliament and subordinate legislation thereunder;

.5 any proceedings giving rise to a question of law (including the interpretation of statutes) in relation to which uniformity throughout the United Kingdom or in more than one jurisdiction within the United Kingdom is, in the opinion of the Supreme Court, desirable;

.6 the validity of any executive decision or act of the Government of the United Kingdom or of any public body exercising powers under this Constitution or an Act of Parliament;

.7 the interpretation and effect of the laws of the European Community and any other international treaties giving rise to rights or obligations enforceable within the United Kingdom;

.8 matters within the jurisdiction of other courts and tribunals of the United Kingdom established under this Part.

98.3 .1 There is a right of appeal to the Supreme Court, without leave, from any decision of a superior court in any part of the United Kingdom holding an Act of Parliament (but not subordinate legislation thereunder) wholly or partly void.

.2 In any other matter in which the Supreme Court has appellate jurisdiction, Act of Parliament or Rules of Court may require that leave be given for all or any category of appeals.

99. ADDITIONAL JURISDICTION

99.1   .1 The Supreme Court may, on the invitation of the country or territory in question, exercise the jurisdiction in relation to appeals from countries or territories outside the United Kingdom which, immediately prior to the coming into force of this Constitution, was exercised by the Judicial Committee of the Privy Council.

      .2 For the purposes of proceedings under this Article, the powers of the President under Article 98.2 include power to invite any person who holds or has held office as a judge of the highest appellate court of any country or territory which has invited the Supreme Court to exercise jurisdiction, to sit as a member of a division of the Supreme Court.

99.2   .1 The Supreme Court may exercise any further jurisdiction conferred upon it by Act of Parliament.

      .2 A Bill for such an Act shall not be presented to the Head of State for Assent, unless —

        .1 it has been approved by resolutions of the Assemblies for Scotland and Northern Ireland; and

        .2 there is endorsed thereon a certificate of the Speaker of the House of Commons to that effect.

100. BINDING FORCE OF DECISIONS

100.1 Any decision of the Supreme Court (including a decision that it has jurisdiction to hear an appeal) is final and conclusive.

100.2 Until overruled by a subsequent decision of the Supreme Court, a decision of the Supreme Court is binding on all other courts in the United Kingdom, except to the extent that a decision on the interpretation or effect of the laws of the European Community is inconsistent with a subsequent decision of the Court of Justice of the European Community.

100.3 The Supreme Court is not bound by its own previous decisions.

101. OTHER UNITED KINGDOM COURTS

101.1 .1 Further courts and tribunals of the United Kingdom may be established by Act of Parliament to exercise

.1 any specialised jurisdiction which may more appropriately be exercised within the United Kingdom as a whole than separately within its parts; or

.2 any extra-territorial jurisdiction of the United Kingdom.

.2 Courts and tribunals so established may be designated as superior, intermediate or inferior courts.

101.2 Judges of courts and tribunals so established shall—

.1 be selected from persons who have such qualifications as Act of Parliament may prescribe; and

.2 be appointed by the Minister of Justice, acting in accordance with the recommendation of the United Kingdom Judicial Appointments Commission.

102. UNITED KINGDOM JUDICIAL APPOINTMENTS COMMISSION

102.1 There is established by this Constitution a United Kingdom Judicial Appointments Commission, which consists of—

.1 10 representatives of the Judicial Services Commission for England and Wales (one of whom is the Chairman of the Welsh Appointments Committee established under Section 2 of Schedule 5);

.2 4 representatives of the Judicial Services Commission for Scotland;

.3 2 representatives of the Judicial Services Commission for Northern Ireland.

102.2 The representatives of the Judicial Services Commissions shall be selected by, and serve on the Commission for the term of office fixed by, the Judicial Services Commission which they represent.

PART 3: JUDICIAL SERVICES COMMISSIONS AND JUDICIAL COUNCILS

---

103. JUDICIAL SERVICES COMMISSIONS AND JUDICIAL COUNCILS

103.1 There are established by this Constitution a Judicial Services Commission and a Judicial Council for each of England and Wales, Scotland and Northern Ireland.

103.2 .1 The membership and structure of the Judicial Services Commission, and the membership of the Judicial Council, for England and Wales are as set out in Schedule 5.

.2 Act of Assembly shall make provision, in like form, with the necessary modifications, for the membership of the Judicial Services Commissions and Judicial Councils for Scotland and for Northern Ireland.

---

104. FUNCTIONS OF JUDICIAL SERVICES COMMISSIONS

104.1 The Judicial Services Commissions shall perform the functions with respect to the appointment of judges, and the authorising of judges to sit, set out in Sections 3 and 4, 10 and 11 or 16 and 17 of Schedule 4, as the case may be.

104.2 The Judicial Services Commissions shall adopt procedures for the identification of candidates for judicial office which will ensure, so far as practicable, that adequate numbers of candidates of both sexes and from diverse racial, religious and social backgrounds are considered for appointment.

104.3 .1 The Judicial Services Commissions shall establish procedures for considering complaints relating to legal proceedings and the capacity and conduct of judges of superior and intermediate courts.

.2 Such procedures shall include powers—

.1 to refer to the Judicial Conduct Tribunal under Part 4 any complaint where a *prima facie* case is shown of circumstances which, if proved, might justify removal of a judge from office;

.2 where a complaint of judicial misconduct or failure in the execution of office does not justify reference to the Judicial Conduct Tribunal—

.1 to investigate it; and

.2 if found proved, to draw the finding to the attention of the judge;

.3 to direct compensation out of public funds.

.3 No complaint of the incorrectness of any judicial decision shall be considered.

104.4 The Judicial Services Commissions shall make an annual report to Parliament or, in the case of Scotland and Northern Ireland, to the appropriate Assembly.

104.5 Further functions may be conferred on a Judicial Services Commission by Act of Parliament or Assembly, as appropriate.

---

105. FUNCTIONS OF JUDICIAL COUNCILS

105. The Judicial Councils shall advise the Minister of Justice or the Executives for Scotland or Northern Ireland, as the case may be, on

.1 policy concerning the administration of and provision of resources for court services; and

.2 any other matter concerning the administration of justice on which the Minister of Justice or Executive requests advice or on which the Judicial Council thinks it appropriate to tender advice.

PART 4: JUDICIAL INDEPENDENCE AND CONDUCT

---
106. APPLICATION OF PART 4
---

106. This Part applies for the purpose of—

   .1 securing the independence of the judiciary;

   .2 dealing with judicial incapacity or misconduct and allegations thereof.

---
107. PROTECTION OF JUDICIAL SALARIES

107.1 A judge's salary shall not be reduced, and no adverse changes shall be made in other conditions of service during tenure of office.

107.2 The salaries of judges of the Supreme Court, and other United Kingdom courts, and of superior and intermediate courts shall be charged on the Consolidated Fund.

---
108. TENURE OF JUDICIAL OFFICE

108.1 .1 A judge ceases to hold office—

   .1 upon attaining the age of 70 years (or, in the case of judges of inferior courts, such lower age as Act of Parliament or of the competent Assembly may prescribe); or

   .2 upon receipt by the Prime Minister, Minister of Justice, or Chief Executive, as the case may be, of a letter of resignation from the judge; or

   .3 upon removal from office in accordance with this Part; or

   .4 upon acceptance of an office which is declared by this Constitution or Act of Parliament to be inconsistent with judicial office; or

.5 in the case of a judge of an inferior court, upon the expiration of any fixed term for which the appointment was made without the appointment having been renewed.

.2 A judge who attains the retiring age may continue to act in any proceedings the hearing of which had commenced before attaining that age.

108.2 No judge may be removed from office except on the ground of —

.1 physical or mental incapacity which is likely to be permanent or prolonged; or

.2 serious judicial misconduct; or

.3 failure in the due execution of office; or

.4 having been placed, by personal conduct or otherwise, in a position incompatible with the due execution of office.

108.3 No judge may be removed from office except by the procedure specified in this Part.

108.4 .1 A judge of a superior or intermediate court who is appointed to hold office for a fixed term which is renewable is entitled to have the appointment renewed unless —

.1 the judge would attain the age of 70 before the expiry of the renewed term; or

.2 the appropriate Judicial Services Commission or the United Kingdom Judicial Appointments Commission, as the case may be, directs that the appointment shall not be renewed.

.2 The Commission making such a direction shall, upon being requested to do so, give reasons to the judge.

109. JUDICIAL CONDUCT TRIBUNALS

109.1 Judicial Conduct Tribunals shall be established by Act of Parliament for England and Wales and by Act of the competent Assembly for Scotland and for Northern Ireland.

109.2 .1 Each Tribunal shall consist of—

.1 a President (who shall be a judge of a superior court);

.2 at least 2 other judicial members (who shall be judges of a superior or intermediate court); and

.3 at least 2 lay members.

.2 For the purposes of this paragraph, the expression—

'judge' does not include a part time, temporary or unpaid judge;

'lay' describes a person who has never qualified as a member of the legal profession or served as a judge (except as a part-time unpaid judge of an inferior court).

109.3 .1 Judicial members of the Judicial Conduct Tribunal for England and Wales shall be selected by the Master of the Rolls and the Chief Justice of the High Court.

.2 Judicial members of the Judicial Conduct Tribunal for Scotland shall be selected by the Lord President.

.3 Judicial members of the Judicial Conduct Tribunal for Northern Ireland shall be selected by the Chief Justice of Northern Ireland.

.4 Lay members shall be appointed by the respective Judicial Services Commissions.

109.4 No member of a Judicial Services Commission may at the same time be a member of a Judicial Conduct Tribunal.

---

110. COMPLAINTS RELATING TO JUSTICES OF SUPREME COURT

110.1 Any complaint relating to a justice of the Supreme Court or any judge of another United Kingdom court shall—

.1 be made to the President of the Supreme Court (or, if the complaint relates to the President, to the senior of the other justices); and

.2 be referred to whichever of the Judicial Services Commissions the President or such other Justice thinks most appropriate.

110.2 If that Judicial Services Commission decides that there are grounds for referring the complaint to a Judicial Conduct Tribunal, a Judicial Conduct Tribunal shall be constituted consisting of the President of each Tribunal and one judicial member and one lay member from each of the three ordinary Tribunals.

---

111. FUNCTIONS OF JUDICIAL CONDUCT TRIBUNALS

111.1 Judicial Conduct Tribunals shall investigate, as the case may be —

.1 complaints relating to justices of the Supreme Court or a judge of another United Kingdom court referred under Article 110; or

.2 complaints relating to judges of superior or intermediate courts referred to them by the respective Judicial Services Commissions under Article 104.3.2; or

.3 complaints relating to a Director of Public Prosecutions or a Director of Civil Proceedings.

111.2 .1 A Judicial Conduct Tribunal shall, if it finds the complaint proved, recommend the removal of the judge from office.

.2 But the Tribunal may, if it finds that there has been judicial misconduct or failure in the due execution of office but that such misconduct is not sufficiently serious to justify removal from office, instead draw the attention of the judge to the finding.

111.3 .1 In the case of a justice of the Supreme Court or a judge of another United Kingdom court, the Supreme Court has an original and exclusive jurisdiction to review the decision of the Judicial Conduct Tribunal under paragraph .2.

.2 In other cases, a decision of a Judicial Conduct Tribunal under paragraph .2 is subject to judicial review but not to appeal.

111.4 A Judicial Services Commission or the United Kingdom Judicial Appointments Commission may apply to the appropriate Judicial Conduct Tribunal for an order for the suspension of any judge (without loss of salary) against whom a complaint is pending, whether or not the complaint has been referred to the Tribunal.

---

112. PROCEDURE FOR REMOVAL OF JUDGES

112.1 Where a Judicial Conduct Tribunal has recommended the removal from office of a Justice of the Supreme Court, a judge of another United Kingdom court or a judge of a superior court —

.1 the Minister of Justice shall lay a resolution for the removal of the judge from office before Parliament; and

.2 the resolution shall take effect upon being passed by both Houses of Parliament.

112.2 Where a Judicial Conduct Tribunal has recommended the removal from office of a judge of an intermediate court, the Minister of Justice (in the case of England and Wales) or the appropriate Chief Executive (in the case of Scotland or Northern Ireland) shall implement the recommendation.

112.3 .1 A judge of an inferior court may —

.1 be removed from office on a ground specified in Article 108.2; and

.2 be suspended pending the investigation of possible grounds for removal,

by the Minister of Justice (in the case of England and Wales) or the appropriate Chief Executive (in the case of Scotland or Northern Ireland).

.2 The Minister, or the Chief Executive, shall give reasons for any proposed removal from office and shall allow the judge to make representations.

.3 The removal is subject to judicial review.

112.4 .1 When a judge is removed from office on a ground other than incapacity, any pension rights in respect of the office may be removed or reduced.

.2 In the case of a justice of the Supreme Court, a judge of another United Kingdom court or a judge of a superior or intermediate court, such rights may be removed or reduced only if, and to the extent, recommended by the appropriate Judicial Conduct Tribunal.

113. JUDICIAL CONTROL OF COURT BUSINESS

113. Distribution of court business and the allocation and listing of cases shall be undertaken in accordance with Rules of Court and shall be under the supervision, and subject to the directions, of designated judges, who shall be selected as the appropriate Judicial Council shall determine.

CHAPTER 10
The Public Services

114. THE PUBLIC SERVICES

114.1 There is established by this Constitution —

.1 a public service under the Government of the United Kingdom;

.2 a public service under the Executive of each nation and region;

.3 a public service under each local authority.

114.2 .1 This Part provides with respect to appointments to, and tenure of office in, the public service under the Government.

.2 Provision shall be made by the Public Services Commission, by regulation, for appointments to, and tenure of office in, the public services under the Executives and local authorities.

114.3 .1 Every public service shall be politically neutral.

.2 Appointment in every public service shall be on the basis of merit only.

114.4 .1 Nothing in this Chapter prevents a Minister from appointing a person to the public service under the Government, as a personal adviser to the Minister.

.2 Such person shall hold office during the Minister's pleasure and on such terms as the Minister shall determine with the consent of the Public Services Commission.

114.5 The first duty of each public service, and of every person appointed to a public service, is to the Constitution.

114.6 Act of Parliament shall provide with respect to the procedures whereby executive agencies under the Government may be held accountable to Parliament.

115. PUBLIC SERVICES COMMISSION

115.1 There is established by this Constitution a Public Services Commission for the United Kingdom.

115.2 The Public Services Commission consists of a Chief Commissioner and such number of other Commissioners (not being fewer than 12) as Act of Parliament shall prescribe.

115.3 The Chief Commissioner and the Commissioners shall be appointed by the Head of State, on the recommendation of such Select Committee as the House of Commons shall designate for the purpose, which shall make its selection from nominations made by the Minister having responsibility for the public service.

115.4 No person may be appointed as a Commissioner who is a member of, or candidate for election to, either House of Parliament, the European Parliament, an Assembly or a local authority.

115.5 A Commissioner ceases to hold office —

.1 at the expiry of 5 years from the date of appointment (which may be renewed); or

.2 upon the Commissioner attaining the age of 65 years; or

.3 on receipt by the Minister having responsibility for the public service of a letter of resignation from the Commissioner; or

.4 if the Commissioner is removed from office by the Head of State, upon grounds of misconduct or incapacity, acting in accordance with a resolution of the House of Commons; or

.5 if the Commissioner becomes a candidate for election to either House of Parliament, the European Parliament, an Assembly or a local authority.

115.6 Commissioners shall receive salaries, and office and administrative facilities, appropriate to the full-time performance of their responsibilities.

116. FUNCTIONS OF PUBLIC SERVICES COMMISSION

116.1 The Public Services Commission has the duty —

.1 to prepare, and from time to time amend, a Code of Professional Conduct for the public services;

.2 to prepare, from time to time, regulations with respect to —

.1 the methods of recruitment to any public service;

.2 the terms and conditions of employment or appointment in any public service;

.3 the principles and procedures governing promotion and transfer within the public services;

.4 vetting of officers in the public services for security purposes;

.5 procedures for the discipline of officers in any public service;

.6 procedures for the hearing and settlement of the grievances of officers in any public service; and

.7 removal from office of officers in any public service.

116.2 The Public Services Commission shall adopt procedures for the identification of candidates for appointment to any public service which will ensure, so far as practicable, that adequate numbers of candidates of both sexes and from diverse racial, religious and social backgrounds are considered for appointment.

116.3 All public appointments, other than appointments to the public services, shall be made by the Head of State acting in accordance with the advice of the Public Services Commission.

117. PUBLIC SERVICES COMPLAINTS COMMISSION

117.1 .1 The Public Services Commission shall establish a Public Services Complaints Commission for the public services.

.2 Act of Parliament shall provide with respect to appointments, tenure of office and conditions of office of members of the Public Services Complaints Commission.

117.2 The Public Services Complaints Commission shall—

.1 investigate complaints, including complaints by officers in a public service, concerning—

.1 breaches or failures to comply with the Code of Professional Conduct or of the regulations governing a public service;

.2 malversation of a public service;

.3 improper conduct towards an officer in a public service by a Minister, a member of an Executive or an elected member of a local authority; and

.2 report its findings and any recommendations to the Public Services Commission and to Parliament.

117.3 No public servant shall suffer any detriment for disclosing information to the Public Services Complaints Commission for the purpose of protecting the Constitution or for making a complaint.

CHAPTER 11
Administrative Justice

118. JUDICIAL REVIEW

118.1 Act of Parliament shall provide for—

.1 judicial review of acts or omissions of persons or bodies in the performance of any public functions; and

.2 a general duty upon public authorities to give reasons for their decisions;

.3 effective remedies (including the payment of compensation) in cases where applications for judicial review are upheld.

118.2 Application for judicial review may be made by any person having a sufficient interest in the matter to which the application relates.

119. COMMISSION FOR PUBLIC ADMINISTRATION

119.1 There is established by this Constitution a Commission for Public Administration—

.1 the composition of which shall be determined by Act of Parliament; and

.2 the members of which shall be appointed by Parliament or, with the consent of Parliament, by the Assemblies.

119.2 The Commission shall act through such Commissioners for Administration, or divisions or committees, concerned with particular categories of public authorities or with public authorities in particular nations or regions, as Act of Parliament shall prescribe.

119.3 The Commission has the duty—

.1 to investigate complaints from persons with sufficient interest in the matter, concerning failures of administration or unfair administration by public authorities;

.2 to investigate, on its own initiative or at the request of a Minister or an Executive, acts or omissions, practices or patterns of conduct of public authorities that appear to constitute failures of administration or unfair administration;

.3 to keep under review the constitution and workings of tribunals and statutory inquiries, and connected administrative procedures;

.4 to undertake research into, and to prepare and promulgate Codes of Conduct and other guidelines for, the promotion of standards of good administration with which public authorities may reasonably be expected to comply.

119.4 All acts and omissions of public authorities, and all public authorities, are subject to investigation under this Article, unless Parliament provides otherwise.

119.5 Act of Parliament shall provide—

.1 for effective redress (including the payment of compensation) for persons whom the Commission finds to have been adversely affected by failure of administration or unfair administration; and

.2 with respect to the powers and procedures of the Commission.

119.6 The Commission shall report, as appropriate, to Parliament, Assemblies or local authorities its findings in relation to its investigations and its recommendations for consequential reforms.

119.7 The Commission shall submit an annual report to Parliament and to the Assemblies, which may include recommendations for improvements in any aspect of administrative justice.

120. COMPLAINTS PROCEDURES

120. Every public authority having dealings with the public shall establish a procedure for the receipt and investigation of complaints by members of the public concerning any such dealing and for redress where the complaint is upheld.

CHAPTER 12
Protection of the United Kingdom

---

121. THE ARMED FORCES

121.1 .1 Acts of Parliament shall provide for, and regulate, the Armed Forces of the United Kingdom, comprising the Royal Navy, the British Army and the Royal Air Force, together with the Territorial and Reserve Forces.

   .2 Each such Act shall expire at the end of the fifth year following its enactment.

   .3 Expenditure with respect to the Armed Forces shall be authorised by annual Appropriation Act.

121.2 .1 There is established by this Constitution a Defence Council, consisting of the Minister having responsibility for defence (who shall chair the Council) and such other Ministers, officers in the public services or in the Armed Forces as Act of Parliament shall prescribe.

   .2 Act of Parliament shall provide with respect to appointments, tenure of office and conditions of office of members of the Council.

---

122. DECLARATION OF WAR

122.1 Declarations of a State of War and declarations of a State of Peace shall be made by the Head of State by Order in Council.

122.2 No such Order in Council shall be made unless a draft of the Order has been approved, by resolution, by a two thirds majority of those voting in each House of Parliament.

123. DEPLOYMENT OF ARMED FORCES

123.1 The deployment of the Armed Forces during and in pursuit of a State of War is the responsibility of the Minister having responsibility for defence, acting in consultation with the Defence Council and subject to the general direction of the Cabinet, and in such manner as Act of Parliament may prescribe.

123.2 Act of Parliament shall regulate the deployment of the Armed Forces in support of the civil authorities and for the maintenance of national security or civil order.

123.3 Act of Parliament shall regulate the deployment of the Armed Forces in support of the civil authorities for —

    .1 the maintenance of essential supplies to preserve life and livelihood in a civil emergency;

    .2 the undertaking of necessary work of urgent national importance.

123.4 Act of Parliament shall regulate the deployment of the Armed Forces in support of the civil community for the alleviation of distress and for connected purposes arising out of natural or other disaster.

123.5 .1 The Minister responsible for national security and civil order may, by order, direct deployment of the Armed Forces under paragraphs .2, .3 or .4 but no such order may be made unless a draft of the order has been approved by each House of Parliament.

    .2 The draft of order shall be accompanied by a certificate signed by at least two-thirds of the members, or, in the case in paragraph .4, four of the members, of the Defence Council stating their assent to such deployment of the Armed Forces.

    .3 The order expires at the end of 14 days after it is made, but it may be renewed in the manner provided in this paragraph.

123.6 Any executive action taken under this Article or under an Act of Parliament made thereunder is subject to judicial review.

123.7 Nothing in this Article prevents the taking of any measures which may be necessary for the purposes of defence against attack by armed force.

---

124. VISITING FORCES

124.1 No armed forces of any country outside the United Kingdom, nor any weapons or equipment for the use of such forces, shall be—

.1 based in the United Kingdom, the other British Islands or a dependent territory, or their territorial waters; or

.2 used from the landspace, airspace or territorial waters of the United Kingdom, the other British Islands or a dependent territory,

without the prior consent of Parliament.

124.2 Act of Parliament shall provide with respect to the armed forces of a country outside the United Kingdom visiting the United Kingdom, the other British Islands or dependent territories, including the status, powers and responsibilities of those forces.

---

125. POLICE

---

125. Act of Parliament or, in the case of Scotland and Northern Ireland, Act of Assembly shall provide—

.1 for the establishment, organisation, governance and financing of such number of police forces, serving such areas, as the Act shall prescribe;

.2 for the selection, appointment and conditions of service of police officers and, in particular, procedures for the identification of candidates which will ensure, so far as practicable, that adequate numbers of candidates of both sexes and from diverse racial, religious and social backgrounds are considered for appointment;

.3 for procedures for the discipline of police officers;

.4 for procedures whereby each police force can be held accountable with respect to the performance of its functions to such body of persons holding elected membership of Parliament, an Assembly or local authority as the Act shall prescribe;

.5 for the establishment of independent bodies with the duty of investigating, both on their own initiative and on complaints, acts, omissions and practices in connection with the performance of their functions by police officers or police authorities;

.6 for effective redress (including the payment of compensation) for persons adversely affected by the defective performance of such functions.

---

126. NATIONAL SECURITY

126.1 For the purposes of this Constitution, the expression 'national security' means —

.1 the protection of the territorial integrity of the United Kingdom and the safety of its citizens; and

.2 the maintenance of the system of government established by this Constitution and of the rights and privileges guaranteed by this Constitution against —

.1 espionage, sabotage or subversion by deceptive or clandestine methods to undermine that system of government; or

.2 the use of violence in pursuit of political ends, or against or between members of any group defined by the race, ethnicity, national origins or religious beliefs of its members.

126.2 .1 No public authority shall be established for the purpose of national security, except as prescribed by Act of Parliament.

.2 No person may undertake activities for the purpose of

national security except as an officer, agent or employee of such a security service.

126.3 .1 The provisions of this Constitution with respect to officers of the public service under the Government apply to the officers of any statutory security service.

.2 But the Public Services Commission may make such special arrangements with regard to the officers of such a security service as may be necessary for the effective performance of its functions.

126.4 .1 The Prime Minister shall establish a National Security Committee of the Cabinet to exercise a general direction over the activities of all statutory security services.

.2 The Prime Minister —

.1 is entitled to have access to all information and all records relating to the activities of any statutory security service; and

.2 is responsible to Parliament for their proper and lawful performance of their functions.

126.5 .1 The Prime Minister shall submit an annual report to Parliament concerning the activities of all statutory security services.

.2 There may be excluded from the report any matter, the publication of which the National Security Committee, after consultation with the Inspector-General of Security Services, considers to be prejudicial to the proper performance of the functions of any such service.

127. INSPECTOR GENERAL OF SECURITY SERVICES

127.1 .1 There is established by this Constitution the office of Inspector General of Security Services.

.2 The Inspector-General shall be appointed by the Head of State on the advice of the Prime Minister, who shall select from nominations made by the Public Services Commission.

127.2 The Inspector-General has the duty, in relation to the statutory security services—

.1 to monitor compliance by them with their operational policies;

.2 to review their operational activities;

.3 to keep under review applications by them for, and the issue and execution of, warrants authorising entry upon or interference with property;

.4 to investigate complaints concerning any of their activities that appear to be unlawful, unauthorised, unreasonable or unnecessary;

.5 to investigate, on the Inspector-General's own initiative or at the request of the Prime Minister, any of their acts, omissions, policies or patterns of conduct that appear to be inconsistent with their operational policies or to constitute the improper performance of their functions;

.6 to make consequential recommendations to the National Security Committee, including recommendations for redress for persons whom the Inspector-General finds, in an investigation under this Article, to have been adversely affected.

127.3 The Inspector-General is entitled to have access to such information under the control of a statutory security service, and to request and receive such explanations from the security service, its officers, agents or employees, as the Inspector-General considers necessary for the performance of the duties of the office.

127.4 .1 The Inspector-General shall—

.1 report, as frequently as circumstances require, to the National Security Committee on the performance of the duties, and the findings of investigations, under this Article; and

.2 submit an annual report to such Select Committee as the House of Commons shall determine.

.2 There may be excluded from any such report, and from any other evidence from the Inspector-General to the

Select Committee, any matter, the publication of which the National Security Committee, after consultation with the Inspector-General, considers to be prejudicial to the proper performance of the functions of any statutory security service.

127.5 The Inspector-General shall receive a salary, and office and administrative facilities, appropriate to the full-time performance of the responsibilities of the office.

---

128. SUSPENSION OF THE CONSTITUTION

128.1 Where, in the opinion of the Prime Minister, in the United Kingdom or any part of the United Kingdom—

.1 a grave threat to national security or public order has arisen or is likely to arise; or

.2 a grave civil emergency has arisen or is likely to arise,

the Head of State may, by Order in Council, make provision, to the extent strictly required by the exigencies of the situation and reasonably justified in a democratic society, suspending, in whole or in part, absolutely or subject to conditions, any of the provisions of this Constitution set out in paragraph .2.

128.2 Subject to paragraph .3, the following provisions may be suspended under this Article—

.1 the provisions of the Bill of Rights contained in Division 1 of Chapter 2;

.2 Article 29.3, with respect to the communication of information to public authorities;

.3 Articles 60.1 and 78.4, with respect to the duration of Parliament and the Assemblies, and Part 3 of Schedule 3, with respect to the electoral cycle;

.4 the provisions of an Act made under Article 70 in so far as it affects any provision of the Bill of Rights or relates to the civic rights of non-nationals under Article 33.

128.3 The following provisions may not be suspended under this Article—

.1 Article 2 (*Right to life*), except in respect of deaths resulting from lawful acts of war;

.2 Article 3 (*Freedom from torture*);

.3 Article 4.1 (*Freedom from slavery*);

.4 Article 5.6 (*Treatment of persons in detention*);

.5 Article 6.2 to 6.6 (*Right to fair hearing in criminal cases*);

.6 Article 7 (*Prohibition of retrospective offences*);

.7 Article 9 (*Freedom of thought*);

.9 Article 19.1 (*Equality*).

128.4 Unless the urgency of the situation makes it impracticable to obtain such approval, an Order in Council under this Article shall not be made, unless a draft of the Order has been approved, by resolution, by a two-thirds majority of those voting in each House of Parliament.

128.5 An Order in Council that has been made without having been approved in draft under paragraph .4 ceases to have effect unless, within 14 days after it is made, it is confirmed, by resolution, by a two-thirds majority of those voting in each House of Parliament.

128.6 The validity of an Order in Council made under this Article may be challenged in proceedings for judicial review.

128.7 .1 An Order in Council made under this Article has effect only for such time as shall be specified in the Order.

.2 The duration of the Order may be extended, by resolution, by a two-thirds majority of those voting in each House of Parliament, if, and to the extent that, the making of a new Order in Council would be justified under this Article.

129. DETENTION IN EMERGENCIES

129.1 Where a person is detained under an Order in Council made under Article 128 —

.1 the person shall, as soon as reasonably practicable and not more than 7 days after commencement of the detention, be provided with a statement in writing, in a language that the person understands, specifying in detail the grounds of the detention;

.2 not more than 7 days after the commencement of the detention, a notification shall be published in newspapers having general circulation in the United Kingdom stating that the person has been detained and the particulars of the provision of law under which the detention is authorised;

.3 not more than 3 weeks after the commencement of the detention and thereafter during the detention at intervals of not more than 6 months, the detention shall be reviewed by an independent and impartial tribunal, the members of which shall be appointed by the appropriate Judicial Services Commission;

.4 the person shall be afforded reasonable facilities to consult a representative of his or her choosing and to appear, in person or through such a representative, before the tribunal.

129.2 .1 The tribunal reviewing a detention under this Article may make recommendations concerning the necessity or expediency of continuing the detention, which shall be communicated to the detainee.

.2 Unless Act of Parliament or the Order in Council otherwise provides, the authority by which the detention was ordered, after consideration of the recommendations, is not obliged to act in accordance with them.

SCHEDULES

SCHEDULE 1

The Areas of the Assemblies

1. Scotland

2. Wales

3. Northern Ireland

4. Northern: Northumberland, Cleveland, Tyne and Wear, Durham

5. North West: Lancashire, Merseyside, Greater Manchester, Cheshire and Cumbria

6. Yorkshire: South, North and West Yorkshire and North Humberside

7. West Midlands: West Midlands, Shropshire, Hereford and Worcester, Staffordshire and Warwickshire

8. East Midlands: Nottinghamshire, Lincolnshire, Derbyshire, Leicestershire and South Humberside

9. Central: Bedfordshire, Buckinghamshire, Hertfordshire and Northamptonshire

10. East Anglia: Norfolk, Suffolk, Essex and Cambridgeshire

11. London

12. South East: East and West Sussex and Kent

13. South Central: Berkshire, Hampshire, Isle of Wight, Surrey and Oxfordshire

14. Wessex: Gloucestershire, Somerset, Avon, Dorset and Wiltshire

15. South West: Cornwall and Devon

SCHEDULE 2
Calculation of Revenue Sharing

1. The personal income tax shall be a United Kingdom tax with a common definition of taxable income and common rates and allowances set annually by Act of Parliament and administered by a United Kingdom Board of Inland Revenue.

2. There shall be allocated to the Assembly for each nation or region the estimated product of the personal income tax accruing to the residents of that nation or region.

3. .1 For the first financial year after the coming into force of this Constitution, the Chancellor of the Exchequer shall calculate for the United Kingdom an average per capita expenditure in relation to the functions to be performed by the Assemblies and their Executives.

    .2 In each following year, that calculation of expenditure —

    .1 shall be adjusted by reference to the growth of the Gross Domestic Product;

    .2 shall not be adjusted to reflect changes in the actual expenditure of the Assemblies and their Executives.

4. .1 The average per capita expenditure for the United Kingdom shall be multiplied by the population of each nation or region to derive the expected expenditure in respect of that nation or region.

    .2 The expected expenditure for each nation or region shall be compared with the allocation under paragraph 2.

5. .1 Any nation or region whose allocation exceeds its expected expenditure shall have the surplus deducted from that allocation.

    .2 Any nation or region whose allocation falls short of its expected expenditure shall receive an additional allocation equivalent to the shortfall.

6.   Act of Assembly may vary the rate of income tax levied within the nation or region by 1 or 2 or 3 pence in the pound below or above the standard rate set by Act of Parliament.

7.   .1 Where an Act of an Assembly reduces the standard rate of income tax, its allocation shall be reduced by an amount equal to the revenue lost in consequence of the reduction.

     .2 Where an Act of an Assembly increases the standard rate of income tax, its allocation shall be increased by an amount equal to the revenue raised in consequence of the increase.

SCHEDULE 3
Elections

PART 1: PARLIAMENTARY CONSTITUENCIES

1. THE HOUSE OF COMMONS

1.   The Electoral Commission shall determine a common electoral quota for the whole of the United Kingdom by dividing the total electorate of the United Kingdom by the number of seats in the House of Commons as fixed for the time being by Act of Parliament.

2.   The number of seats in the House of Commons for each nation and region shall be determined by—

   .1 dividing the electorates of Scotland, Wales, Northern Ireland and each of the regions of England by the common electoral quota; and

   .2 allocating to Scotland, Wales, Northern Ireland and each of the regions of England that number of the total number of the seats in the House of Commons that is in direct proportion to the product of the relevant division.

3.   The number of constituencies shall be equivalent to half the total number of seats in the House of Commons as fixed for the time being by Act of Parliament.

4.   In making its recommendations with respect to boundaries of House of Commons constituencies, the Electoral Commission shall—

   .1 as far as possible, have regard to the boundaries of local authorities;

   .2 ensure that no boundary of any House of Commons constituency crosses a boundary of a nation or region; and

.3 subject to those considerations and the factors of distance and density of population, ensure that the electorate of each House of Commons constituency is as near as is practicable equivalent to that of every other such constituency.

5. The recommendations of the Electoral Commission with respect to boundaries of House of Commons constituencies —

    .1 shall be laid before the House of Commons by its Speaker; and

    .2 shall not take effect until approved by resolution of the House.

---

2. SECOND CHAMBER

---

6. The Electoral Commission shall determine a common electoral quota for the whole of the United Kingdom by dividing the total electorate of the United Kingdom by the number of seats in the Second Chamber as fixed for the time being by Act of Parliament.

7. The number of seats in the Second Chamber for each nation and region shall be determined by —

    .1 dividing the electorates of Scotland, Wales, Northern Ireland and each of the regions of England by the common electoral quota; and

    .2 allocating to Scotland, Wales, Northern Ireland and each of the regions of England that number of the total number of the seats in the Second Chamber that is in direct proportion to the product of the relevant division.

8. In making its recommendations with respect to the number of constituencies, and their boundaries, in respect of the seats in the Second Chamber allocated to each nation or region, the Electoral Commission shall ensure that —

    .1 no boundary of any constituency crosses a boundary of a nation or region; and

    .2 subject to that consideration and the factors of distance and density of population, the electorate of each Second

Chamber constituency in a nation or region is as near as is practicable equivalent to that of every other such constituency in that nation or region;

.3 the number of seats in each Second Chamber constituency is within the limits set by Article 85.2.

9.   Nothing in this Part prevents the constitution of a nation or a region as a single constituency.

10.   The recommendations of the Electoral Commission with respect to the numbers and boundaries of Second Chamber constituencies —

.1 shall be laid before the Second Chamber by its Speaker; and

.2 shall not take effect until approved by resolution of the House.

PART 2: ELECTION OF MEMBERS OF PARLIAMENT

---
1. THE HOUSE OF COMMONS
---

1.   At each general election, and in any by-election, for the House of Commons, the candidate who has secured the largest number of votes in a constituency shall be declared elected.

2.   As soon as is practicable after the declaration of the final results of a general election for the House of Commons, the returning officer for each nation or region shall—

.1 compare the votes cast for each political party contesting the election in that nation or region with the number of seats won in the House by that party; and

.2 declare the number of additional members in the House for each political party, in order that the proportion of the seats held by that party in the House in respect of that nation or region corresponds as closely as possible to the proportion that the votes cast for that party in the nation or region bear to the total votes cast there.

3.   No additional member of the House of Commons in respect of any nation or region shall be declared for any political party for which the number of votes cast in that nation or region in respect of that House is less than 5 per cent of the total of all such votes.

4.   The additional members for the House of Commons in respect of a nation or region shall be determined as Act of Parliament shall prescribe.

---

2. SECOND CHAMBER

5.   At each general election, and in any by-election, for the Second Chamber, the candidate who receives the necessary quota of votes under a system of single transferable voting shall be declared elected.

6.   A system of single transferable voting is one in which each vote —

   .1 is capable of being given so as to indicate the voter's order of preference for the candidates for election for the constituency; and

   .2 is capable of being transferred to the next choice —

      .1 when the vote is not required to give a prior choice the necessary quota of votes; or

      .2 when, owing to the deficiency in the number of votes given for a prior choice, that choice is eliminated from the list of candidates.

7.   Act of Parliament shall prescribe the method of voting, and the method of counting and transferring votes, and different provision may be made in those respects in relation to general elections and by-elections.

PART 3: THE ELECTORAL CYCLE

1.   .1 A general election for both Houses of Parliament shall be held on the first Thursday following 1 October 199-.

.2 Notwithstanding Article 60.1, the term of the first Second Chamber is 2 years, and accordingly a general election for the Second Chamber shall be held on the first Thursday following 1 October [199– + 2].

.3 Subsequent general elections shall be held, in respect of each House, on the first Thursday following 1 October in the fourth year following that in which the previous general election was held.

.4 In the case of a dissolution of the House of Commons, a general election of members of the House shall be held within 3 months following the Proclamation made under Article 60.5.1.

2. Elections for the Assemblies shall be held on the first Thursday following 1 October in [199– + 1] and thereafter in the fourth year following that in which the previous elections were held.

3. Elections for local authorities shall be held on the first Thursday following 1 October in [199– + 3], and thereafter in the fourth year following that in which the previous local authority elections were held.

SCHEDULE 4
National Courts

PART 1: COURTS IN ENGLAND AND WALES

---

1. COURTS IN ENGLAND AND WALES

1.1. The courts for England and Wales are—

.1 a Court of Appeal (which is a superior court);

.2 a High Court for civil and public proceedings (which is a superior court);

.3 a Crown Court for criminal proceedings (which is a superior court);

.4 such other courts and tribunals as may be established by Act of Parliament (which may be designated either as intermediate or inferior courts).

1.2 The Court of Appeal consists of—

.1 the Master of the Rolls; and

.2 such number of other justices (not being less than 20) as Act of Parliament may prescribe.

1.3 The High Court consists of the Chief Justice and such number of other justices (not being less than 50) as Act of Parliament may prescribe.

1.4 .1 The Crown Court consists of the justices of the High Court and such number of other judges as may be prescribed by Act of Parliament.

.2 Notwithstanding the status of the Crown Court as a superior court, judges of the Crown Court (other than justices of the High Court) shall not be treated for the purposes of this Constitution as judges of a superior court.

1.5 Except for the duration of any vacancy—

.1 the justices of the Court of Appeal shall include at least 2 persons; and

.2 the justices of the High Court shall include at least 4 persons,

who have been judges of intermediate courts in Wales or have substantial experience of legal practice in Wales.

1.6 The number and title of judges of intermediate and inferior courts shall be such as Act of Parliament may prescribe.

---

2. JUDICIAL QUALIFICATIONS

2.1 .1 Judges of superior and intermediate courts shall be selected from—

.1 persons who have rights of audience in the courts to which they are to be appointed; or

.2 in the case of judges of a superior court, persons who have served as judges of another superior court or of an intermediate court; or

.3 in the case of judges of an intermediate court, persons who have served as judges of another intermediate court or an inferior court and who have such further qualifications (if any) as may be prescribed by Act of Parliament.

.2 Nothing in this Section prevents the appointment of lay members of a court of specialised jurisdiction to sit with a presiding judge qualified under this Section.

2.2 Judges of inferior courts shall be selected from persons who have such qualifications as may be prescribed by Act of Parliament.

3. APPOINTMENT OF JUDGES

3.1   .1 The Master of the Rolls, the Chief Justice of the High Court and the other justices of the superior courts in England and Wales shall be appointed by the Minister of Justice.

       .2 The Minister of Justice shall make the appointment to fill any vacancy by selecting one out of two persons whose names shall be submitted for consideration by the Judicial Services Commission (subject to the right to invite the Commission to reconsider the submission).

3.2   Subject to this Section, judges of intermediate and inferior courts shall be appointed by the Minister of Justice, acting in accordance with the recommendation of the Judicial Services Commission.

3.3   .1 Judges of intermediate or inferior courts who are appointed to sit in districts wholly within Wales shall be appointed by the Minister of Justice, acting in accordance with the recommendation of the Welsh Appointments Committee.

       .2 Judges of inferior courts who are appointed to sit in districts wholly within a region of England shall be appointed by the Minister of Justice, acting in accordance with the recommendation of the Regional Appointments Committee for that region.

4. SUPPLEMENTARY APPOINTMENTS

4.1   .1 The Judicial Services Commission may authorise—

       .1 a judge of any court to sit as a judge of a court of equal or lesser jurisdiction;

       .2 any person who is eligible for appointment as a judge of any court or who is a retired judge of any court to sit as a temporary judge of that court;

       .3 any person who is eligible for appointment as a judge of any court to sit as a part-time judge of that court.

.2 But at least half the members of any division of the Court of Appeal shall consist of persons currently holding office as Justices of the Court of Appeal or permitted by this Constitution to act after attaining retiring age.

.3 Authorisation under this Section may be given by general rules and may be delegated to such persons as appear to the Judicial Services Commission to be appropriate.

4.2 .1 Assistant judges of any court may be appointed for the purpose of dealing with interlocutory, uncontested or other subsidiary matters.

.2 For the purposes of appointment and tenure, assistant judges of a superior court shall be treated as judges of an intermediate court and assistant judges of an intermediate court shall be treated as judges of an inferior court.

5. JURISDICTION OF COURT OF APPEAL

5.1 The Court of Appeal is the highest appellate court in England and Wales.

5.2 The Court has jurisdiction to hear appeals from any decision of the High Court or the Crown Court or an intermediate or inferior court, subject to—

.1 Article 94.2;

.2 the giving of leave to appeal, where required by Act of Parliament or Rules of Court;

.3 any Act of Parliament excluding or limiting rights of appeal in any class of proceedings;

.4 in the case of appeals from an inferior court, any intermediate appeal procedures which may be established by Act of Parliament.

6. CONSTITUTIONAL JURISDICTION OF HIGH COURT

6.1 Any reference made in England and Wales under Article 94.1 shall be made to the High Court.

6.2 There is a right of appeal to the Court of Appeal without leave from any decision of the High Court, or of a Crown Court, that an Assembly Act is wholly or partly void.

6.3 Any proceedings in which —

.1 the plaintiff, applicant or accused claims that there has been a contravention of the Bill of Rights, contained in Chapter 2; or

.2 the plaintiff, applicant or accused challenges the validity of —

.1 any subordinate legislation made under an Act of Parliament or of an Assembly; or

.2 any executive decision of the Government of the United Kingdom or of the Executive for Wales or for a region or of any body exercising powers under this Constitution; or

.3 a substantial issue as to the interpretation of this Constitution arises,

may be commenced in the High Court, without prejudice to the exercise of any power of the High Court to transfer such proceedings to another court.

6.4 In —

.1 any such proceedings as are mentioned in subsection .3; or

.2 any proceedings in which a claim that an Act of Parliament or of an Assembly is wholly or partly void has been dismissed,

no restriction may be placed on any right of appeal to the Court of Appeal unless the claim or challenge is frivolous, vexatious or an abuse of the process of the court.

7. SITTINGS OF HIGH COURT AND CROWN COURT

7.   Provision shall be made for regular sittings of the High Court and the Crown Court at one or more places in Wales and in each region.

8. RULES COMMITTEES

8.   There shall be Rules Committees, the membership of which shall be prescribed by Act of Parliament, which shall make, amend and keep under review Rules of Court for practice and procedure.

PART 2: COURTS IN SCOTLAND

9. COURTS IN SCOTLAND

9.1   The courts for Scotland are —

.1 a Court of Session, comprising an Inner House and an Outer House (which is a superior court);

.2 a High Court of Justice (which is a superior court);

.3 Sheriff's courts (which are intermediate courts);

.4 District courts (which are intermediate courts);

.5 such other courts and tribunals as may be established by Act of the Assembly for Scotland (which may be designated either as intermediate or inferior courts).

9.2   The Court of Session consists of —

.1 the Lord President (who shall preside over the First Division of the Inner House);

.2 the Lord Justice Clerk (who shall preside over the Second Division of the Inner House); and

.3 such number of other judges (who shall compose the Outer House) as Act of the Assembly for Scotland may prescribe.

9.3 The High Court of Justice consists of the Lord President, as Lord Justice General, and the other judges of the Court of Session.

9.4 The number and title of judges of intermediate and inferior courts shall be such as may be prescribed by Act of the Assembly for Scotland.

10. QUALIFICATIONS AND APPOINTMENT OF JUDGES

10.1 Judges shall be selected from persons who have such qualifications as may be prescribed by Act of the Assembly for Scotland.

10.2 Judges shall be appointed by the Chief Executive for Scotland, acting in accordance with the recommendation of the Judicial Services Commission for Scotland.

11. SUPPLEMENTARY APPOINTMENTS

11.2 The Judicial Services Commission for Scotland may authorise —

.1 a judge of any court to sit as a judge of a court of equal jurisdiction;

.2 any person who is eligible for appointment as a judge of any court or who is a retired judge of any court to sit as a temporary judge of that court.

11.2 Authorisation under this Section may be given by general rules or delegated to such persons as appear to the Judicial Services Commission for Scotland to be appropriate.

12. CONSTITUTIONAL PROCEEDINGS

12.1   Any proceedings in which —

.1 the pursuer, applicant or accused claims that there has been a contravention of the Bill of Rights, contained in Chapter 2; or

.2 the pursuer, applicant or accused challenges the validity of —

.1 any subordinate legislation made under an Act of Parliament or of the Assembly; or

.2 any executive decision of the Government of the United Kingdom or of the Executive for Scotland or of any body exercising powers under this Constitution; or

.3 a substantial issue as to the interpretation of this Constitution arises,

may be commenced in the Court of Session or High Court without prejudice to the exercise of any power of that court to transfer such proceedings to another court.

12.2   In —

.1 any such proceedings as are mentioned in subsection .1; or

.2 any proceedings in which a claim that an Act of Parliament or of the Assembly is wholly or partly void has been dismissed,

no restriction may be placed on any right of appeal to the Inner House unless the claim or challenge is frivolous, vexatious or an abuse of the process of the court.

13. RULES COMMITTEES

13.   There shall be Rules Committees, the membership of which shall be prescribed by Act of the Assembly for Scotland, which shall make, amend and keep under review Rules of Court for practice and procedure.

PART 3: COURTS IN NORTHERN IRELAND

---

14. COURTS IN NORTHERN IRELAND

14.1   The courts for Northern Ireland are—

.1 a Court of Appeal (which is a superior court);

.2 a High Court for civil and public proceedings (which is a superior court);

.3 a Crown Court for criminal proceedings (which is a superior court);

.4 such other courts and tribunals as may be established by Act of the Assembly for Northern Ireland (which may be designated either as intermediate or inferior courts).

14.2   The Court of Appeal consists of—

.1 the Chief Justice of Northern Ireland; and

.2 such number of other Justices (not being fewer than 3) as may be prescribed by Act of the Assembly for Northern Ireland.

14.3   The High Court consists of the Chief Justice of Northern Ireland and such number of other Justices (not being fewer than 6) as Act of the Assembly for Northern Ireland may prescribe.

14.4   .1 The Crown Court consists of the Justices of the High Court and such number of other judges as Act of the Assembly for Northern Ireland may prescribe.

14.5   .2 Notwithstanding the status of the Crown Court as a superior court, judges of the Crown Court (other than Justices of the High Court) shall not be treated for the purposes of this Constitution as judges of a superior court.

14.6   The number and title of judges of intermediate and inferior courts shall be such as Act of the Assembly for Northern Ireland may prescribe.

15. JUDICIAL QUALIFICATIONS

15.1   .1 Judges of superior and intermediate courts shall be selected from —

      .1 persons who have rights of audience in the courts to which they are to be appointed; or

      .2 in the case of judges of a superior court, persons who have served as judges of another superior court or of an intermediate court; or

      .3 in the case of judges of an intermediate court, persons who have served as judges of another intermediate court or an inferior court and who have such further qualifications (if any) as Act of the Assembly for Northern Ireland may prescribe.

    .2 Nothing in this Section prevents the appointment of lay members of a court of specialised jurisdiction to sit with a presiding judge qualified under this Section.

15.2 Judges of inferior courts shall be selected from persons who have such qualifications as Act of the Assembly for Northern Ireland may prescribe.

16. APPOINTMENT OF JUDGES

16.1   .1 The Chief Justice of Northern Ireland and the other Justices of the superior courts in Northern Ireland shall be appointed by the Chief Executive for Northern Ireland.

    .2 The Chief Executive shall make the appointment to fill any vacancy by selecting one out of two persons whose names shall be submitted for consideration by the Judicial Services Commission for Northern Ireland (subject to the right to invite the Commission to reconsider the submission).

16.2 Judges of intermediate and inferior courts shall be appointed by the Chief Executive for Northern Ireland, acting in accordance with the recommendation of the Judicial Services Commission for Northern Ireland.

17. SUPPLEMENTARY APPOINTMENTS

17.1 .1 The Judicial Services Commission for Northern Ireland may authorise —

    .1 a judge of any court to sit as a judge of a court of equal or lesser jurisdiction;

    .2 any person who is eligible for appointment as a judge of any court or who is a retired judge of any court to sit as a temporary judge of that court;

    .3 any person who is eligible for appointment as a judge of any court to sit as a part-time judge of that court.

  .2 Authorisation under this Section may be given by general rules and may be delegated to such persons as appear to the Judicial Services Commission for Northern Ireland to be appropriate.

17.2 .1 Assistant judges of any court may be appointed for the purpose of dealing with interlocutory, uncontested or other subsidiary matters.

  .2 For the purposes of appointment and tenure, assistant judges of a superior court shall be treated as judges of an intermediate court and assistant judges of an intermediate court shall be treated as judges of an inferior court.

18. JURISDICTION OF COURT OF APPEAL

18.1 The Court of Appeal is the highest appellate court in Northern Ireland.

18.2 The Court has jurisdiction to hear appeals from any decision of the High Court or the Crown Court or an intermediate or inferior court, subject to —

  .1 Article 94.2;

  .2 the giving of leave to appeal, where required by any Act of Parliament or the Assembly for Northern Ireland or Rules of Court;

.3 any such Act excluding or limiting rights of appeal in any class of proceedings;

.4 in the case of appeals from an inferior court, any intermediate appeal procedures which may be established by any such Act.

---

19. CONSTITUTIONAL JURISDICTION OF HIGH COURT

19.1 Any reference made in Northern Ireland under Article 94.1 shall be made to the High Court.

19.2 There is a right of appeal to the Court of Appeal, without leave, from any decision of the High Court that an Act of the Assembly for Northern Ireland is wholly or partly void.

19.3 Any proceedings in which —

.1 the plaintiff, applicant or accused claims that there has been a contravention of the Bill of Rights, contained in Chapter 2; or

.2 the plaintiff, applicant or accused challenges the validity of —

.1 any subordinate legislation made under an Act of Parliament or of the Assembly for Northern Ireland; or

.2 any executive decision of the Government of the United Kingdom or of the Executive for Northern Ireland or of any body exercising powers under this Constitution; or

.3 a substantial issue as to the interpretation of this Constitution arises,

may be commenced in the High Court, without prejudice to the exercise of any power of the High Court to transfer such proceedings to another court.

19.4 In —

.1 any such proceedings as are mentioned in subsection .3; or

.2 any proceedings in which a claim that an Act of Parliament or of the Assembly for Northern Ireland is wholly or partly void has been dismissed,

no restriction may be placed on any right of appeal to the Court of Appeal unless the claim or challenge is frivolous, vexatious or an abuse of the process of the court.

20. RULES COMMITTEES

20. There shall be Rules Committees, the membership of which shall be prescribed by Act of the Assembly for Northern Ireland, which shall make, amend and keep under review Rules of Court for practice and procedure.

SCHEDULE 5

Judicial Services Commission and Judicial Council for England and Wales

---

1. JUDICIAL SERVICES COMMISSION FOR ENGLAND AND WALES

1.1   .1 The Judicial Services Commission for England and Wales consists of —

     .1 a lay President;

     .2 5 judges (who shall include at least one justice of the Court of Appeal, at least one justice of the High Court and at least one judge of an intermediate court) who shall be elected by the judges by such method as Act of Parliament shall prescribe;

     .3 2 persons who have regularly exercised rights of audience in the superior courts for not less than 15 years;

     .4 1 lay member resident in Wales;

     .5 6 other lay members, who shall be broadly representative of the community.

   .2 The Judicial Services Commission may act notwithstanding any vacancy in its membership.

   .3 For the purposes of this Section, the expressions 'judge' and 'lay' have the meanings given by Article 109.2.2.

1.2   .1 The members of the Judicial Services Commission (other than judicial members) shall be appointed by the Minister of Justice after consultation with the Master of the Rolls and the Chief Justice of the High Court.

   .2 The lay members shall be selected by the Minister of Justice from a list of names submitted by the Public Services Commission.

.3 If either of the Master of the Rolls or the Chief Justice records dissent from a proposed appointment, the fact of the dissent shall be published if the Minister proceeds with the appointment.

1.3 The members of the Judicial Services Commission shall be appointed for such terms (being not less than 5 years) as Act of Parliament may prescribe.

1.4 No person may be appointed for a term which would expire after that person attains the age of 70 years.

1.5 A member of the Judicial Services Commission ceases to hold office —

.1 upon the expiry of the terms of the appointment (which may be renewed);

.2 if the member ceases to have the qualification necessary for appointment;

.3 on receipt by the Minister of Justice of a letter of resignation from the member;

.4 in the case of a judicial member, if the member is removed from office under Part 4 of Chapter 9;

.5 in the case of a non-judicial member, if the member is removed from office by the Public Services Commission;

.6 if the member accepts an office which is declared by the Constitution or Act of Parliament to be inconsistent with membership of the Judicial Services Commission.

---

2. WELSH AND REGIONAL APPOINTMENTS COMMITTEES

2.1 There is established by this Constitution a Welsh Appointments Committee of the Judicial Services Commission.

2.2 .1 The members consist of —

.1 the member of the Judicial Services Commission appointed under Section 1.1.4 (who shall chair the Committee);

.2 2 judges of intermediate courts in Wales, who shall be elected by the body of such judges;

.3 one member of the legal profession practising in Wales who has practised there for not less than 15 years;

.4 3 other lay members resident in Wales.

.2 The Welsh Appointments Committee may act notwithstanding any vacancy in its membership.

2.3 Section 1.2 to .5 applies to the Welsh Appointments Committee as it applies to the Judicial Services Commission, except that—

.1 the Minister of Justice shall also consult the Chief Executive for Wales; and

.2 an expression of dissent by the Chief Executive has the same effect as an expression of dissent by the Master of the Rolls or the Chief Justice of the High Court.

2.4 .1 Regional Appointments Committees shall be established by Act of Parliament for each region of England.

.2 Such Act shall make provision for appointments to, and cessation of, office of members of the Committees in like form, with necessary modifications, to subsections .2 and .3.

2.5 The Welsh Appointments Committee and the Regional Appointments Committees shall report to the Judicial Appointments Commission which may give them directions as to administration and procedure.

---

3. CONDITIONS OF SERVICE OF COMMISSION MEMBERS

3.1 Membership of the Judicial Services Commission, the Welsh Appointments Committee and Regional Appointment Committees shall be part-time, except that the President of the Judicial Services Commission shall serve full-time.

3.2 Non-judicial members shall receive such pay as may be determined by the Minister of Justice in consultation with the Treasury.

4. ADMINISTRATION OF COMMISSION

4.   The Judicial Services Commission shall —

.1 employ its own staff (subject to the approval of the Treasury as to the numbers and salaries of staff); and

.2 provide the administration services required by the Welsh Appointments Committee and Regional Appointments Committees.

5. JUDICIAL COUNCIL

5.1   The Judicial Council consists of representatives of justices of the Court of Appeal, of justices of the High Court, of judges of intermediate courts and of judges of inferior courts (including at least one judge of an intermediate or inferior court in Wales).

5.2   Act of Parliament shall provide for the method of selection and terms of office of the members.

SCHEDULE 6
Words of Enactment

1. In every Bill presented to the Head of State for Assent, other than a Bill mentioned in paragraphs 2 to 6, the words of enactment shall be as follows —

   Be it enacted by the Head of State by and with the advice and consent of the House of Commons and the Second Chamber of the United Kingdom and by the authority of the same, as follows —.

2. In every Bill presented to the Head of State for Assent under Article 67 or 68, the words of enactment shall be as follows —

   Be it enacted by the Head of State by and with the advice and consent of the House of Commons of the United Kingdom in accordance with the provisions of Article 67 (*or Article 68, as the case may be*) of the Constitution of the United Kingdom and by the authority of the same as follows —.

3. In every Bill to amend this Constitution to which Article 69.1 or Article 69.2 applies that is presented to the Head of State for Assent, the words of enactment shall be as follows —

   Be it enacted by the Head of State by and with the advice and consent of the House of Commons and the Second Chamber of the United Kingdom in accordance with the provisions of Article 69.1 (*or Article 69.2, as the case may be*) of the Constitution of the United Kingdom, and by the authority of the same as follows —.

4. In every Bill to amend this Constitution to which Article 69.3 also applies, to the words of enactment set out in paragraph 3, there shall be added, immediately before the expression 'of this Constitution', the following expression —

, and after being duly ratified by Assemblies in accordance with Article 69.3,.

5. In every Bill to amend this Constitution to which Article 69.4 also applies, to the words of enactment set out in paragraph 3, there shall be added, immediately before the expression 'of this Constitution', the following expression —

, and after approval by referendum in accordance with Article 69.4,.

6. In every Constitutional Bill to which Article 70 applies that is presented to the Head of State for Assent, the words of enactment shall be as follows —

Be it enacted by the Head of State by and with the advice and consent of the House of Commons and Second Chamber of the United Kingdom in accordance with the provisions of Article 70 of the Constitution of the United Kingdom and by the authority of the same, as follows —.

PART II

Commentary

CHAPTER 1

The Constitution

ARTICLE 1: CONSTITUTION AS FOUNDATION OF POWER IN UNITED KINGDOM

This Article has several fundamental functions. First, it affirms the Constitution's most radical characteristic: that it *is* a written Constitution for the United Kingdom which wholly replaces the former, unwritten constitutional order. Though the revolution in practice and action contemplated by the Constitution is partial, in the sense that, while vital reforms are made, not everything is changed, the revolution in constitutional thought required is total. Henceforth, authority for legislative, judicial or executive action must be sought not in common law principles such as parliamentary sovereignty or prerogative power, nor in constitutional conventions, such as ministerial responsibility, but in the written provisions of this Constitution. If the authority cannot be found there, the action is invalid, whatever the traditional conceptions might suggest.

Second, the Article places the Constitution in the context of the United Kingdom's international and European commitments. The statement in this Article is deliberately drafted in general terms; specific implementation of the commitment referred to is provided in later Articles, notably Article 51.3 on international relations. So far as the European Community is concerned, Article 50 secures the direct application and effect of European Community law by giving constitutional force to the appropriate provisions of the European Communities Act 1972, as amended. By this means, a constitutional base for European Community law in the United Kingdom is secured, which is compatible with the 'sole foundation' claim of Article 1.1; at the same time, the open texture of Article 1.2 provides a constitutional mandate for the United Kingdom's participation in whatever course of development the Community might pursue, whilst not *constitutionally* committing it to anything beyond respect of its existing Community obligations. So far as the broader international order is concerned, Article 1.2 is designed not to exclude the recognition of general international law (as opposed to our treaty obligations, dealt with under Article 51.3 as part of the law of the United Kingdom), but to leave to the courts the question of whether and with what effect such international law obligations are to be recognised as operative in the United Kingdom in any given case.

Third, the Article lays down, in 1.3, the general principle of application and interpretation of law which is appropriate to a written Constitution. So far as possible laws are to be interpreted in harmony with the Constitution. Should it be impossible to interpret a law so as to bring it into conformity with the Constitution, then Article 1.4 on inconsistency will apply. Article 1.3 deliberately distinguishes between 'Acts of Parliament' and 'laws'. The latter, broader term includes not only Acts of Parliament but also legislation passed by the Assemblies.

Fourth, the Article lays down the general principle of transition from the unwritten Constitution era to the written Constitution era. It deprives of effect all existing law (including, for the purposes of this provision, common law) and other constitutional practice to the extent of its inconsistency with the Constitution. By necessary implication it preserves all other law in full force, and it also preserves the legal effect of things done prior to the enactment of the Constitution under laws, conventions and practices which are rendered invalid after that date.

CHAPTER 2
Rights and Freedoms

PART 1: FUNDAMENTAL RIGHTS AND FREEDOMS

Division 1: The Bill of Rights

The Bill of Rights set out here draws on the European Convention on Human Rights and Fundamental Freedoms ('the Convention') and on the United Nations International Covenant on Civil and Political Rights ('the Covenant'), by both of which the United Kingdom is legally bound. Our Bill is compatible with both but in some respects goes further in its definition and protection of rights. As a general principle we have relied on the provisions of the Convention, in some instances limiting the circumstances in which a right may be curtailed, but in others replacing the provision with its equivalent in the Covenant where the wording is preferable.

In Article 2 (right to life), for instance, which is based on Article 2 of the Convention, we have removed the exception which permits the death penalty during time of war. In Article 5 (right to liberty), which is based on Article 5 of the Convention, we have deleted references to the detention of alcoholics, drug addicts and vagrants. Their imprisonment for specific criminal offences would, of course, still be permitted. From Article 8 (respect for private and family life), which is based on Article 8 of the Convention, we have removed 'economic wellbeing of the country' as grounds for infringing privacy. In the case of Article 11 (freedom of expression) we have relied almost entirely on the stronger protection provided by the Covenant. Similarly, Article 15 (right to participation in public life and service) draws on the Covenant in preference to the more limited protection provided by Protocol 1 to the Convention.

In one instance, Article 18, which provides a right of asylum, we have drawn on the American Convention of Human Rights because there is no equivalent provision in either the Convention or the Covenant. In other cases we have added to the protection provided by the international instruments, as in our Article 19 (equality), which includes within the grounds for non-discrimination homosexuality, age and disability.

The UK government has entered a number of reservations to provisions of the Convention and Covenant and failed to ratify some Protocols to the Convention. Where we consider the government should accept these provisions we have included them within our text and indicated where we have done so.

Both of these international instruments permit derogations from certain rights and freedoms during periods of serious public emergency. Article 128 of this Constitution permits derogations (or 'suspensions') in similar circumstances but provides that a decision to suspend a right requires an affirmative resolution of both Houses of Parliament, with periodic votes to renew it. Furthermore, the courts (like courts in other Commonwealth countries) are empowered to review whether the facts of the situation justify suspension. In practice the courts would give considerable weight to the government's view on a decision of this kind, but it would not necessarily be decisive.

The Bill of Rights applies to any act (or omission) by any person or body in the performance of any public function (see Article 20). We envisage that the normal method of challenging legislation or the actions of public authorities will be by application to the High Court for judicial review (or the Scottish Court of Session or the Northern Ireland High Court), with a right of appeal to the Supreme Court. In other circumstances, however, Bill of Rights issues would not be dealt with exclusively by judicial review. For example, defendants to a charge of obstructing the highway might raise as a defence the claim that they were exercising their right to freedom of assembly protected by the Bill of Rights. We envisage that the trial court would rule on the validity of the defence.

Deciding on the validity of a statute, however, would always be a matter of public importance and it would be essential to avoid conflicting decisions in different lower courts. Accordingly, if a defendant challenged the validity of the Act of Parliament under which he or she was being prosecuted in a magistrate's court, that court would have to refer the challenge for decision by the High Court, with a right of appeal to the Supreme Court, unless the challenge was clearly hopeless. If the High Court dismissed the challenge, the case would then continue in the magistrate's court. Individuals would retain the right to complain to the European

Commission of Human Rights in Strasbourg if they believed that their rights under the Convention had been infringed and they had been unable to obtain a remedy under the provisions of the Bill of Rights in the UK Constitution.

If the Bill of Rights is to be effective, the legal remedies in administrative law need to be rectified, in particular the bar on obtaining an injunction against the Crown and the absence of financial compensation (in most instances) for loss caused by administrative action where a public authority has exceeded its powers or acted improperly or unreasonably. This argument, the historical development of support for a Bill of Rights, the arguments for and against its introduction, and related issues are set out in *A British Bill of Rights* (London: IPPR, 1990), which first published the draft Bill of Rights contained in this Constitution (with minor amendments).

The text of the Bill of Rights consists of 18 Articles which contain the substantive rights protected by the Bill of Rights and 6 Articles which define the operation and effect of the Bill. Throughout the commentary on the Bill of Rights 'EC' refers to the European Convention on Human Rights and Fundamental Freedoms and 'IC' to the International Covenant on Civil and Political Rights.

ARTICLE 2: RIGHT TO LIFE

This is EC 2, with the omission of para. 2(b), which states: 'in order to effect a lawful arrest or to prevent the escape of a person lawfully detained'. Escaping from arrest or detention cannot justify intentional killing unless it involves life-threatening violence, in which case 2.3.1 would apply.

The EC allows the death penalty 'in respect of acts committed in time of war or imminent threat of war', to be applied 'only in the instances laid down in the law'. There is no restriction in respect of the type of crimes for which the death penalty can be imposed. IC allows a reservation 'which provides for the application of the death penalty in times of war pursuant to a conviction for a most serious crime of a military nature committed during war time'. This reservation is unsatisfactory as it seems to allow the death penalty for desertion but not for civilian genocide. It is our view that the death penalty is wrong in any circumstances and these provisions have therefore been omitted.

The European Court of Human Rights has not yet had occasion to interpret the words 'everyone has the right to have his life respected' which open Article 2 of the Convention. The Commission has however examined their application to a number of issues including euthanasia, sterilisation, and the duty to safeguard life as well as to refrain from taking it intentionally. The European Commission expressly left open the question whether the unborn child is covered by EC 2 in *Bruggemann and Scheuten v FRG* (Application 10 D & R 100), a case brought under EC 8 (right to respect for private life) alleging that the rules restricting a woman's access to abortion constituted a violation of that Article. The Commission held that pregnancy and its termination cannot be considered solely a matter of the private life of the mother, observing that in the domestic law of all parties to the EC certain rights are attributed to a conceived but unborn child (for example, in relation to inheritance).

In the case of *X v UK* (Application No. 8416/79; 19 D & R 244) the applicant complained of the refusal by the High Court to grant an injunction to prevent the termination of his wife's pregnancy. His complaint was that the Abortion Act 1967 violated Articles 2, 5 (right to liberty and security), 6 (right to a fair hearing), 8, and 9 (freedom of thought). The Commission rejected the view that a foetus has an absolute right to life and found the UK abortion laws compatible with EC 2(1), which they considered contained an implied limitation protecting the woman's life and health at her early stage of pregnancy. The applicant (the father of the child) also claimed violations of EC 8 because he was excluded from all the decisions relating to the abortion. The Commission held that the father's rights did not embrace procedural rights to be consulted where the woman intended to have an abortion.

ARTICLE 3: FREEDOM FROM TORTURE

This is EC 3, with the addition of 'cruel' from IC 7.

ARTICLE 4: FREEDOM FROM SLAVERY AND ENFORCED LABOUR

This is EC 4, omitting 'in countries where they are recognised' after 'objectors' in section 4.3.2. IC 8 is very similar.

ARTICLE 5: RIGHT TO LIBERTY AND SECURITY

The listed exceptions to the right to liberty and security are those set out in EC 5 with the deletion of references to detention of minors for educational supervision, alcoholics, drug addicts and vagrants. This does not, of course, make it unlawful to imprison drug addicts for drug offences, etc. In 5.1.2.4, the words 'constituting a serious threat to public health' and 'where necessary for the prevention of harm to themselves or others' have been added to narrow the exception. A reference to 'persons suffering from mental disorder' is substituted for 'persons of unsound mind'.

5.2 is IC 9(2) with part of EC 5(2).

5.3 is mainly a rearranged IC 9(3). 5.3.2 is from IC 9(3) with the addition at the end of the words 'pending trial' from EC 5(3). 5.3.3 is also from IC 9(3) but omits the words at the end 'and, should occasion arise, for execution of the judgement', which seem unnecessary.

5.4 is IC 9(4). EC 5(4) is very similar.

5.5 is IC 9(5). EC 5(5) is very similar.

5.6 is IC 10(1). There is no EC equivalent.

5.7 is IC 10(2)(a). There is no EC equivalent.

5.8 is IC 10(2)(b) and the second sentence of IC 10(3), slightly reworded. This arrangement seems better than that in IC 10. There is no EC equivalent. The UK has reserved the right not to apply this provision where there is a lack of suitable prison facilities or where the mixing of adults and juveniles is deemed to be mutually beneficial. In our view this reservation should not be retained.

5.9 is IC 11. EC Protocol 4 is very similar.

The UK has also generally reserved 'the right to apply to members of and persons serving with the armed forces of the Crown and to persons detained in penal establishments of whatever character such laws and procedures as they may from time to time deem to be necessary for the preservation of service and custodial discipline'. This has particular application to this Article. In our view this reservation should not be retained.

ARTICLE 6: RIGHT TO FAIR AND PUBLIC HEARING

This is EC 6 with some additions from IC 14. 'Morals' has been deleted from the grounds for removing the press and public from a trial, in 6.1, as we do not consider that it could be justified to exclude the press or public on those grounds.

6.3.6 is IC 14(3)(g) and has no equivalent in EC 6.

6.4 is a modified version of IC 14(6). There is no EC equivalent (Article 5.5 above does not apply because the detention is not unlawful). IC 14(6) is clumsily and too narrowly worded – it applies only if it is 'conclusively' shown by a 'newly discovered fact' that there has been a miscarriage.

6.5 is section (5) of IC 14. There is a similar provision in EC Protocol 7.

6.6 is section (7) of IC 14. There is a similar provision in EC Protocol 7.

ARTICLE 7: RETROSPECTIVE OFFENCES PROHIBITED

7.1 is EC 7(1), complete. IC 15 is similar, except that it adds a sentence at the end of para. 1 enabling an offender to have the benefit of any reduction in penalties made subsequent to the offence. This would seem to be unnecessary.

7.2 is based on EC 7(2). (IC 15(2) is similar.) However, EC 7(2) allows trial 'for any act or omission which, at the time when it was committed, was criminal according to the general principle of law recognised by civilised nations'. We think that this restriction should be tightened up and limited to genocide or crimes against humanity.

ARTICLE 8: RESPECT FOR PRIVATE AND FAMILY LIFE

This is EC 8, slightly reworded, with the removal of 'economic wellbeing of the country' as grounds for infringing privacy. We consider that there is no justification for this exception, inspection of financial records in a fraud investigation, or VAT inspection, for instance, falling within the exception for 'prevention of crime'.

EC 8 does not give any right to privacy as such, but only the right to respect for private and family life, home and correspondence.

In the *Leander* case (9 EHRR 433), which concerned security monitoring, the State was found to have interfered with the negative obligation imposed by EC 8 by compiling, storing, using and disclosing private information about the applicant, but it was held that such interference was justified in the interests of national security in that, in the circumstances, it corresponded to a pressing social need and was proportionate to the legitimate aim pursued. In *Malone v UK* (7 EHRR 14), which concerned telephone tapping in the course of police investigations, the Court found it unnecessary to make a finding as to whether this practice could be justified under EC 8(2) since in this case the interferences were not 'in accordance with the law', there being no written law on the matter. As a result of the judgment, the UK government introduced the Interception of Communications Act 1985.

In *Gaskin v UK* (12 EHRR 36), the applicant himself wanted access to the information held and compiled by the State authority when he was in care during his early childhood and formative years. The Court stated that a 'fair balance has to be struck between the general interest of the community and the interests of the individual'. Whilst an applicant had an interest protected by the Convention in receiving this information, the 'confidentiality of public records is of importance for receiving objective and reliable information . . . and necessary for the protection of third persons'. The Court decided that the lack of procedure for balancing those interests in the British system constituted a violation of the right to respect for private and family life.

ARTICLE 9: FREEDOM OF THOUGHT

This is, with the exception of 9.3, EC 9 complete but slightly reworded. It is very similar to IC 18(1) and (3). IC 18(2) provides that 'No one shall be subject to coercion which would impair his freedom to have or to adopt a religion or belief of his choice.' This does not seem to add anything to 9.1 above.

9.3 is a general prohibition applying both to Parliament and the Assemblies against making laws which interfere with freedom of religion. The implication of this prohibition, along with the reform of the Second Chamber, is that the established position of the Church of England and Church of Scotland will be brought into question. We have not examined the implications in any depth, but believe that the logic of the Bill of Rights and the development in the United Kingdom of a variety of religious faiths as well as denominations should in the long run result in disestablishment and a secular constitution.

ARTICLE 10: RIGHT TO EDUCATION

This Article is based on EC Protocol 1 para. 2. The opening words of 10.2 are altered; the original is 'In the exercise of any functions which it assumes in relation to education and to teaching, the State shall respect . . .'. This is not wholly appropriate to the UK, where education is mainly a local authority function.

IC contains no equivalent to 10.1. This should clearly be included as a basic right.

IC 18(4) is fairly similar to 10.2. It contains a number of textual differences. These are:

IC 18(4) speaks of the 'liberty of parents', not the 'right of parents'.

IC 18(4) refers to legal guardians as well as parents.

IC 18(4) refers to 'religious and moral education of their children in conformity with their own convictions'. The words 'moral' (IC) and 'philosophical' (EC) are not entirely synonymous.

The words following 'convictions' follow the wording of a reservation by the UK on the ratification of the Protocol. We think that the reservation is reasonable and should be retained.

The extent of a State's duty to protect the right to education has been a subject of concern in a number of EC Member States. The UK has accepted the duty to protect this right only so far as is compatible with the provision of efficient instruction and training and the avoidance of unreasonable public expenditure.

The State has no obligation under Article 2 of EC Protocol 1 to establish or subsidise private schooling, or any particular type of schooling, for example grammar schools (7 EHRR 135). Nor need it conform education to the linguistic preferences of the parents. However, in the *Belgian Linguistics* case (1 EHRR 241) the Court found a violation of Article 2 read in conjunction with EC 14 (non-discrimination) because Dutch-speaking children residing in the French unilingual region had access to Dutch schools but French-speaking children in the Dutch area had no access to French schools.

In *Campbell and Cosans* (4 EHRR 293) it was held that Article 2 of Protocol 1 does not prevent states from imparting through teaching or education information or knowledge of a directly or indirectly religious or philosophical kind but they must take care that such information is conveyed in an objective and pluralistic manner. The Court has also held (*Kjeldsen, Busk, Madsen and Pedersen v Denmark*, 1 EHRR 711) that the State is forbidden to pursue an aim of indoctrination that might be considered as failing to respect parents' religious and philosophical convictions.

IC 18 refers to freedom of thought, conscience and religion and the State's obligation to ensure the moral education of children. The Human Rights Committee has held (*Communication 40/1978 v Finland*) that Finnish legislation requiring the study of the history of religion did not violate the rights of parents who objected to religious instruction, provided the courses were given in a neutral and objective way.

ARTICLE 11: FREEDOM OF EXPRESSION

This is IC 19 with the addition of part of EC 10(1). Unlike EC 10, IC 19 clearly separates the right to hold opinions and does not make it subject to any restrictions. The expression of opinions can be regulated but not the right to possess them. In contrast, EC 10 legitimates interference with the possession of views as well as their expression. The formulation of the scope of freedom of expression in IC 19 para. 2 is also more elaborate and comprehensive than EC 10. Most significantly, it includes the right to 'seek' information, the root of freedom of information. There have been calls to amend EC 10 to provide that right but no such amendment has yet been made. Para. (3) (our 11.3) also seems preferable to the detailed list of exceptions in EC 10(2).

In contrast to the decision we have taken in relation to Articles 6 and 16, we have not deleted the exception 'morals' from this Article. This is because we do not think that necessary controls on freedom of expression, for instance on pornography, should always fall within the criminal law. Where regulation, such as cinema or sex shop licensing, is the most appropriate form of control, rather than the criminal law, it would not be covered by the 'crime prevention' exception, but would be covered by 'morals'. We note that the

European Court of Human Rights has not interpreted 'morals' as grounds for interfering in the values and mores of private individuals.

Traditionally in the English legal system, since the right to free speech has no enforceable constitutional protection, the protection of the interests of the State or its agents can override the freedom of the individual. The Strasbourg approach is quite the reverse, guaranteeing the individual the right to freedom of expression unless a restriction on it can be shown to be justified.

The right to express ideas that offend, shock or disturb the State or any sector of the population has been firmly upheld in the case of *Handyside v UK* (1 EHRR 737). In the *Sunday Times* case (2 EHRR 245), which concerned an injunction issued by the Attorney General to prevent a newspaper from publishing an article about an issue which was the subject of legal proceedings but which had not yet proceeded to trial, the Court stated that the principle of freedom of the press applied even to the administration of justice. Whilst courts are a forum for the settlement of disputes, this does not mean that there could be no prior discussion of those disputes elsewhere. For a restriction on that freedom to be 'necessary in a democratic society' it must correspond to a pressing social need and be proportionate to the legitimate aim pursued.

In a case brought under the International Covenant (*Wernberger v Uruguay* 28/1978), the applicant was arrested and held incommunicado for many months. He was later convicted of being a member of a subversive association. He claimed that the real reason for his arrest and conviction was that he had contributed information on trade union activities to a newspaper opposed to the government. The Committee found that he had indeed been detained for having disseminated information relating to trade union activities and therefore found a violation of IC 19.

ARTICLE 12: FREEDOM OF ASSEMBLY AND ASSOCIATION

This is EC 11, with the substitution of 'the preservation of public order' in 12.2 for 'the prevention of disorder or crime'.

The IC separates freedom of assembly (IC 21) from freedom of association and trade unions (IC 22). Otherwise, the IC and EC versions are very similar, except that in the IC the armed forces and police exceptions do not apply to freedom of assembly.

Whilst EC 11 protects the right to form and join trade unions, it does not secure any particular treatment of unions or their members by the State, such as an obligation on the State to conclude any collective agreement with them. Not only is this latter right not mentioned in EC 11(1), but neither can it be said that all Contracting States should incorporate it in their national law or practice, or that it is indispensable for the effective enjoyment of trade union freedom (*Swedish Engine Drivers' Union* 1 EHRR 617 para. 1).

EC 11 is unclear as to whether an individual has the freedom not to associate. Nevertheless, the Court ruled that 'compulsion to join a particular trade union may not always be contrary to the Convention. However, a threat of dismissal involving loss of livelihood . . . strikes at the very substance of freedom guaranteed by Article 11' (case of *Young, James and Webster* 4 EHRR 38).

Limitations on the right to associate include those listed in EC 11. Military personnel and student unions are not granted the same protections as trade unions. The Court has held that Belgian law, which required all medical practitioners to be registered under an 'Order', did not interfere with freedom of association because the purpose of the 'Ordre' was to protect the general health of the public. However, the 'Ordre' could not prevent practitioners from forming together or joining professional associations (*Le Compte, Van Leuven, de Meyere* 4 EHRR 1).

In the case of the *Council of Civil Service Unions v UK* (known as the GCHQ case, 10 EHRR 269), the Commission found that the government's action in removing the right of individual employees to belong to a union was an interference with the rights protected by EC 11(1), but that it was justified under EC 11(2); and that the restrictions were 'lawful' under the second part of EC 11(2) as GCHQ employees were deemed to be members of the administration of the State and the regulations were introduced in accordance with national law.

Finally, EC 11 leaves to each state a 'free choice' in limiting the means used to protect the occupational interests of trade union members by trade union action (*Swedish Engine Drivers' Union* 1 EHRR 617 para. 1). For example, 'the grant of a right to strike . . . may be subject under national law to regulation of a kind that limits its exercise in certain instances' (*Schmidt and Dahlstrom* 1 EHRR 632 para. 1).

ARTICLE 13: RIGHTS IN RESPECT OF MARRIAGE

13.1 is EC 12, omitting words at the end which are inappropriate in a domestic charter. IC 23(2) is similar. 'Everyone' has been substituted for the EC wording, 'men and women'.

13.2 is IC 23(3). There is no EC equivalent.

13.3 is based on IC 23(4), which requires States to take steps to ensure these rights. There is no EC equivalent.

13.4 is IC 24(1), with the substitution of 'public authorities' for 'the State' at the end. There is no EC equivalent and we have omitted the non-discrimination provisions as being covered by Article 19 below.

IC 24(3) provides that every child has the right to acquire a nationality. In our Articles 30–32 we have provided for the basic right to acquire nationality. Were the Bill of Rights to be enacted in isolation it would need to include a domestic equivalent of IC 24(3) and probably extend it.

ARTICLE 14: RIGHT TO ENJOYMENT OF POSSESSIONS

14.1 is EC Protocol 1 Article (1), omitting at the end 'and by the general principles of international law' as being unnecessary in a domestic charter, but providing for compensation for British citizens and aliens if deprived of their possessions under the exceptions allowed. There is no IC equivalent.

14.2 is EC Protocol 1 Article 1(2), with the substitution of 'to enforce such laws as may be necessary' for 'of a State to enforce such laws as it deems necessary'.

Article 1 of the First Protocol to the European Convention protects the peaceful enjoyment of possessions. The term 'possessions' includes any property right or interest recognised in domestic law. Compulsory contributions to social security schemes and pension rights may create property rights over a portion of the assets in the fund (*Müller v Austria* 5849/72 3 DR 25). But a State may alter the terms of a statutory pension and forego repayment by acting in the 'public interest'. The Commission has often found measures aimed at monetary and economic stability to be in the public interest, a term which has been held to include: taxation, customs duties, impositions of fines, orders for attachment of unlawful property, and redistribution of land in clearance schemes (511/59 3 *Yearbook* 395; *Handyside v UK* 1 EHRR 737). Whilst no one may be deprived of his or her possessions except in the public interest, the Article does not expressly provide for compensation, nor does it create any obligation for the State to secure the value of property against inflation; nor does it extend to future earnings (*X v Federal Republic of Germany* 8724/78 20 DR 226).

In deciding whether to compensate an individual for a property interest taken, there must be a determination 'whether a fair balance was struck between the demands of the general interest of the community and the requirements of the individual's fundamental rights' (*Sporring and Lonnroth v Sweden* 5 EHRR 35 para. 1). The *Lithgow* case (8 EHRR 329) concerned compensation for shareholders in industries that were being nationalised by the UK government. The Court held that the state had a wide margin of appreciation as regards not only the decision to nationalise but also the compensation terms and concluded there had been no violation. A similar approach was taken in the *James* case (8 EHRR 121) concerning leaseholders' rights to purchase their freeholds. The Court upheld the domestic law, but emphasised that such law in addition to being appropriate and proportionate must also be accessible and precise.

ARTICLE 15: RIGHT TO PARTICIPATE IN PUBLIC LIFE AND SERVICE

This is essentially IC 25, with the omission of a cross-reference to IC 2 (on discrimination). EC Protocol I Article 3 is more limited and gives a right to vote (but not to stand for election) in terms similar to those in 15.2 above.

ARTICLE 16: FREEDOM OF MOVEMENT

This is based on EC Protocol 4 Article 2, adapted for domestic use. The UK has not ratified this Protocol because of the exclusion order powers conferred by the Prevention of Terrorism Act. IC 12(1)–(3) is very similar.

'Morals' has been deleted as a grounds for restricting these rights as it is capable of wide interpretation and we do not consider it justified in this case, given the remaining exceptions for the prevention of crime and the protection of the rights and freedoms of others.

In 16.2 we have added the provision that anyone holding British nationality is entitled to a passport, believing this right to be of such importance that it ought to have a constitutional guarantee.

ARTICLE 17: FREEDOM FROM EXPULSION FROM UNITED KINGDOM

17.1 is based on IC 12(4) and EC Protocol 4 Article 3. It is our intention that those British citizens who do not currently have a right of abode in the UK should be covered by this provision. There is currently a reservation under IC 12(4) in respect of persons not having a right of entry under current UK law.

The Convention and Covenant contain no exception for extradition, which is not treated as expulsion.

17.2 is IC 13, adjusted for a domestic charter. In relation to the right to submit reasons against expulsion, we have added the requirement that the right to submit reasons be 'prior to expulsion', and have omitted the exception to this right 'where compelling reasons of national security otherwise require', for which there is no justification. There is no EC equivalent to IC 13.

ARTICLE 18: RIGHT OF ASYLUM

Article 18 is paras (7) and (8) of the American Convention on Human Rights, with minor textual amendments. There is nothing comparable in either the EC or IC.

ARTICLE 19: EQUALITY

19.1 is EC 16.

19.2 and 19.3 are essentially an amalgam of EC 14 and IC 26, with the addition of three further grounds for non-discrimination: homo-sexuality, age and disability.

Division 2: Application and interpretation

ARTICLE 20: APPLICATION OF BILL OF RIGHTS

This is based (rather loosely) on cl. 3 of the draft New Zealand Bill of Rights. See also s. 32 of the Canadian Charter of Rights and Freedoms. Article 20 does not cover Parliament, which is covered by Article 21. It makes explicit the government's obligation to take positive steps to ensure compliance with the Bill of Rights.

A Bill of Rights is mainly intended to protect individuals and minorities against the misuse of power by government bodies and other public authorities It is not designed to be a direct source of rights and obligations as between *private* persons – for example, so as to enable a disaffected worker to sue a trade union, an employee to sue his or her employer for discrimination, or an individual to sue a peeping Tom neighbour for breach of privacy.

Sometimes, however, it is possible to argue that a private body is in reality so powerful and so governmental in its activities that it is really a 'private government' which should be as amenable to judicial review as government itself. The courts have recently developed criteria for deciding whether 'private' bodies, such as the Stock Exchange, the Advertising Standards Authority and profes-sional disciplinary committees, are subject to judicial review. Article 20 makes it clear that the Bill of Rights imposes duties upon any person or body to comply with its terms when performing any public function. The primary remedies would clearly be for infringements by public authorities but there would also be the possibility of remedies against other bodies which, because of the special powers or public funds they enjoy, would be regarded as within the sphere of 'State action'.

The Bill of Rights would also be a legitimate source of guidance upon where the public interest lies in private law cases.

ARTICLE 21: SCOPE OF EXCEPTIONS

Article 21 is intended to ensure that the courts allow exceptions to any right only if it is 'strictly necessary in the circumstances'.

ARTICLE 22: INTERPRETATION

This is an interpretation section. It makes it clear that the Bill of Rights is meant to give effect to and be interpreted in conformity with the International Covenant and the ECHR, and that the courts will take notice of the judgments and opinions of the two bodies which adjudicate on the Covenant and Convention: the Human Rights Committee, and European Court and Commission of Human Rights, respectively.

22.2 and 22.3 are based on the equivalent provisions of the European Communities Act 1972.

The interpretation of a Constitution guaranteeing fundamental rights and freedoms calls for a different approach from the traditional (and increasingly outmoded) approach to the interpretation of ordinary statutes. Even in the absence of a Bill of Rights, British courts, influenced by Community law concepts, are much more purposive than in the past. When construing the Bills of Rights of other Commonwealth countries, the Privy Council has recognised that a generous interpretation is called for, which has regard to the character and genesis of the Constitution and avoids what has been called 'the austerity of tabulated legalism'.

The Supreme Court of Canada, however (like the Supreme Courts of India, the United States and Zimbabwe), is more contextual in approach than our courts and more willing to have regard to a wide range of evidence of the relevant social context. One question which arises is whether Parliament should, in relation to the Bill of Rights, specifically direct the courts to have regard to special principles of interpretation. For example, the Hong Kong Bill of Rights Ordinance provides that, in interpreting and applying the Ordinance, the rules of interpretation applicable to other legislation may (but not must) be disregarded, and that regard shall be had to:

(a) the fact that the purpose of the Ordinance is to implement further the International Covenant on Civil and Political Rights as applied to Hong Kong; and

(b) the international origin of that Covenant and the need for
uniformity in interpretation of rights recognised in that Covenant
and similar rights recognised in other international agreements.

We have considered it appropriate to include similar guidance
for the interpretation of a UK Bill of Rights. Article 22 therefore
states that it is intended to give effect in the UK to the International
Covenant and the European Convention and requires the courts
to interpret it accordingly (but without prejudice to any rights in
the Bill of Rights which are more extensive than those contained
in those international texts – see Article 23). This will necessarily
require the UK courts to have regard to the decisions of the UN
Human Rights Committee and the European Court of Human
Rights respectively. In addition, however, there are the numerous
decisions, opinions and reports of the European Commission on
Human Rights, the Human Rights Committee, and of the more
specialist international human rights commissions and committees
which will be of relevance to their decisions. The judgments and
advisory opinions of the Inter-American Court of Human Rights are
also of strongly persuasive value on the international plane, as are
the judgments of strong national constitutional courts in common
law and civil law systems.

ARTICLE 23: RIGHTS UNDER OTHER AGREEMENTS

Article 23 is EC 60 and is intended to ensure that, where the UK
is party to other international human rights treaties, such as the
United Nations Convention on the Elimination of All Forms of
Discrimination Against Women or International Labour Organisation
Conventions, nothing in the Bill of Rights can be interpreted as
limiting the rights an individual enjoys under those Conventions.

ARTICLE 24: ABUSE OF FREEDOMS

This is IC 5(1) from which the words 'or at their limitation to a greater
extent than is provided for in the present Covenant' have been
deleted from the end of the Article to ensure that the Article is
not used to restrict lawful political activities or to justify state

surveillance and restrictions on state employees such as in former West Germany's *Berufsverbot*.

Division 3: Remedies

ARTICLE 25: REMEDIES

This Article gives a right to damages (as well as other remedies) for infringement of rights under the Bill of Rights.

ARTICLE 26: HUMAN RIGHTS COMMISSION

26.1 sets up a new body, the Human Rights Commission, appointed by the Secretary of State. However, as provided for elsewhere in the Constitution, the Commissioners are appointed only on the recommendation of the Public Services Commission, which is intended to ensure that they are appointed because of their expertise or other qualification for the post rather than because of any political views they may hold.

In 26.2 the Commission's duty is restricted to promoting compliance with the Bill of Rights but Parliament could confer additional responsibilities, e.g. to encourage good practice by private individuals and bodies not bound by the Bill of Rights. The wording of this clause is based on section 14(b) of Bermuda's Human Rights Act 1981.

The intention is that the primary role of the Commission will be to take legal proceedings against those who contravene the Bill of Rights and to assist individuals who initiate such proceedings. Clearly, the Commission should also have a duty to advise Parliament, the Assemblies, public authorities and those other bodies subject to the Bill of Rights whether their current policies or practices contravene its provisions and if proposed legislation or policies are likely to do so. The following clauses provide for these specific functions.

26.3 empowers the Commission to investigate practices and procedures which may be incompatible with the Bill of Rights. Following an investigation which disclosed actions contrary to the Bill of Rights, the Commission's advice to the body concerned could be sufficient to stop the offending behaviour, thus avoiding any need for litigation.

In 26.4 the Commission's role in assisting individuals who want to take cases under the Bill of Rights is intended to reduce the number of cases which go unlitigated because individuals cannot afford to take the case, to provide complainants with more support and expertise, and to ensure that the Court is presented with the full implications of the case. The Commission can, however, initiate proceedings without receiving any complaint, necessary in a situation in which individuals may not be aware of their rights or in a position to take action publicly to defend them. The intention is that the Commission should have considerably wider powers to initiate legal proceedings than the existing Equal Opportunities Commission, Commission for Racial Equality or Fair Employment Commission. In the case of the EOC and CRE it was thought that their powers to initiate investigations would compensate for limited powers to initiate proceedings, but the limitations on their investigation powers have meant that they have proved largely ineffective. The Human Rights Commission should not be hampered in this way.

26.5 empowers the Commission to challenge in Court a provision of an Act of Parliament or of an Assembly which, in its view, contravenes the Bill of Rights. It would be asking the Court to declare that part of the Act null and void.

26.6 is based on section 11(1)(o) of the Australian Human Rights and Equal Opportunities Commission Act. It enables the Commission to contribute to court proceedings in which it is not a litigant, for instance by submitting an *amicus curiae* brief.

26.7 and 26.8 are based on s. 11(1)(e) and s. 11(1)(k) of the Australian Human Rights and Equal Opportunities Commission Act 1986 respectively.

26.9 empowers the Commission to provide Codes of Practice on some or all of the provisions of the Bill of Rights to assist those who are bound to uphold it. The Codes would not be legally binding but could be cited as relevant in legal proceedings under the Bill of Rights. Under the sex discrimination, race relations and fair employment legislation, such Codes require the approval of the Secretary of State, but this would not be appropriate for Codes which are intended to ensure that the government, *inter alia*, does not itself contravene the Bill of Rights. Based on s. 11(1)(u) of the Australian Human Rights and Equal Opportunities Commission Act 1986.

PART 2: SOCIAL AND ECONOMIC RIGHTS

ARTICLE 27: SOCIAL AND ECONOMIC RIGHTS

The international covenants and charters which are particularly relevant at the present time are the United Nations International Covenant on Economic, Social and Cultural Rights (1966), the Council of Europe Social Charter (1961) and the Community Charter of Fundamental Social Rights for Workers (1990). The seven rights which are cited in Article 27.1.1–7 are drawn from these covenants, by which the UK is already legally bound:

.1   based on Council of Europe Social Charter, Article 1

.2   International Covenant, Article 9

.3   International Covenant, Article 11

.4   International Covenant, Article 12

.5   International Covenant, Article 13

.6   Community Charter of Fundamental Social Rights for Workers, Article 13

.7   Community Charter of Fundamental Social Rights for Workers, Article 19.

27.2 requires Parliament and the Assemblies of Scotland and Northern Ireland to provide access to the legal system and adequate legal aid, and is based on section 39A of Part IV (Directive Principles of State Policy) of the Indian Constitution.

27.3 precludes the intervention of the courts in enforcing social and economic rights. This reflects the view that, whilst the Constitution should state the general principles on which public policy is to be conducted, it would not be appropriate for the courts to judge whether or not the government or Parliament had provided, for example, an adequate level of income maintenance. Unlike the rights secured in the Bill of Rights, such matters are essentially political and best determined by political means. The same argument would apply to the determination of what is an adequate level of legal aid.

PART 3: FREEDOM OF INFORMATION

ARTICLE 28: ACCESS TO OFFICIAL INFORMATION

Article 28 concerns the fundamental rights of the citizen in relation to information required of them by public authorities. The basic principle of freedom of information is encapsulated in sections 28.1 and 28.2: namely that there is a general right of access to official information, subject to exemption on specific grounds. These exemptions are common to most existing freedom of information legislation in other countries, with the exception of that covering the constitutional position of the public service. This is included to cover the difficult question of policy advice, whose disclosure is thought by some to threaten the relationship between Ministers and civil servants and by others to deny government the privacy it requires for its own policy discussions. 28.3 and 28.4 require Parliament to legislate to make the right of access practicable and to provide a Commissioner to enforce it.

ARTICLE 29: USE OF INFORMATION BY PUBLIC AUTHORITIES

Article 29 deals with information required of citizens by public authorities and requires that they should be informed of the purposes for which such information may be used and likewise in regard to the transfer of any information to another authority, except where the investigation of fraud or other misdemeanours is involved. This exception would allow public authorities to compare or check the information received from a citizen with that held by another public authority where there was a reasonable suspicion of deceit. On the basis of this Article aggrieved persons would be able to seek judicial review of the actions of public authorities which had contravened its provisions.

The provisions of Articles 28 and 29 are intended to strengthen citizens in relation to public authorities both by increasing the information available to them to judge their actions and by protecting them from improper use of personal information by public authorities. These are necessary but not sufficient conditions for effective political influence by the citizen.

CHAPTER 3
Nationality

ARTICLE 30: BRITISH NATIONALITY

The four Articles in Chapter 3 establish who, on the coming into force of the Constitution, will be holders of 'British nationality', and how individuals can acquire (or lose) that status subsequently; make provision for individuals to hold dual nationality; and require Parliament to determine the civic rights of non-nationals.

The phraseology of 30.1 comes from the Hong Kong (British Nationality) Order 1986/948 (made under the Hong Kong Act 1985), which creates the status of British National (Overseas). 'British national' has previously only been used loosely in the United Kingdom to describe individuals possessing one of the confusing collection of sub-categories of British citizenship without right of abode in the UK created by the British Nationality Act 1981.

30.2 automatically reclassifies as British nationals all those holding one of the six sub-categories of citizen which exist under the 1981 Act. Whereas in other countries, right of abode in that country, civic rights and civic duties are normally attached to nationality status, so that there is a clear dividing line between nationals and aliens, this does not currently apply in the UK, where no right of abode is attached to any of the categories of citizenship except 'British citizenship'. The anomalous British position is particularly obvious in the context of the European Community. A person with the nationality of a Member State is a Community national and, as such, has important rights deriving from Community law. The other Member States have had no difficulty in stating who their nationals are; the United Kingdom has had to produce a peculiar definition which includes British citizens, British Dependent Territories' citizens connected with Gibraltar, and those British subjects who have right of abode (e.g. because they have a parent born in the United Kingdom). All other British passport-holders and all Commonwealth citizens are excluded (by the UK's own definition of its nationals) from the EC's freedom of movement provisions.

The object of 30.2 is to end this anomaly and establish a single 'British national' status to which the rights and duties in the Constitution are attached. For instance, this is necessary in order to know to whom Article 17.1 ('No British national shall be expelled from the United Kingdom or deprived of the right to enter the United Kingdom') applies.

30.3 establishes who holds British nationality by descent and who holds it otherwise than by descent. This is important as it determines whether British nationals can pass on their status to their children (see Article 31.2).

ARTICLE 31: ACQUISITION AND LOSS OF BRITISH NATIONALITY

31.1 re-enacts the so called *ius soli* rule that was used in British nationality law at all times prior to the coming into force of the British Nationality Act 1981. The rule is simple and certain and states that a person is a British national if he or she is born in the territories with which that status is associated, with the very limited exceptions set out in 31.2.1 and .2. The advantage of the *ius soli* rule is its certainty. There is no need, for instance, to establish the immigration status of the parents before determining the child's nationality. Its removal in 1983 has left some children born in the UK stateless.

31.2 retains the current rule that British citizenship automatically passes (as a general rule) only to the first generation born outside the territory.

31.3 and 31.4 state that Parliament shall provide for and regulate the further acquisition of British nationality (e.g. by naturalisation). It would undoubtedly be necessary and desirable for there to be exceptions to the general rule that British nationality can be transmitted automatically only to the first generation born outside the territory. For example, exceptions should take into account the position of British nationals working for institutions of the European Community. Parliament could also provide for the automatic reclassification of British nationals by descent as British nationals otherwise than by descent upon fulfilment of a residence requirement.

ARTICLE 32: ALLEGIANCE AND DUAL NATIONALITY

32.1 provides that every British national owes a duty of allegiance to the Constitution rather than, as now, to the Crown.

32.2 gives constitutional protection to the freedom to hold dual nationality, a right denied in many countries but granted in the UK since 1949.

32.3 provides that any British national has the right to live in the United Kingdom. This is a basic tenet of international law, breached in spirit by the British Nationality Act 1981, which withdrew that right from those citizens it reclassified into one of the sub-categories of citizenship abolished by this Constitution. 32.3 does not provide for British nationals to have a right of abode in British Dependent Territories, as this would not be appropriate for a Constitution which is for the United Kingdom only. The United Kingdom government cannot presume to grant anyone the right of abode in a colony. The British Dependent Territories' citizens of the remaining colonial possessions (Hong Kong and a few small territories in the Caribbean, Atlantic and Pacific) do not in fact have right of abode in their respective territories; they depend on the immigration laws of each territory for the opportunity to live there. Under 32.3 they would gain a right of abode, in the UK.

The United Kingdom has been unable to ratify Article 12 (4) of the International Covenant on Civil and Political Rights and Article 3 to Protocol 4 of the European Convention because it denies individuals the right to enter the State of which they are nationals. The distinctions created by the Immigration Act 1971, under which some British nationals and some Commonwealth citizens had right of abode whilst others in both categories did not, were translated into categories of citizenship by the British Nationality Act of 1981. Recreating one category of British national therefore has implications for 'immigration' – except that it is not appropriate to describe the arrival of a country's own nationals as immigration. The majority of those given British national status and therefore right of abode are unlikely to choose to exercise that right. There is a large number of white British citizens, believed to be between two and three million, who are entitled to live in the United Kingdom and choose not to do so. Moreover, many of those who do want to come to Europe may choose to use their British nationality to settle, as Community nationals, in other European countries where the economic opportunities and welfare benefits are preferable.

ARTICLE 33: CIVIC RIGHTS OF NON-NATIONALS

Most of the rights enshrined in the Bill of Rights (Articles 2–19) apply to anyone within the jurisdiction of the United Kingdom, not only to its nationals. However, certain rights such as the right to a passport and to vote are granted by the Constitution to British nationals only. Article 33 requires Parliament to determine the extent to which non-nationals should be entitled to civic rights and subject to the civic duties attached to British nationality. Such rights and duties might include the right to apply for work in the public service, to vote and stand for office in local and national elections, and the duty to serve on a jury. The European Community is currently considering the harmonisation of the rights of non-EC nationals across the Community and, when an EC directive is forthcoming, the government will be required to introduce the agreed provisions.

33.2 states that Parliament *may* provide for Irish and Commonwealth citizens to retain their existing civic rights, for instance to vote, but these rights are not enshrined in the Constitution.

CHAPTER 4

The Head of State

Articles 34 to 38 establish the position, functions, duties and powers of the Head of State. The effect is to preserve the Monarchy but with all its powers derived from the Constitution and with no remaining prerogative powers of political significance. The replacement of the Sovereign by an appointed or elected official, should it ever be thought desirable, could be achieved by a constitutional amendment replacing this Article, but without alteration to the structure of the Constitution as a whole.

ARTICLE 34: HEAD OF STATE

Article 34 establishes the office of the Head of State, which is held by the Queen and her heirs and successors.

34.1.2 incorporates into the Constitution the arrangements under the Act of Settlement 1700 with two important exceptions. The Act of Settlement disqualifies Roman Catholics, and those who marry Roman Catholics, from succession to the throne. Secondly, the principle of the line of descent contained in the Act of Settlement is that preference is given to males over females, whilst recognizing the right of primogeniture. 34.1.2 removes discrimination on grounds of religion or gender, but only as regards persons born after the coming into force of the Constitution. The order of succession for those already born is thus preserved, to avoid uproar and confusion. 34.1.3 permits the Head of State to abdicate in favour of the Heir to the Throne.

34.2 provides for a Regent in the event of the Head of State's incapacity or minority. It reflects the present arrangement as contained in the Regency Act 1937–53, but does not continue the provisions of section 4 of the Regency Act 1937 which prevent a Regent assenting to a Bill for changing the order of succession to the throne or for altering the Scottish Act of 1706 for securing the

Protestant religion and Presbyterian Church Government. Under 34.2.2 Parliament is to legislate concerning the performance of the functions of the Head of State during absence abroad or temporary incapacity.

34.4.2 gives the Head of State immunity from taxation in respect of the Civil List, but not in relation to income or property held in his or her private capacity. The present practice of granting immunity from taxation on the Sovereign's personal wealth is of relatively recent origin and we do not believe it should receive constitutional protection, whatever Parliament may decide from time to time.

Under 34.3 the Head of State enjoys in person immunity from all civil suits for actions done in a private capacity and from criminal proceedings for actions in both public and private capacities. The immunity is *personal* and does not extend to anyone purporting to act on the Head of State's behalf. 34.4 and 34.5 provide for the Civil List to be provided by Act of Parliament and for the appointment of the Head of State's household. 34.5 is original: European constitutions are full of articles on the Royal Household, British independence constitutions are not. The formulation here seeks to ensure some independence for the Sovereign but at the same time to provide some role for the elected government, which is responsible for footing the bill.

ARTICLE 35: FUNCTIONS OF THE HEAD OF STATE

Article 35 makes it clear that the Head of State acts on the authority of the Constitution rather than the Royal Prerogative. No one can hide behind the Sovereign's skirts and take extra-constitutional powers claiming to do so in the name or under the authority of the Sovereign.

ARTICLE 36: DUTIES OF THE HEAD OF STATE

Article 36 lists the duties of the Head of State. It is modelled on the relevant provisions of the Spanish constitution and seeks to set out the principal prerogative powers of the Sovereign. Commonwealth monarchical constitutions do not have any such list but rely instead on conventions derived from the United Kingdom. The Article provides no scope for the exercise of discretion by the Head of State.

ARTICLE 37: PERSONAL POWERS OF THE HEAD OF STATE

Article 37 lists the personal powers of the Head of State, which include offering advice to the Prime Minister, conferring personal honours and making statements as Head of the Commonwealth.

Though the exercise of these rights is fully discretionary, and may not be questioned by any court, the Head of State is bound not to manifest preference for any political party.

ARTICLE 38: THE POWER OF MERCY

Under Article 38 the Head of State may on the advice of the Minister of Justice exercise the power of mercy.

ARTICLE 39: THE PRIVY COUNCIL

The final Article in this chapter preserves in a modified form the Privy Council. The essential purpose is to provide the equivalent of a Council of State for situations involving war or other emergencies. Orders in Council which deal with the declaration of war (Article 122) and the suspension of the Constitution (Article 128) are to be made by the Sovereign on the advice of the Privy Council. The primary function of the Privy Council, and the reason for maintaining it under the Constitution, is that it remains an important method of giving the force of law to acts of government through Order in Council. This power should remain, as should the Statutory Instruments Act 1946 under which many Orders in Council are made.

39.1 establishes the Council and its membership, which includes the Heir to the Throne and persons who hold or *have held* various offices, including the Speakers of either House of Parliament, the Prime Minister, members of the Cabinet and Leader of the Opposition. Others may be appointed on the advice of the Prime Minister for life.

39.2.2 provides for Parliament to legislate for other functions of the Privy Council. It now has supplementary functions which include a number of committees which act as appeal committees from numerous professional bodies and the universities, such as the Scottish Universities Committee under section 9 of the Universities (Scotland) Act 1889. Under Article 99 the functions of the Judicial Committee as an appellate court are transferred to the Supreme Court.

CHAPTER 5
The Executive

Division 1: The Government of the United Kingdom

Division 1 makes provision for the Executive for the United Kingdom, for the offices of Prime Minister and Deputy Prime Minister, for Ministers including the Chancellor of the Exchequer, Minister of Justice and Minister for International Relations, for the Cabinet, for ministerial responsibility to Parliament, and for codes of conduct for Ministers.

ARTICLE 40: THE EXECUTIVE POWER FOR THE UNITED KINGDOM

Article 40 provides that the executive power shall be exercised by the government of the United Kingdom, comprising the Prime Minister and members of Parliament appointed as Minister. 40.3 provides a general power of action in addition to the powers conferred directly by the Constitution and by Acts of Parliament. Since Article 1 states that the Constitution provides the sole foundation for the exercise of executive authority, there is no residue of Crown prerogative or common law powers available to the government as at present. This Article provides a general competence for the government to act within the provisions of the Constitution. This provision is loosely based on clause 135 of a draft Constitution for the state of Israel drawn up by members of the Tel Aviv University Law School under the chairmanship of Professor Uriel Reichman, which demonstrates a concise and workmanlike approach to many difficult points of constitutional law.

ARTICLE 41: THE PRIME MINISTER

Article 41 establishes the office of Prime Minister, who is to be elected from among its members by the House of Commons and who will cease to hold office if no longer a member or candidate in a forthcoming election.

This is a major departure from current constitutional law, convention and practice. The appointment of the Prime Minister by the Head of State becomes a formality and all the questions about who shall be summoned to form a government are thrown in to the House of Commons. It is a question whether the procedures for this election ought also to be specified by the Constitution. In line with our general policy of leaving Parliament to establish its own procedures, we have decided against their inclusion in the Constitution. But others may well think this is too important a matter to be excluded.

41.2.4 provides for a personal vote of no confidence in the Prime Minister, which is deliberately distinguished from a vote of no confidence in the government under Article 60.3, leading to a dissolution of the House of Commons. The aim is to provide for changes of government without the need for elections, which may be advantageous in the more fluid parliamentary situation under an electoral system based on some form of proportional representation (PR).

Again, opinions may divide sharply on this point: some believe that the personal vote of no confidence would encourage irresponsible behaviour by small parties, which will have the prospect of bringing down governments without the prospect of having to fight an election. It is not clear however that the prospect of an election would hold any terrors under a PR system.

ARTICLE 42: DEPUTY PRIME MINISTER

Article 42 provides for a Deputy Prime Minister to perform the functions of the Prime Minister when the Prime Minister is unable to perform them or the office is vacant. The last provision would cover death in office or the loss of a vote of confidence and provide continuity of the government until a new Prime Minister could be elected.

ARTICLE 43: MINISTERS

Article 43 establishes the office of Minister. Ministers' numbers and responsibilities are determined by the Prime Minister, but must include the Chancellor of the Exchequer, the Minister for Justice and the Minister for International Relations, who are to be members of the House of Commons. Other Ministers may be drawn from either House. Those in the Second Chamber will stand for election at different times from their colleagues in the Commons, but are subject to the same conditions for ceasing to hold office.

The Article specifies that there shall be a Minister of Justice because he or she has responsibilities under the Constitution in relation to the appointment of the judiciary (see Schedule 5). 43.1.3.2 cites the Minister's responsibilities as 'courts and legal services' and, although we have not felt it appropriate to set out the responsibilities in detail in the Constitution, it is our intention that the Ministry of Justice would take over the legal functions now carried out by the Lord Chancellor's Department (which would cease to exist) and those of the Home Office. We take the view that the Home Office's current responsibility for criminal law and procedure, and for the enforcement by statutory bodies of aspects of the civil law protecting individual rights such as the race discrimination legislation, sit uneasily with its control functions such as responsibility for the police and immigration services. Likewise, the Lord Chancellor's direct responsibility for the appointment of the judiciary and his position as a Law Lord sit uneasily with his political role as a member of the government. This fragmented, and in some instances inappropriate, distribution of functions should be brought to an end with the creation of a single strong ministry responsible for all of the 'justice' functions, separate from any responsibility for law enforcement. At present, some legal functions are the responsibility of the law officers – the Attorney-General and Solicitor-General. Under the Constitution the role of the Attorney-General is defined in Article 46 and that of the Directors of Public Prosecutions and Civil Prosecutions, offices within the Ministry of Justice, in Articles 48 and 49.

ARTICLE 44: THE CABINET

Article 44 establishes the Cabinet and its membership, gives it general direction and control of the government, and makes it collectively responsible to Parliament. This limits collective responsibility to the Cabinet, that is to those Ministers who are in fact collectively involved in making government decisions. Other Ministers will be bound by other ties and loyalties. The present convention which extends to every Tom, Dick and Harry associated with a Minister would lapse.

The term 'general decision and control' is drawn from the Constitution of Malta, one among many Commonwealth independence constitutions in which draftsmen have tried to capture the essence of the unwritten constitution.

44.3 gives a constitutional basis for Cabinet committees and requires that Parliament must be informed of their purposes, terms of reference and duration. Much government business is effectively discharged by committees, and the present mystery surrounding their existence is as dangerous as it is absurd.

ARTICLE 45: MINISTERIAL RESPONSIBILITY

45.1 affirms the full accountability of the Head of Government (i.e. the Prime Minister) both to Parliament and to the Head of State. It complements provisions relating both to open government and to individual ministerial responsibility elsewhere in the Constitution. Failure by the Head of Government to abide by the terms of this provision might form the basis of a complaint to the Constitutional Commission (Article 76).

Much current ministerial and civil service practice, and most parliamentary procedure, is based upon the antique constitutional convention of individual ministerial responsibility. This means, in theory, that Ministers are accountable to Parliament for all that happens in their departments (see below) and must carry the blame for any maladministration, misconduct, etc. on the part of their civil servants. However, most contemporary commentators agree that there is a huge gap between theory and practice. In part this is because the growth of government functions, and of the size and organisational complexity of the civil service, has made it impossible for Ministers to know about, let alone control, more than a small fraction of what goes on in their departments. In part it is also because Ministers and civil servants find it both convenient and easy (in the absence of freedom of information legislation, and because of the government's capacity to shelter behind its parliamentary majority) to get away with telling Parliament as little as possible.

45.2, whilst recognising that the scale and complexity of modern government means that Ministers cannot be expected to exercise detailed control of all departmental business (hence the phrase *general* direction and control'), reaffirms their present obligation to give 'regular, full and accurate account' to Parliament. This provision is linked to others in this Constitution dealing with the relationship between Executive and legislature.

Thought was given to the desirability of including, alongside Departments, explicit reference to Executive Agencies, such as those being set up under the 'Next Steps' programme. The development of such bodies raises important issues to do with ministerial account-ability and parliamentary scrutiny. However, it was felt that giving such agencies special constitutional status would result in undue rigidity; also, more generally, that it would be a mistake to start making special provisions in respect of such institutional 'nuts and bolts' of public administration. Agencies would clearly be covered by the terms of Articles 118 and 119 (administrative justice).

45.3 reinforces 45.2 by imposing positive constitutional obligations upon Ministers to spell out fully to Parliament the scope of their responsibilities. Failure to do so might form the basis of a complaint to the Constitutional Commission. In this and other contexts it should also be noted that a likely by-product of changes in the elec-toral system, as provided elsewhere, would be to weaken the expec-tation that Ministers wishing to evade responsibility could usually hide behind the government's hitherto more or less guaranteed parliamentary majority.

ARTICLE 46: CODE OF MINISTERIAL CONDUCT

Since the Second World War, Ministers have been issued with succes-sive editions of a document entitled *Questions of Procedure for Ministers*. This is treated as a highly confidential document, though its contents have been extensively leaked. Much of it has to do with the preservation of Cabinet secrecy and collective ministerial responsibility. Article 46 recognises the need for a formal code of ministerial conduct (not necessarily confined to the ground covered in *Questions of Procedure*); also that such a document should be in the public domain and subject to parliamentary approval (including approval of any revisions or amendments). Failure to abide by the code might form the basis of a complaint to the Constitutional Commission (Article 76).

The Constitutional Commission would consider complaints by members of both Houses (including parliamentary committees) concerning alleged constitutional transgressions by the Prime Minister or Ministers. Complaints would be 'filtered' by the Speakers of the two Houses, thus reducing the risk that the procedure would be abused for routine political point-scoring. Such complaints might, for instance, concern the withholding of information from Parliament or breaches of the Code of Conduct for Ministers.

Division 2: Legal officers

ARTICLE 47: ATTORNEY-GENERAL

Departing from the current practice, Article 47 requires the Attorney-General to be a professional appointment; a senior lawyer who is *not* a member of Parliament. The intention is to end the Attorney-General's dual function as both a member of the government and legal adviser to that government, to separate the political and legal roles. As a professional he or she will advise the government, attending Cabinet meetings but not voting. The Attorney-General, under 47.4.2, has responsibility for the conduct of litigation to which the government is a party, but has no part in criminal prosecutions; responsibility for authorising certain prosecutions under the Official Secrets Act or Public Order Act, for instance, passes to the Director of Public Prosecutions (Article 48). The Attorney-General is appointed by the Prime Minister and can be removed by the Prime Minister at any time (47.3.3). He or she ceases to hold office if a new Prime Minister is elected (47.3.4).

ARTICLE 48: DIRECTOR OF PUBLIC PROSECUTIONS

Article 48 establishes the office of Director of Public Prosecutions (DPP) within the (newly created) Ministry of Justice and requires the Scottish and Northern Ireland Assemblies to establish an office with equivalent powers. The DPP, a senior lawyer, is appointed by the Minister of Justice (see Article 43) on the recommendation of the Judicial Services Commission (48.2) and has the same security of tenure as a judge.

The Director of Public Prosecution's role, under 48.4, acting in the public interest, is to initiate, authorise or take over criminal proceedings before any United Kingdom court or court in England and Wales, or to discontinue any such proceedings (except an appeal by someone who has been convicted). In exercising these powers he or she is not subject to anyone's direction. That is, although the office is within the Ministry of Justice, the Director of Public Prosecutions is not subject to the Minister's instruction or accountable to the Minister for his or her decisions.

ARTICLE 49: DIRECTOR OF CIVIL PROCEEDINGS

Article 49 establishes an entirely new office, that of Director of Civil Proceedings (DCP), a step advocated by Sir Harry Wolff in 'Public Law–Private Law: Why the Divide? A Personal View'. *Public Law* (1986), 220–38.

As in Article 48, the Scottish and Northern Ireland Assemblies are required to make similar provision in their areas. The DCP, an office within the Ministry of Justice, is appointed by the Minister of Justice on the recommendation of the Judicial Services Commission, again from persons having rights of audience in the superior courts of the UK. The DCP has the same tenure as a judge and is not subject to the Minister's control nor accountable to the Minister for his or her decisions.

Under 49.4, the DCP, acting in the public interest, has the power to initiate or intervene in civil proceedings (before a UK court or court in England and Wales). 49.4.1 cites in particular the DCP's role in relation to initiating or intervening in proceedings under the Bill of Rights, proceedings in which the UK's compliance with treaty obligations or EC law is at issue, or judicial review cases.

Division 3: International relations

ARTICLE 50: EUROPEAN COMMUNITY LAW

In conjunction with Articles 1.2 and 53.2 this Article ensures the direct application and effect of European Community law by giving constitutional force to the appropriate provisions of the European Communities Act 1972, as amended by the European Communities (Amendment) Act 1986. As indicated in the commentary on Article 1, this does not commit the United Kingdom beyond the present obligations, but allows for further development. It also ensures that any such development must be treated as a constitutional amendment which could not be included except by the special procedures established by Article 69. Together with Article 51, requiring the approval of Parliament for treaties, this would prevent a repetition of the remarkable way in which the original European Communities Act 1972 was put through Parliament with a bare majority, to be subjected after the event to an advisory referendum in 1975.

ARTICLE 51: INTERNATIONAL RELATIONS

This Article gives the government powers to conduct international relations, maintain diplomatic representatives and conclude treaties subject to parliamentary approval. Again the need for this provision arises from the absence of the prerogative powers of the Crown. It is modelled on clauses 103 to 109 of the draft Israeli Constitution cited above (see commentary for Article 40), but 51.3 goes further by providing that a treaty once approved by Parliament takes effect as part of domestic law. Parliamentary participation in treaty-making removes the need for legislation and perhaps also removes the temptation from government to sign treaties to which it has no intention of giving effect.

CHAPTER 6
The Legislatures

PART 1: THE LEGISLATIVE POWER

Part 1 of Chapter 6 vests the legislative power in the United Kingdom in Parliament and in elected Assemblies for Scotland, Wales, Northern Ireland and twelve English regions, and provides for the division of legislative competence between Parliament and the Assemblies and for the resolution of conflicts between them.

What is proposed is a modified form of federalism which attempts to realise the principle of subsidiarity. Parliament is given exclusive competence in certain matters but these are matters on which it has now or will in the future have to share its powers with the European Community. It can if it wishes delegate any of its extensive powers to the Assemblies. On the other hand, the competences given to the Assemblies are not exclusive because Parliament can legislate in these matters under Article 55, if legislation by an Assembly would either be inadequate or have spillover effects outside its own jurisdiction. This formula recognises the fact that whatever federal constitutions may say, there is seldom a clear-cut division of competence in practice. The aim is not to determine what is the appropriate level for a particular function to be carried out, such as the protection of the environment, but to determine which aspects of that function are best carried out at what level. Under the system proposed here, environmental protection falls within the competence of the Assemblies because that is the level at which the bulk of legislation would have to be implemented. But both the European Community and Parliament would have power to legislate on matters such as air pollution where national or regional boundaries are irrelevant to the problems to be addressed.

ARTICLE 52: THE LEGISLATIVE POWER

Article 52 vests the legislative power in Parliament and the Assemblies. The Assemblies therefore have constitutional standing, unlike local authorities at present, and their powers cannot be altered save by a process of amendment which requires their consent (Article 69.3). Parliament and the Assemblies may delegate their legislative powers, but may not alienate them.

ARTICLE 53: EXCLUSIVE LEGISLATIVE POWERS OF PARLIAMENT

Article 53 sets out the exclusive powers of Parliament on a range of matters affecting the internal unity and the external relations of the United Kingdom, which include the Head of State, Parliament itself, elections generally, membership of the European Community, international relations, defence and security, citizenship, taxation and social security and a variety of matters affecting the United Kingdom as a common market.

These are based on the exceptional matters listed in the Northern Ireland Constitution Act 1973 and subsequent proposals for Scotland.

Parliament also has exclusive powers to legislate where necessary to give effect to treaties or European Community obligation and can delegate to an Assembly on any matter falling within its exclusive powers (53.3).

ARTICLE 54: LEGISLATIVE POWERS OF ASSEMBLIES

Article 54 provides the Assemblies with powers to make laws over a wide range of policy areas from agriculture to transport. Under 79.4 executive powers are granted on the same matters. The bulk of those are matters which fall within the powers of the Northern Ireland Assembly and the executive responsibilities of the Scottish Office. Recent proposals for Scotland, e.g. Mr Dewar's 1987 Bill, specify those matters in detail. Here the powers are given in general terms subject to important conditions under Articles 54.4 and 55.

Under 54.2, the Assemblies for Scotland and Northern Ireland are given additional powers to legislate for their own legal systems, including police and prisons. England and Wales are for this purpose retained as a single jurisdiction, which creates an anomaly, a special instance of the 'West Lothian question'. We concluded that there would be serious disadvantages in breaking up the court system and no compensating advantages in terms of local administration and accountability. Under Article 125 Parliament may provide for a decentralised structure of governance for the police.

ARTICLE 55: CONCURRENT LEGISLATIVE POWERS

Assemblies may amend or repeal laws made by or under Acts of Parliament before the Constitution comes into force, but may not legislate beyond their own boundaries, or in a way which amends the Constitution or is inconsistent with any provision of European Community law. But the most important constraint in practical terms on the Assemblies' power of legislation is the provision in Article 55 for the exercise of concurrent powers by Parliament under certain conditions. These provisions are based on Article 72 of the Constitution of the Federal Republic of Germany (1949). The two conditions for the exercise of concurrent powers by Parliament essentially concern boundary problems: where Assemblies either cannot regulate adequately by themselves or create external repercussions by so doing. Intervention by Parliament might be disputed by Assemblies on the facts and it would no doubt take some time to establish what 'adequately' meant in any particular circumstance or what level of external repercussion merited intervention. Subsidiarity is bound to involve conflict, but at least Assemblies will have a secure constitutional base from which to argue, negotiate or litigate with central government and the European Community.

55.2 provides that when Parliament exercises concurrent powers of legislation, the executive power shall remain with the Assemblies or local authorities, unless expressly provided otherwise. The aim here is to keep the administration as far as possible decentralised. Article 85 (1) of the German Constitution provides an inspiration if not a model.

ARTICLE 56: CONFLICTS OF LEGISLATION

Assembly Acts do not require the consent of the Head of State, nor is there any pre-assent scrutiny by the UK government or any other body. This removes potential conflicts from the political to the judicial arena, a feature of the Constitution discussed in the Introduction. Article 56 provides for the superiority of Acts of Parliament over Assembly Acts where there are inconsistencies between them. This is a standard provision of federal constitutions and should assist the courts to resolve cases involving conflict of laws in the matters covered by concurrent powers. Where proceedings are initiated by the United Kingdom government or an Assembly executive questions of vires would be subject to the original jurisdiction of the Supreme Court under Article 98.4.

PART 2: PARLIAMENT

Part 2 establishes Parliament, provides for its membership, the qualifications and disqualifications for membership, expiry and dissolution of the two Houses, powers and privileges, Speakers, salaries and facilities, declaration of interest and legislative powers.

Many of the provisions represent a continuation of existing law practice and convention. The main improvements in Parliament's position, such as the election of the Prime Minister by the House of Commons or the power to approve treaties, are dealt with elsewhere (Articles 41 and 51). Important changes in the method of electing Parliament are introduced in Chapter 8. The most important innovations in this chapter are the replacement of the House of Lords by an elected Second Chamber and the enhanced powers which this Chamber has in relation to legislation to amend the Constitution or to give direct effect to its provisions. The House of Commons retains its primacy in relation to Money Bills and ordinary legislation, though the period by which the Second Chamber can delay ordinary legislation is extended.

Division 1: Composition of Parliament

ARTICLE 57: PARLIAMENT

Article 57 establishes Parliament. It consists of the Head of State and two Houses, and its general constitutional function is to legislate and to hold the government of the United Kingdom to account.

ARTICLE 58: MEMBERSHIP

Elections are to be conducted in accordance with other provisions of the Constitution, at fixed times and subject to supervision by the Electoral Commission, an enhanced constitutional version of the Boundary Commission (Articles 83 and 88, and Schedule 3).

58.2 reduces the number of members for the Commons to between 475 and 525, the exact number to be determined by Act of Parliament. This reflects the view that with the substantial transfer of domestic responsibilities to the Assemblies fewer members will be necessary to shoulder the legislative and constituency burden. Likewise 58.5 fixes the number of Ministers at not more than one-tenth of the membership of either House, rather less than the maximum figure of 95 Ministers now imposed on the House of Commons by the House of Commons Disqualifications Act 1975. The limitation is necessary to avoid executive domination, or collective ministerial regimentation, of parliamentary debates and proceedings. Whereas the existing House of Lords contains over 1,100 peers entitled to sit, the Second Chamber would have a much smaller membership of between 225 to 265, but as these will be elected full-time politicians this should provide an adequate working House.

58.6 states the existing practice that members vote only in person. 58.4 is a new provision, arising from the election of the Second Chamber, which prevents a member of one House standing for election or sitting as member of the other (the model is Article 43 of the Australian Constitution).

ARTICLE 59: QUALIFICATIONS AND DISQUALIFICATIONS FOR MEMBERSHIP

Article 59 deals with qualifications and disqualifications for member-ship of the either House. Eligibility for membership is similar to existing law affecting the Commons, except that the age limit is reduced from 21 to 18 years and candidates must be citizens of the United Kingdom, thus excluding Commonwealth and Republic of Ireland citizens (at present qualified), and also nationals of other European Community states. Other grounds for disqualification are public office, bankruptcy, mental illness, conviction for a criminal offence, responsibilities for elections, or conviction of an electoral offence.

59.3 makes plain that membership of either House ceases at the next expiry or dissolution of that House, and that the existing power of the Commons to expel any of its members is expressly extended to cover both Houses (a resolution of the House of Lords as a legis-lative body could not exclude a member of that House permanently: see Erskine May, 21st edition, p. 40). Any member would be permit-ted to vacate his or her seat by way of a simple letter of resignation to the Speaker of the member's House, in place of the existing Com-mons method of fictitious acceptance of the offices of Bailiff or Steward of the Chiltern Hundreds or the Manor of Northstead.

ARTICLE 60: EXPIRY AND DISSOLUTION OF HOUSES OF PARLIAMENT

Article 60 establishes a fixed term of four years for each House. Under Schedule 3 the elections of the two Houses will be staggered after the first general election following the adoption of the Constitu-tion. Elections to each House will take place every four years, at a time known to all in advance whereas at present a Prime Minister is enabled under the prerogative to choose any date for an election within a five year maximum limit.

60.2 and 60.3 provide for early dissolution of the House of Com-mons in the event of the failure of the House to elect a Prime Minister, or the loss of a vote of confidence in the government.

60.4 seeks to avoid misuse of these provisions by limiting the duration of a newly elected House to the remainder of the term of its predecessor. A similar provision may be found in Mr Benn's Commonwealth of Britain Bill (1991). The Second Chamber will not be dissolved.

In place of the anachronism of the 1694 Triennial Act providing a three-year maximum between the termination and summoning of Parliament, 60.5 puts into legal form the requirement for the simultaneous termination and summoning of the House of Commons and sets a time limit of a month for the first meeting of the House following a general election, in order to keep the period in which no House of Commons exists to a minimum.

Division 2: Powers and procedure

ARTICLE 61: POWERS AND PRIVILEGES OF PARLIAMENT

At present 'the law and custom of Parliament' is a matter of common law and in part it is based on the internal practice of the two Houses. Article 61 provides for the continued existence of the unwritten law and the inherent jurisdiction and power of both Houses to determine their own proceedings and privileges. Whilst this is expressed to be subject to any modifications made in the Constitution, 61.1.2 states that the freedoms and restrictions contained in the Bill of Rights shall not affect parliamentary practice.

61.2 restates Article 9 of the 1689 Bill of Rights governing the freedom of members of Parliament to speak out in the conduct of parliamentary business without fear of reprisal.

61.3 gives constitutional recognition to the inherent power of Parliament to summon witnesses and request the production of documentary evidence. We expect that the Commons' Select Committee system will grow in importance and there will be a marked development of Select Committees in the Second Chamber, so that this power to send for persons, papers and records will be increasingly central to the task of supervising government policy and administration.

ARTICLE 62: THE SPEAKERS

Article 62 requires the election of a Speaker for each House of Parliament. Standing orders of both Houses will regulate procedure, including the provision of deputies for the Speakers, the election of the Speakers and their deputies and the appointment of Counsel as legal advisers. The Speaker of the Second Chamber will operate by analogy with the traditions of the Speaker of the Commons, rather than of the Lord Chancellor, who presides in the House of Lords. The Speakers will represent their respective Houses with political impartiality, and their general functions will be to regulate debates and enforce the rules of their House, and to exercise such powers as their House through standing orders confers upon them or are otherwise conferred by law. They have for instance an important responsibility in the certification of Bills: Money Bills under Article 67, public Bills under Article 66, Bills for amendment of the Constitution under Article 69 and Constitutional Bills under Article 70. Their certificates are conclusive and may not be challenged except in the Supreme Court.

ARTICLE 63: SALARIES AND FACILITIES

Article 63 emphasises the full-time nature of a member's responsibilities. Assessment of members' salaries should be on this basis so that members may rely upon their parliamentary salary as their sole source of income and not be compelled to seek outside work, which diminishes the time available for parliamentary and constituency responsibilities.

63.2 requires that the standing orders of both Houses shall ensure that their sittings are held at times convenient to all persons who are eligible to be members. The main beneficiaries should be women, many of whom cannot contemplate membership under the present arrangements.

ARTICLE 64: DECLARATIONS OF INTEREST

Outside work will continue to be permitted including the holding of consultancies and directorships in commerce and industry, and also sponsorship of MPs by trade unions. Article 64 lays down the existing regulations for the declaration of all outside financial interests of members. 64.1 adopts the resolution of the House of Commons on oral declarations in 1974 (slightly modified) for both Houses. 64.2.1 extends the existing Commons register of members' interests to both Houses and 64.2.2 requires that there shall be a joint Select Committee of both Houses to examine matters connected with the register and to make recommendations to Parliament about them.

Division 3: Legislative powers

Division 3 makes provision for the legislative powers of the two Houses. The most important innovation lies in the powers of the Second Chamber with regard to amendments to the Constitution and Constitutional legislation, that is, statutes giving direct effect to provisions of the Constitution, such as those concerning elections. In these matters the Second Chamber has equal status with the House of Commons and can in effect veto amendments to the Constitution. The Second Chamber is also given extended delaying power over Public Bills other than Money Bills. In other respects the relationship between the Houses follows the provisions of the 1949 Parliament Act.

ARTICLE 65: INTRODUCTION OF BILLS

Article 65 codifies the current rules governing the introduction of Bills: namely that public Bills may be introduced by any member (65.1.1), but that any Bill which involves taxation, public expenditure or debt requires the consent of the Cabinet (65.3). This is a fundamental principle of the present Constitution and guarantees the government's control over fiscal and economic policy. The government is not however given a monopoly over the introduction of legislation, as in many other Constitutions, and provision is made in 65.2 for the continuance of private legislation subject to the standing orders of both Houses. 65.1.2 encapsulates the regular procedure for Bills to become law, which is departed from for purposes of constitutional amendment and legislation under Article 69, for Money Bills under Article 67, and for certain other Bills under Article 68.

ARTICLE 66: SUBORDINATE LEGISLATION

Article 66 extends parliamentary scrutiny of subordinate legislation. Under 66.1 a Standing Committee is set up in each House with specific responsibilities for advising members on enabling clauses in draft primary legislation, as recommended in the Donoughmore Report on Ministers' Powers in 1932 but never adopted, and on certain statutory instruments laid before Parliament under terms of reference similar to those of the Joint Select Committee on Statutory Instruments.

66.2 preserves the existing powers of either House to annul or disapprove subordinate legislation. We have also considered the inclusion of a power to amend subordinate legislation, but have not been able to explore the ramifications sufficiently to recommend it with confidence.

ARTICLE 67: RESTRICTIONS ON POWERS OF SECOND CHAMBER AS TO MONEY BILLS

The provisions of the Parliament Act 1911 over Money Bills are retained in Article 67, consistent with the principle that national finance is the special responsibility of the House of Commons, so that the Second Chamber may only delay such Bills for a period of one month.

ARTICLE 68: RESTRICTIONS ON POWERS OF SECOND CHAMBER AS TO CERTAIN BILLS

Under Article 68 the revising role of the Second Chamber over ordinary public legislation, with a power of delay of one year over measures passed by the Commons, is retained but the terms of the Parliament Acts 1911 and 1949 are replaced by the more sophisticated machinery provided for in the Parliament (No. 2) Bill 1969 prepared by the Labour government at that time (withdrawn after securing its second reading under pressure of parliamentary time).

68.5.3 extends the period of delay proposed in that Bill from 60 to 120 parliamentary days, thus strengthening the power of the Second Chamber to reflect its new position as an elected rather than hereditary and appointed body.

Division 4: Constitutional amendments and legislation

The Second Chamber is entrusted by the Constitution with special responsibility for the review of Bills which include constitutional matters or human rights. Bills to amend the Constitution require the approval of the Second Chamber with a special two-thirds majority under Article 69. Other Bills of a constitutional nature, as defined in Article 70 and certificated as such by the Second Chamber's Speaker, will require the consent of the Second Chamber by simple majority. This category of legislation will include all Bills affecting human rights and freedoms, as well as measures affecting the structure of government or giving detailed effect to the Constitution.

ARTICLE 69: AMENDMENT TO THE CONSTITUTION

Article 69 provides that Parliament may amend the constitution by legislation, but that this must be passed by a qualified majority (two-thirds) in both Houses. In addition to creating a higher hurdle for constitutional legislation than for ordinary statutes, this gives the Second Chamber a veto over amendments, as a safeguard against temporary majorities in the Commons. This provision should be read alongside the powers of the Second Chamber in relation to quasi-constitutional legislation, that is, legislation on elections and so forth which Parliament is obliged by the Constitution to provide (Article 70). Together these provisions give the Second Chamber a strong constitutional role, backed by the legitimacy of direct elections, which may go some way to restoring its reputation as the watchdog of the Constitution.

Article 69 provides two levels of qualified majority. Under 69.1 the core provisions of the Constitution can only be amended by a two-thirds majority of all the members of both Houses. The provisions include:

Chapter 1:	The Constitution as foundation of power in the United Kingdom	
Chapter 2:	Fundamental Rights and Freedoms	
Chapter 3:	Nationality	
Chapter 4:	Articles 34–36	Head of State
Chapter 5:	Articles 40	Executive
	Articles 41	Prime Minister
	Articles 44	Cabinet
	Articles 47–49	Legal officers
	Article 50	European Community law
Chapter 6:	Articles 52–57	Legislative powers and Parliament
	Article 70	Constitutional Bills
Chapter 7:	Article 78 and 79 Schedules 1 and 2	Assemblies
Chapter 8:	Articles 83–86, 88 89 and Part 1 of Schedule 3	Elections
Chapter 9:	and Schedules 4 and 5	Judiciary
Chapter 10		The public services
Chapter 11		Administrative justice
Chapter 12		Protection of the United Kingdom

Other provisions of the Constitution may be amended by a two-thirds majority of both Houses present and voting, provided the two-thirds constitutes at least half the membership of each House.

69.3 provides that no amendment to the Constitution which affects the powers and responsibilities of the Assemblies shall come into force unless it has been ratified by a majority of the members of two thirds of the Assemblies. Parliament cannot therefore change the position of the Assemblies without their consent.

69.4 deals with the question of secession: no part of the United Kingdom may be allowed to secede or be excluded without a referendum of its voters, conducted and supervised by the Electoral Commission. This Article does not provide any method to initiate an amendment for secession other than a Bill introduced into Parliament like other amendments. But 69.7 provides that these provisions as they affect Northern Ireland must be read subject to Article I of the Anglo-Irish Agreement, which states:

The two Governments
(a) affirm that any change in the status of Northern Ireland would only come about with the consent of a majority of the people of Northern Ireland;

(b) recognise that the present wish of a majority of the people of Northern Ireland is for no change in the status of Northern Ireland;

(c) declare that, if in future a majority of the people of Northern Ireland clearly wish for and formally consent to the establishment of a united Ireland, they will introduce and support in the respective Parliaments legislation to give effect to that wish.

This supposes a means of consulting the wishes of the people of Northern Ireland *prior* to legislation and commits the government of the United Kingdom to introduce and support such legislation. It cannot commit Parliament to passing the legislation to which the qualified majorities in both Houses might prove a formidable obstacle. It is a question whether the position of Northern Ireland should be treated differently for purposes of amendment in the light of the treaty obligations. The significance of Article I is discussed at length in T. M. Hadden and Kevin Boyle, *The Anglo-Irish Agreement: Commentary, Text and Official Review* (London: Sweet & Maxwell, 1989, pp. 18–22).

ARTICLE 70: CONSTITUTIONAL BILLS

Article 70 provides a special procedure for the passage of Constitutional Bills, that is, Bills as defined in 70.3 which are required to be enacted by the Constitution, which give detailed effect to any Article of the Constitution, which affect any Article of the Bill of Rights (Chapter 2), or affect the principal institutions established by the Constitution: e.g. Head of State. Such Bills are required to be passed by a majority of all members of both Houses on their final reading. As noted above, this gives the Second Chamber equality with the Commons on constitutional questions.

Division 5: Public finance

ARTICLE 71: PUBLIC FUNDS

Article 71 defines and regulates the Consolidated Fund, which is currently governed by the Exchequer and Audit Departments Act 1806 as amended by the National Loans Act 1968. The Consolidated Fund is defined as the 'Account of Her Majesty's Exchequer' and forms one general fund kept by the Treasury at the Bank of England.

The Article also seeks to clarify other accounts or funds which are provided for by the Constitution. Currently the National Loans Fund Act 1968 provides that all money raised by the creation of debt is payable into the National Loans Fund. The constitutional importance of the Article is the attempt to regulate all such funds by statute. Thus funds outside the supply system such as Trading Funds (the Government Trading Funds Act 1973) or the National Insurance Fund (Social Security Act 1965) are required to have statutory authority under the Constitution.

71.3 provides the authorization requirements for expenditure from the Consolidated Fund. The House of Commons votes the necessary supply and agrees to payments out of the Consolidated Fund. The estimates must be approved by the House of Commons.

71.4.1 and .2 seek to place all public funds under the Constitution and the authority of statute.

ARTICLE 72: CONTINGENCIES FUND

Article 72 provides for a Contingencies Fund, and the legal authority for such a fund is therefore provided under the Constitution. The Treasury authorises issues out of the Fund subject to the limits set on the capital of the Fund by the Contingencies Fund Act 1974. Currently the maximum cost is set at 2 per cent of the total of authorised supply expenditure in the preceding financial year. No final charge is permitted to rest on the Fund. The necessary parliamentary authority is required to enable repayment to be made. When advances from the Fund are repayable from rates, the necessary provision should normally be sought in the next batch of Supplementary Estimates.

The Treasury will continue to exercise its system of internal control and regulation over the Fund.

ARTICLE 73: APPROPRIATION

Article 73 regulates withdrawals from the Consolidated Fund, in the Treasury's terms 'issues out of the Consolidated Fund'. An important element in the regulation of the fund is the internal control exercised by the Treasury. This includes the submission to the Treasury of the annual estimates and supplementary estimates. 73.5 permits virement. This arises when the total expenditure on any service may not exceed that granted by Parliament, but a trade-off may be allowed between subheads of expenditure within the main head. The exercise of virement is subject to Treasury control and is now recognised by the Constitution. For the rest the Article encapsulates present procedures for appropriations.

ARTICLE 74: BUDGET

Article 74 requires the Chancellor of the Exchequer, in presenting his or her budget to the House of Commons, to present details of government policy in relation to the raising of revenue at the same time as presenting the government's policy in relation to expenditure. Revenue can be raised only under the authority of an Act of Parliament.

ARTICLE 75: COMPTROLLER AND AUDITOR GENERAL

Article 75 recognises the importance of the Comptroller and Auditor General under the Constitution. By statute (the Exchequer and Audit Departments Acts 1866 and 1921 and the National Audit Act 1983), the Comptroller and Auditor General enjoys independence. This is recognised in the Constitution, and his or her mode of appointment remains regulated by the National Audit Act 1983. The functions of the Comptroller and Auditor General are provided under the

National Audit Act 1983 to include powers to certify accounts of all government departments and a wide range of public sector bodies; to examine revenue and store accounts; and to report such examinations to Parliament. He or she also has a wide range of powers to examine the economy, efficiency and effectiveness (i.e. a VFM audit) in the use of the resources by those bodies he or she audits or to which he or she has rights of access.

Division 6: Constitutional Commission

ARTICLE 76: CONSTITUTIONAL COMMISSION

Article 76 establishes a Constitutional Commission which is in effect a joint committee of the two Houses of Parliament, but with the power under 76.1.3 to coopt additional members up to one-third of its membership. The aim is to allow the Commission to avail itself of the services of learned and distinguished persons and thus to add weight and impartiality to its scrutiny of constitutional behaviour. Its general responsibility is to monitor the working of the Constitution and to review and investigate, through its Integrity Committee, complaints about the propriety, constitutional and otherwise, of Ministers. The Commission is not intended to preclude and pre-empt legal proceedings before the courts, and rules may need to be worked out to define the functional relationship between the Commission and the courts. The establishment of the Commission however reflects our general view that the business of Parliament should be left as much as possible to Parliament and an expectation that an adverse report from the Commission would prove a sufficient sanction on errant Ministers.

ARTICLE 77: INTEGRITY COMMITTEE

Under Article 77 an Integrity Committee is drawn from among members of the Constitutional Commission who are members of Parliament to investigate complaints of impropriety either upon complaint or on its own initiative. The Committee has the powers of a tribunal of inquiry and reports to the relevant House of Parliament which must consider the report within 60 days of receiving it.

CHAPTER 7
National and Regional Government

ARTICLE 78: ASSEMBLIES

78.1 and Schedule 1 provide that there shall be Assemblies for Scotland, Wales, Northern Ireland and the regions of England. The Schedule provides that there should be twelve regions for England. The proposals for the English regions are bound to be controversial and require detailed justification which we will provide in a separate report. In brief, we have put more emphasis on cultural factors such as regional or local identity and on social and economic geography than on uniformity of population or areas; in fact we have assumed that a uniform system is not only unnecessary but would run counter to the purpose of decentralisation. This is reflected in the provisions for local government, which allow also for regional diversity. The range of population size is from 1.5m for Northern Ireland and the South-West to 6.5m for London and the North-West. This range of population is considerably smaller than for provinces in Germany (650,000 to 16.5m), Italy (100,000 to 8.8m), Australia (450,000 to 5.5m) or France (235,000 to 10m). We have also assumed that there is no optimum size of population for the performance of any government functions and no categorical need to tailor regions to produce a particular population. We have followed existing county boundaries, unless there is a strong case for departure. We have tried to ensure that there is no place in any region which is more than 100 miles or two hours' travelling time from the regional capital. We have concluded that a system of small city regions would not suit the geographical diversity of England and that the fact that an area looks towards London should not determine whether or not it is included in a London region. In fact for political reasons we have decided against a mega-region for London and the South-East, and plumped for the old GLC boundaries for London, with consequent difficulties for the rest of the South-East. These will be explored more fully in a separate report. The boundaries of Scotland, Wales and Northern Ireland remain as at present.

Article 78 further provides for the functions of the Assemblies, their election, members and qualifications, term, procedures and standing rules, general competence and legislation.

78.1.1 confirms the legislative power granted under Article 54 of Chapter 6. Under 78.2.2 Assemblies are also responsible for holding their executives to account.

78.1.3 allows each Assembly to legislate for the names of the Assembly and its members. It is therefore possible for the Scottish Assembly to call itself the Scottish Parliament, if it chooses, but for the purposes of the Constitution to avoid confusion the name Parliament is reserved to the Parliament of the United Kingdom.

Under 78.2 and 78.3 Parliament controls elections to the Assemblies and the number of members and their qualifications. The franchise, boundaries and election procedures are all UK matters and subject to the supervision of the Electoral Commission.

The Assemblies have a fixed four-year term, with no power of dissolution. Elections will take place in the second year of the electoral cycle established in Part 3 of Schedule 3.

The standing orders of the Assemblies are to provide for the election of a presiding officer, the election of the Chief Executive and other matters (78.5).

78.6 gives a general competence to the Assemblies to do anything which is calculated to assist in the performance of any of their functions.

78.7 provides that laws passed by Assemblies shall be called Acts of Assembly, when passed by an affirmative vote of a majority of the members voting and certified by the presiding officer and the Clerk to the Assembly. There are thus none of the mechanisms provided in earlier legislation for the intervention of the UK government in the proceedings of Assemblies before their legislation receives assent. The tutelary role of the Secretary of State contained in the Northern Ireland Constitution Act 1973 and the Scotland and Wales Acts 1978 disappears. Governments will deal with each other at arm's length and questions of vires and conflicts of laws will be resolved in the courts rather than by use of the reserve political power of the UK government or pre-assent reference to the Judicial Committee of the Privy Council.

ARTICLE 79: EXECUTIVES

Article 79 provides for an Executive or government to be drawn from each Assembly and for a Chief Executive to be elected by the Assembly; for the Standing Orders of the Assembly; for the election of the Chief Executive and the appointment of other members of the Executive by the Chief Executive; for the appointment of officials by the Executive; for the exercise of executive powers within the legislative competence of an Assembly and over any other matters which Parliament may determine.

These provisions establish the Assemblies and their Executives and the basic relationship between them. This replicates the provisions for Parliament and the government of the United Kingdom with a Chief Executive elected by the legislature with powers to appoint his or her colleagues. The details of the relationship as contained in the Standing Orders of the Assemblies are for the Assemblies themselves. The powers of the Assemblies and hence of the executives are governed by provisions of Article 54 (legislative powers) and by Article 80 (revenue sharing). All matters concerning the election to Assemblies are matters for Parliament under Article 87.

ARTICLES 80 AND 81: ASSEMBLY FINANCE AND REVENUE SHARING

Articles 80 and 81 provide for the establishment of a Consolidated Fund and a Loans Fund for each Assembly and the rules governing their use and any borrowing by members of an Executive; Schedule 2 also provides a formula for revenue sharing as a source of finance for the Assemblies. This is an attempt to find a constitutional device to overcome the conundrum of regional and local government: how to find a tax base which provides a substantial proportion of local revenue and at the same time provides for the equalisation of resources between richer and poorer areas. Tax raising powers are commonly held to be essential to any genuine political independence, but if regional and local governments are left to their own resources there will be great inequalities in standards of public services between different areas. If on the other hand central government provides a substantial proportion of local resources in the form of equalisation grants, it will inevitably become involved in prescribing the ways in which 'its money' is spent, and local autonomy or self-government will be undermined. This has proved the case even where redistribution has been carried through by elaborate formulae based on measurements of need. These do not remove the occasions for political judgments or the temptations to political manipulation. The suggestion here is to assign major tax revenues to the regions as of right with an entrenched formula for redistribution, while keeping the administration and control of the tax itself with central government.

The experience of most countries has been that the buoyant sources of revenue (income taxes, excises, corporation taxes) have been appropriated by central government. The assignation of indirect taxes to regional or local government (sales tax, excise, VAT) runs into difficulties with 'common market' constraints both within the UK and the European Community. In the longer term there are pressures to harmonise such taxes across the EC. This leaves income and property taxes as the most appropriate taxes for local and regional government. Article 82 assigns property taxes (rates on domestic and commercial property) directly to local authorities.

Schedule 2 provides that the whole of the personal income tax shall be assigned to the Assemblies. The personal income tax would remain a United Kingdom tax with the definitions of taxable income, rates and allowances all established by Parliament and administered by the Inland Revenue. The provision in Section 7 that each Assembly be allowed to vary the standard rate of tax levied in its jurisdiction within established limits must require tax payers to furnish the Inland Revenue with their addresses and add to administration and compliance costs of the tax, but to a much lesser extent than would be required for a local income tax.

Section 2 of Schedule 2 refers to the *estimated* product of the personal income tax accruing to residents. This will allow the Inland Revenue to include investment income and its distribution by means of surveys rather than requiring detailed individual returns for all taxpayers and potential taxpayers. Pinpoint accuracy is not required as long as the general approach to distribution is seen to be fair.

Sections 3, 4 and 5 of the Schedule provide the formula for distribution among the Assemblies. This would work as follows:

1. a baseline per capita expenditure in the UK on devolved functions is calculated for year 1;
2. the average per capita expenditure for the UK is multiplied by the population of each nation or region;
3. this expected expenditure for each Assembly is compared with its share of revenue from income tax and its allocation is adjusted to match any excess or deficit.

Section 3.2 of the Schedule provides that after year 1 the average expenditure shall be adjusted in line with the growth of the Gross Domestic Product, which should provide buoyancy, without being linked to inflation, but not adjusted to reflect the actual expenditure of Assemblies. The Assemblies cannot therefore raise the baseline by spending more, though increasing yields from income tax may provide additional resources.

It should also be noted that the system of equalisation is not self-contained and the UK government would be obliged to make up the allocations of the deficit regions if the income tax revenue from the surplus regions was not adequate. There is thus no incentive for the UK government to lower income taxes as a means of controlling the Assemblies.

There are, of course, serious problems in entrenching a financial formula in the Constitution and the political difficulties may outweigh any advantages, quite apart from persuading central government to diminish its dominant fiscal position. A full exposition and defence of this proposal will be made in a separate report. A number of points should however be made in the interim:

1. The personal income tax yields about 25 per cent of current UK government revenue (£55bn, 1990–91 estimate). National Insurance contributions yield £36bn and would remain as a second UK income tax, levied on the working population and employers and available as a macro-economic instrument for the Chancellor.
2. The current level of central government grant to local government is about £42bn and local government income from community charge and uniform business rate £23.5bn.
3. The transfer of functions (and expenditure) to the Assemblies, including health at £22bn, would still leave central government with the lion's share of revenue and a substantial surplus, so that it would retain an important role in equalisation. Preliminary calculations suggest that only the South-East of England would have a revenue surplus and that the UK government would have to make

up roughly 10 per cent of Assembly and local government expenditure. This would be done through the equalisation formula for the Assemblies and would not allow the UK government to intervene in specific areas of policy. If the UK government wants to do that it would have to do so by legislation under the concurrent powers in Article 55.

4. An equalisation formula based on population as proposed does not produce startlingly different results from one based on a more sophisticated needs-based formula. The calculations have to be based on estimates for the standard regions of England and extrapolations of expenditure on devolved functions. The figures suggest that Scotland, which presently enjoys considerable advantages under the Barnett formula for the distribution of public expenditure, would fare substantially worse from a population-based formula and the poorer English regions slightly better. These calculations will be described more fully in a separate report.

5. The formula proposed must give a greater degree of independence to the Assemblies, which would in turn be responsible for equalisation between their local authorities, at the expense of rough justice in the present and the risk of inflexibility in the future. The system would certainly be more transparent than the present one and transfer some of the more difficult political problems from the UK government to Assemblies and local authorities. There is no way of avoiding conflict in these matters: the role of the Constitution is to provide means to minimise the incentives for conflict and to create a more equal balance between central and subordinate governments.

ARTICLE 82: LOCAL GOVERNMENT

Article 82 makes important changes from present constitutional law and practice under which local government is entirely a creature of statute, to be created, altered or abolished at will by Parliament:

1. It provides a constitutional position for local government, without laying down a uniform system for the United Kingdom. Each Assembly will be able to devise arrangements suited to the character and needs of its area.

2. In addition to whatever powers and responsibilities an Assembly may give to its local authorities, each local authority will also have a general competence to carry out within the law and the constitution whatever activities it thinks will be of benefit to its citizens. The idea of a general competence for local authorities has been mooted in a number of reports (e.g. that by the Maud Committee on the *Management of Local Government* (1967) and by the Wheatley Commission in the *Report of the Royal Commission on Local Government in Scotland* (1969)) either in the form used here or as a general power of expenditure not limited to statutory purposes. The idea is to encourage independent initiatives in the interests of the local community, although no doubt the undertakings would be modest, given financial constraints.

3. The boundaries of the local authorities proposed by each Assembly would be subject to review by the Electoral Commission to prevent gerrymandering and other malpractices, and all matters concerning local elections would be controlled by Parliament and supervised by the Electoral Commission. These provisions, along with the Bill of Rights, are intended to prevent the abuse of power by local majorities. It is likely that even with a system of proportional representation several Assemblies will be dominated for long periods by one party.

4. Local authorities are guaranteed by the Constitution an independent source of taxation in the form of rates on property, whose virtues of certainty of collection and simplicity of administration have been painfully rediscovered by experiment, quite apart from the sound economic reasons for taxing property as such. This revenue would provide a good part of local authority expenditure, but how substantial would depend on each Assembly's decisions on the division of functions between itself and its local authorities. These would be likely to differ considerably with size of population and area. The Assemblies would replace central government as the source of equalisation grants.

82.5.2 enables Parliament to authorise further local tax powers through the Assemblies.

CHAPTER 8
Elections

ARTICLE 83: ELECTORAL LAW AND QUALIFICATIONS

Article 83 provides the basis for the law governing elections. 83.1 is a general statement of the principles repeating Article 15 of the Bill of Rights. 83.2 establishes the qualification both to vote and to stand for elections as being a British national who is at least 18 years old, though Parliament may extend the franchise to others (the likely classes are citizens of the Irish Republic or Commonwealth citizens, who are entitled to vote now, and other EC nationals).

ARTICLE 84: ELECTIONS TO HOUSE OF COMMONS

Article 84 and Schedule 3 set out the main elements of the electoral system for the House of Commons, which is also to be the model for Assembly and local authority elections, and for the Second Chamber. The system proposed for the House of Commons is a variant of the Additional Member System. It follows closely the recommendations of the *Report of the Hansard Society Commission on Electoral Reform* (June 1976) with differences of detail in relation to the number of regions in England; of members of the House of Commons and the proportion of additional members (half rather than a quarter), which would produce greater proportionality, but much larger constituencies; and in the allocation of additional members to constituencies. The Commission's report recommends a similar system for European elections and for devolved assemblies for Scotland and Wales. The general case for a system of proportional representation has been made in the Introduction. The choice of this system for the House of Commons arises from considerations of a number of sometimes competing criteria:

(a) *Proportionality*
- a close relation between the proportion of votes cast for a party and its representation in the electoral body;

- a low probability of a party with less than 50% of the total vote having more than half of the seats.

(b) *Locality*
- a close link between elected representatives and particular geographical areas;

- a close relation between local voting and local representation.

(c) *Representativeness*
- the possibility that elected representatives may be drawn from a wide variety of occupational, social, denominational, religious and ethnic backgrounds.

(d) *Discrimination*
- the opportunity for voters to choose among candidates of the same party or to determine how their votes shall be allocated in the absence of a clear winner.

(e) *Simplicity*
- a voting system which is easy to understand and where the relation between the vote and the result is clear;

- a system which does not require second elections or long-drawn-out calculations to arrive at the result;

- a system which does not require additional machinery for the nomination or adoption of candidates.

(f) *Coherence*
- a system which is the same at different levels of government and where the constituencies at different levels are related to each other in a consistent way.

MAIN FEATURES OF THE SYSTEM

(a) The UK is treated as a whole for the purposes of establishing an electoral quota.
(b) Each nation or region receives seats in proportion to its share of the electorate.
(c) Each nation or region is divided up into constituencies, as near

as possible equal in electors, for half the number of seats to which it is entitled.

(d) The candidate with the largest number of votes is elected in each constituency.

(e) The other half of the seats are allocated to parties in proportion to the total vote they receive in the election within each nation or region, subject to a threshold of 5 per cent.

(f) The method for appointing additional members is left to Parliament. We had originally considered a provision that additional members should be drawn from the candidates nominated but not elected in the constituencies of each nation or region, thus avoiding a party list or a separate nomination process. In most regions this would not create a problem, but in some regions one party may well gain over 50 per cent of the vote, win all the directly elected seats and be entitled to additional members as well. In this case some form of party list seems unavoidable.

(g) Vacancies for directly elected members are filled at elections by simple majority.

The proposed system does not perform ideally on any of the criteria outlined above. It could be modified in various respects to alter the emphasis between them. Its advantages and disadvantages are as follows:

(a) *Proportionality*: half the seats are reserved for additional members: this produces a greater degree of proportionality than the present system and makes it less likely that a party with less than 50 per cent of the vote will have a clear majority of seats, but falls short of strict proportionality.

A rough calculation based on the 1987 General Election is shown below in Table 1 on the basis of redistributing half the seats in proportion to votes cast in Scotland, Wales, Northern Ireland and 12 English regions, with a threshold of 5 per cent and a 500-member House of Commons.

(b) *Locality*: Half the members are elected for a constituency in the traditional manner. The constituencies for the House of Commons would be on average more than double the size of present constituencies. But the constituency link would be preserved and if practicable we would prefer that the additional members should be drawn from the unsuccessful candidates in the constituency election, rather than a separate party list, and

Table 1 500-Seat House of Commons under AMS with Regional Thresholds

	(1)	(2)	(3)	(4)			(5) Vote 1987		
	Region	Electorate	Shares	HofC	%Con	%Lab	%SLD	%Oth	
01	Northern	2,001,807	4.63	12	29.21	49.02	21.48	0.29	
02	North-West	5,219,626	12.08	30	38.66	41.12	20.02	0.20	
03	Yorkshire	3,729,670	8.63	22	37.28	41.03	21.42	0.27	
04	West Midlands	3,942,925	9.13	23	45.46	33.34	20.85	0.35	
05	East Midlands	2,575,795	5.96	15	48.00	31.32	20.29	0.39	
06	Central	2,008,846	4.65	12	53.50	21.46	24.64	0.40	
07	East Anglia	2,663,392	6.16	15	53.20	20.39	26.03	0.37	
08	London	5,120,379	11.85	30	46.55	31.58	21.16	0.71	
09	South-East	2,240,707	5.19	13	56.40	16.48	26.51	0.60	
10	South Central	2,999,691	6.94	17	56.40	14.71	28.48	0.41	
11	Wessex	2,391,080	5.53	14	51.42	17.32	30.87	0.39	
12	South-West	1,114,761	2.58	6	48.77	12.91	37.66	0.66	
13	Wales	2,151,352	4.98	12	29.52	45.06	17.92	0.22	7.28 (PC)
14	Scotland	3,953,497	9.15	23	24.03	42.39	19.21	0.34	14.03 (SNP)
15	Northern Ireland	1,089,160	2.52		(see below under note *)				
	Total	43,202,688	99.98	250					

Notes:

Column (2) is the 1987 electorate; column (3) is the electorate in each region as a percentage of the 1987 total UK electorate. The quota of votes per seat is the total electorate divided by 250, about 178,000.

Column (3) is used to calculate the number of constituencies per region; this is shown for the House of Commons in column (4), and is the number of seats contested as single-member constituencies under FPP; the total number of seats per region is twice this, the other representatives being added under AMS. The percentage of votes cast per party for each region at the 1987 election is given in column (5). The listing of seats won by the parties, in column (6), reflects a judgment as to the likely outcome in the elections for the new, larger constituencies given reasonable assumptions about the constituency boundaries *and* assuming that voters behave in the same way as in 1987.

(6) Seats won				(7) Add. seats				(8) Total seats			
Con	Lab	SLD	Oth	Con	Lab	SLD	Oth	Con	Lab	SLD	Oth
1	10	1	-	6	2	4	-	7	12	5	-
14	16	-	-	9	9	12	-	23	25	12	-
9	13	-	-	7	5	10	-	16	19	10	-
16	7	-	-	5	8	10	-	21	15	10	
12	3	-	-	3	6	6	-	15	9	6	
11	1	-	-	2	4	6	-	13	6	6	
15	-	-	-	1	6	8	-	16	6	8	
18	11	1	-	10	8	12	-	28	19	13	
13	-	-	-	2	4	7	-	15	4	7	
17	-	-	-	2	5	10	-	19	5	10	
12	1	1	-	2	4	8	-	14	5	9	
5	-	1	-	1	2	3	-	6	2	4	
1	9	1	1	6	2	3	1	7	11	4	2
3	15	3	2	8	5	6	4	11	20	9	6

Total:

Con	Lab	SLD	Oth	Con	Lab	SLD	Oth	Con	Lab	SLD	Oth
147	86	8	3	64	70	105	5	211	156	113	8

Notes continued

Column (7) uses the figures from column (5) to calculate the additional seats for each party per region, and column (8) shows the total seats won by each party under these assumptions.

* In Northern Ireland the vote shares for the various parties in 1987 were:

37.83 (UU); 11.73 (DUP); 5.28 (Oth U); 9.95 (All); 21.10 (SDLP); 11.42 (SF); 2.68 (Oth)

If the 'others' below 5% are eliminated, with 'Other U' including more than one party, this gives vote shares:

41.10 (UU); 12.74 (DUP); 10.81 (All); 22.93 (SDLP); 12.41 (ST)

So the 12 Northern Ireland seats would be distributed as in Table 2.

again as far as practicable be assigned to the constituency which they had contested.

(c) *Representativeness*: This depends on the method adopted for appointing additional members. The proposals do not score well here: a party list for additional members would probably be a better means of getting a greater variety of candidates than the ordinary adoption process by constituency parties.

(d) *Discrimination*: The system does badly here as well. Electors vote for a single candidate or party and do not get the opportunity to distinguish between candidates of the same party as they can do under STV, or to give a second preference as under the Alternative Vote; nor do they have opportunities for tactical voting as in a second ballot system. Their single vote does however count twice and is less likely to be wasted.

(e) *Simplicity*: The system does well here: the voter is required to vote once only and for a single candidate. If it were possible to draw the additional members from among the defeated candidates for direct election, a separate selection process would also be eliminated. But there may be circumstances in which all the candidates of one party are directly elected and some topping up mechanism would be required.

Table 1 is an attempt to estimate the effect of this system on the House of Commons based on the aggregate votes cast in existing constituencies at the 1987 General Election.

ARTICLE 85: ELECTIONS TO SECOND CHAMBER

Elections to the Second Chamber are also governed by Article 83 and by Article 85 and Schedule 3. The system of election proposed is different from that for the House of Commons, the Assemblies or local government, namely the Single Transferable Vote in multi-member constituencies. The Second Chamber will also be elected on a different cycle after the initial general election following the adoption of the Constitution and will not be dissolved between general elections. All those features are intended to distinguish the Second Chamber from the House of Commons and to strengthen its independence. Its prime function is to defend the Constitution, though there is much other useful work of revision and scrutiny for it to do. Any of this work will be aided by the enhanced legitimacy of election.

Table 2 Distribution of the 12 Northern Ireland seats under AMS

Party	OUP	DUP	Other U	SDLP	All	SF	Other
Seats won	4	2	0	2	0	0	0
Regional vote (%)	37.8	11.7	5.3	21.1	10.0	11.4	2.7
'Entitlement'	5	2	0	3	1	1	0
Additional seats	1	1	0	2	1	1	0

Composition of 500-seat House of Commons under AMS:

			1987 (650 members)
Conservative	211		374
Labour	156		229
SLD	113		22
PC	2		
SNP	6		
OUP	5		
DUP	2	20	24
SDLP	3		
Alliance	1		
SF	1		
Total	500	Total	650

Table 3 gives the distribution of seats among the nations and regions, along with the aggregate votes for 1987. It is not possible to calculate what the outcome might have been using this system in 1987. There are too many unknowns, including the size and distribution of constituencies.

Suggestions are made in the final column for dividing up the nations and regions, on the basis of constituencies of 5 to 9 members, but this will be a matter for the Electoral Commission.

The House of Commons would be elected by AMS in year X; the Second Chamber by STV in year $(X + 2)$. The Commons has 250 constituencies whose apportionment across the nations and regions is shown in column 4 of Table 1. The same allocation is used for the Second Chamber. The Commons constituencies would be

Table 3 1987 votes

Region	Seats	Con	Lab	SLD	Other		Seats/Districts
01	12	436,657	732,909	321,195	4,316		5 + 7
02	30	1,543,438	1,641,832	799,532	7,863		6 + 5
03	22	1,036,145	1,140,226	595,302	7,456		3 × 5 + 1 × 7
04	23	1,342,505	984,667	615,699	10,401		2 × 7 + 1 × 9
05	15	960,282	624,483	405,889	7,854		3 × 5
06	12	827,898	332,081	381,388	6,214		5 + 7
07	15	1,092,215	418,485	534,400	7,592		3 × 5
08	30	1,680,141	1,139,660	763,756	25,525		6 × 5
09	13	951,191	277,996	447,018	10,176		6 + 7
10	17	1,288,892	326,258	650,872	9,269		2 × 5 + 1 × 7
11	14	958,489	322,938	575,476	7,260		2 × 7
12	6	428,369	113,390	330,812	5,788		1 × 6
13	12	501,316	765,209	304,290	3,742	123,699 (PC)	5 + 7
14	23	713,081	1,258,132	570,053	10,069	416,073	2 × 7 + 1 × 9
15	6						1 × 6

| Total: | 250 | | | | | | |

Summary:

	Number	Total reps.
5-member seats	26	130
6-member seats	3	18
7-member seats	12	84
9-member seats	2	18
Total seats		250

aggregated to form multi-member districts. In some cases (Northern Ireland, the South-West) this would be the entire region, but in most regions there would be more than one district. Members of the Second Chamber are not constituency representatives like members of the Commons, they are regional representatives.

The suggested size of districts is between 5 and 9 members. Anything smaller is unsatisfactory: 3 would disfranchise a fourth party with up to 25% of the first preference votes; 4 is theoretically undesirable. 6 is also not good but may be unavoidable; odd numbers are preferred. On the other hand if districts are too large then the whole exercise becomes difficult both for voters and parties. The 9-member districts suggested are in Scotland and the West Midlands in fairly densely populated urban areas. Previous suggestions for STV districts (the SDP/Liberal report of 1982) are based on the present size of the House of Commons. The reduced size proposed in this Constitution reflects the view that much domestic business will be transferred to the Assemblies and that MPs' constituency responsibilities will be somewhat reduced.

ARTICLE 86: BY-ELECTIONS

Article 86 provides for a by-election to take place if the seat of an *elected* member becomes vacant. There is no provision for a by-election if the seat of an 'additional member' becomes vacant. Nor does the Constitution specify whether that vacancy would be filled by a candidate who had failed to be elected or from a party list.

ARTICLE 87: ELECTIONS TO EUROPEAN PARLIAMENT, ASSEMBLIES AND LOCAL AUTHORITIES

Article 87 requires that an Act of Parliament under Article 83 shall make provision for the constituency boundaries and elections for these elected bodies, in line with the provisions of Articles 84 to 86 and Schedule 3.

ARTICLES 88–90: ELECTORAL COMMISSION

Article 88 establishes a new body, the 'Electoral Commission', to supervise elections at all levels of the political system. In some of its responsibilities it supersedes the existing Boundary Commission but its broader scope is similar to the electoral commission established in the Constitution of Malta and the Federal Election Commission in the United States.

The structure and membership of the Commission are set out in Article 88, which establishes its status as an independent parliamentary agency. The power and duties of the Commission are covered in Article 89 together with Schedule 3 Parts 1–3 and the provisions for Assembly and local elections in Articles 78.2 and 82.3 respectively. These powers and duties fall broadly under three heads: the structure of the electoral system; electoral practices; and complaints of malpractice.

The structure of the electoral system: the Commission is responsible for establishing the number of representatives returned by the various regions to the European Parliament, the House of Commons and the Second Chamber. It also draws up the constituency boundaries for the election of representatives to the House of Commons, the Second Chamber, Regional Assemblies, local elections and elections to the European Parliament. Reference to this function can be found under the appropriate articles of the Constitution but it is restated in Article 89 and Schedule 3 Part 1, and a new Act with new guidelines will be enacted. The intention is to minimise political interference in these key aspects of the electoral system.

Electoral practices: Schedule 3 outlines the role of the Commission in relation to returning officers, the election of members of Parliament and particularly the additional members. Article 90 establishes its function for regulating political parties and finance, and the overall review of the electoral process. Apart from continuously adjusting regulatory practice to the changing electoral environment its broad function is to make electoral practice more transparent and open to greater public scrutiny than has been the case previously. This is particularly important in relation to political parties, which play an important role in public life and the democratic process. Reports and recommendations from the Commission would play a major part in the framing of future legislation in areas such as finance, broadcasting and political campaigning.

Malpractice: the Commission has a role in relation to electoral malpractice and can either initiate actions itself or associate itself with the actions of others (89.2). 89.3 gives the Commission further powers to act in exercising this quasi-judicial function. It does not however have the powers to nullify election results but could refer cases to the appropriate court.

ARTICLE 91: REGISTRATION OF POLITICAL PARTIES

The intention of Articles 90 and 91 is to allow political parties to be known to the Constitution. It does not require that parties should be registered or prescribe that only registered parties may put up candidates at elections. The incentive for parties to register with the Electoral Commission, which involves the submission to the Commission of the party constitution and its annual accounts, is that only registered parties will be eligible for public financial support and for access to political broadcasting. The aim is to recognize the constitutional status of political parties and to insist that parties which receive public support should act as public bodies, and in particular reveal their sources of finance.

Article 91 provides that the right to freedom of expression guaranteed by the Article 11 of the Bill of Rights should not be used to evade restrictions placed by Parliament on election expenditure of candidates, parties, whether registered or not, or other groups. Protection of the electoral process against corruption by money is essential to the integrity of the Constitution. This measure is taken in the light of recent cases under the Canadian Bill of Rights. Parliament is also required to put into statutory form the rules governing political broadcasting, which at present are the result of an informal concordat between the major parties and are regarded in some quarters as discriminating against smaller parties.

CHAPTER 9
The Judiciary

This chapter of the Constitution provides with respect to the judicial power in the United Kingdom. It is intended to secure, more firmly than is possible under an unwritten Constitution, a separation of that power from legislative and executive powers and the independence of those exercising that power from those who exercise the law-making and governmental powers of the State.

If courts are to have responsibility for resolving disputes impartially and in ways which attract confidence both of the parties (including the Executive) and of the public, it is necessary to secure that such decision-making can only be undertaken by those in whom the judicial power is vested and that those courts are independent and free from pressure and improper influences exerted by the legislature or government.

This chapter (and Schedules 4 and 5), therefore, establishes the institutions that are to exercise the judicial power in the United Kingdom and the limits on the authority of Parliament and the Assemblies to establish courts. Parliament will, in consequence, no longer have unlimited authority to create new courts. That power will be confined to the establishment of lesser courts of limited jurisdiction and to tribunals.

This chapter also allocates the jurisdiction to exercise the judicial power among the courts established by or under the Constitution. That allocation may be altered only by Parliament within the authority conferred by the supreme law of the Constitution.

To the courts will fall the responsibility of ensuring that these constitutional principles are respected. A major new function is to interpret and enforce the Constitution, and most particularly the Bill of Rights, Article 6 of which guarantees decision-making by impartial and independent courts and tribunals. For the first time, the superior courts and, in particular, the new Supreme Court of the United Kingdom created by the Constitution are vested with the power to render invalid any legislation enacted in the country which infringes the Constitution.

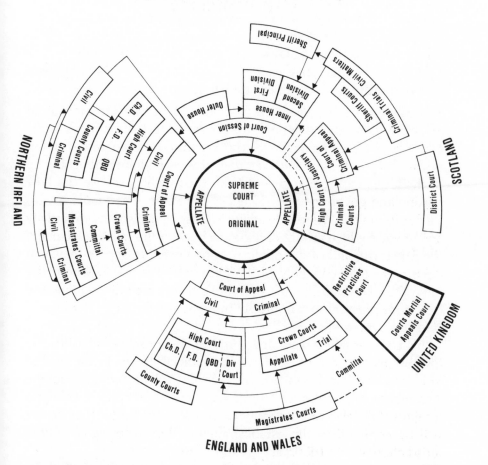

COURTS OF THE UNITED KINGDOM

Important changes to the existing law are made by this chapter (and Schedule 5) with respect to the appointment of the judiciary. There is general agreement about the need for reform, which will be accentuated as the judicial role is extended by the vesting of new functions in the senior judiciary, in particular with regard to the enforcement of the Bill of Rights. If there is to be confidence that the judiciary is sensitive to the broader social implications of its decisions, the narrow base from which judges are largely drawn at present must be broadened. The judiciary must be seen fairly to reflect, not only the nations and regions of the United Kingdom, but more importantly all sections of the society. In particular, there must be a significant increase in the numbers of women and people from ethnic and other such minority groups. A major innovation made by this chapter to these ends is the establishment of independent Judicial Services Commissions for England and Wales (working through Welsh and Regional Committees for intermediate and inferior court judges), for Scotland and for Northern Ireland, with responsibility for all judicial appointments (including lay magistrates and tribunal members). The Commissions are expressly charged with duties which are designed to broaden the bases of judicial selection (Article 104.2). Their power to authorise, for the first time, appointment as a judge of any court on a part-time basis (Schedule 4, Section 4.1.3) should materially increase the number of women judges.

This chapter also contains the principal legal provisions designed to assure the collective independence of the judiciary as the body which exercises the judicial power, and the individual independence of the members of the judiciary from governmental or legislative interference that may threaten their ability to act impartially. Some of these provisions are comparable to those provided by ordinary statute law; some, notably those relating to the appointment, removal and disciplining of the judiciary, are new. In these respects, the Constitution introduces an element of judicial accountability which should be the counterbalance to judicial independence.

It is intended that most of the existing court system (with the notable exception of the House of Lords, which is abolished) will continue within this constitutional framework. Substantial changes in the present law, structure and organisation and officials, or in jurisdiction, practice and procedure, are not a necessary part of the process of constitutional restructuring. On the other hand, some administrative reorganisation will be needed if the High Court is to meet the demands that will be made by establishing Assemblies with legislative powers in Wales and the regions of England.

This chapter is premised on the continuation of three legal systems in the United Kingdom. That for England and Wales will remain a unitary system. The practice and substance of the law, the legal professions and the institutions of law in England and Wales have been unified for some 450 years. Although the National Assembly of Wales will enact legislation that will have effect only in respect of Welsh matters, this does not necessitate a formal division of the legal system into two separate units. Indeed, it is likely to be to the disadvantage of Wales to separate the Principality and practitioners which a legal system of the present size has to offer. There is no reason why, in principle, any court in England and Wales should not have the jurisdiction to apply Welsh legislation if in the circumstances before it that law contains the rules that govern. Similar considerations apply with respect to legislation enacted by the Regional Assemblies in England.

PART 1: THE JUDICIAL POWER

This Part and Schedule 4 contain the central principles governing the legal systems of the United Kingdom and the formal establishment provisions for the courts and authorities that are to derive their existence from the Constitution. The implementing provisions are contained in other Parts or legislation authorised by the Constitution.

ARTICLE 92: THE JUDICIAL POWER

Article 92 vests the judicial power for the United Kingdom in the courts established by or in accordance with the Constitution. Allocation of any part of that power to a body other than one of these courts, as for example to an executive authority, will have no legal effect. These provisions ensure that decisions of a judicial nature will at all times remain in the hands of those appointed, as provided for by the Constitution, to be the judges of these courts.

A primary feature of the division of governmental powers by the Constitution must be the independence of the court system from interference with the performance of its responsibilities by the Executive or the legislative branches. Article 5 of the Bill of Rights guarantees that —

> In the determination of their civil rights and obligations or of any criminal charges against them, everyone is entitled to a fair and public hearing within a reasonable time by an independent and impartial tribunal established by law.

92.2 provides the guarantee of independent courts established by law. Other provisions of the chapter make more particular provision for the independence both of individual judges and collectively of the judiciary, for example with respect to the distribution of the judicial power, security of tenure, appointment and removal and conditions of service and to rights in relation to the administration and the provisions of resources for the court system.

92.3 provides that new bodies to discharge part of the judicial power may be established only in accordance with the Constitution.

Parliament's hitherto unfettered power to establish courts and tribunals must now be exercised in accordance with the Constitution. So, for example, no new superior court can be established without first amending the Constitution. This provision does not preclude the creation of courts or tribunals whose functions are not of a public nature.

ARTICLE 93: ESTABLISHMENT OF COURTS

Article 93 is the source of authority for all the courts entitled to exercise jurisdiction in the United Kingdom and in each of the legal systems with the Kingdom. The principal innovation is the Supreme Court of the United Kingdom, whose primary responsibility will be as a constitutional court for United Kingdom matters.

93.3 provides that the collective jurisdiction currently vested in existing courts is taken over by the courts established by the Constitution. The allocation of that collective jurisdiction between those courts is to be determined by Act of Parliament except where Schedule 4 of the Constitution expressly allocates matters to particular courts.

Parliament would also be expected to respect the distinction made by the Constitution between superior courts and intermediate and inferior courts. In particular, there must be allocated to the former unlimited original jurisdiction in all substantial civil cases and in respect of all serious criminal offences and any supervisory jurisdiction over the latter.

The establishment by the Constitution of distinct court systems requires provisions to be made to determine the territorial limits of their jurisdiction and the extent to which jurisdiction may be exercised by the courts of one part in respect of activities or actions that occur in another part. Under 93.4 these matters must be provided for by Act of Parliament. At present such legal provisions as exist are scattered through specialist legislation (but for civil matters see Civil Jurisdiction and Judgments Act 1982, Parts II and III and Schedules 3 and 4).

ARTICLE 94: LIMITATIONS ON INVALIDATING OF LEGISLATION

The power to invalidate primary legislation will rest only with the superior courts of the three legal systems. Challenges arising in other courts must be referred to those superior courts for decision. There is a right of appeal to the Supreme Court from any such decision that invalidated an Act of Parliament (98.3.1), without the need to pursue an appeal to the appeal court in the particular system. In the case of primary legislation enacted by an Assembly, an appeal must go to those courts (which are the final courts in this respect), as of right, against any decision that invalidated the statute and, with limited exceptions, where such a challenge has been dismissed.

ARTICLE 95: FULL FAITH AND CREDIT

Article 95 is a standard federal provision requiring Assembly legislation and judicial proceedings in the nations to be recognised throughout the United Kingdom.

The important question of enforcement in one part of the United Kingdom of judgments and court orders made in another must be dealt with by Act of Parliament. With respect to criminal matters, present provisions are fragmentarily provided for. Civil judgments are largely dealt with by the Civil Jurisdiction and Judgments Act 1982 (sections 18 and 19).

SCHEDULE 4: COURTS IN ENGLAND AND WALES

Schedule 4 (Part 1) provides for the establishment of the courts and the legal system of England and Wales, the judiciary attached to them and their jurisdictional competence. In large measure, the existing system of courts and jurisdiction is retained. In consequence, much of the existing legislation on these matters is intended to continue, subject to the power of Parliament to make changes within its competence as described by this Schedule.

Section 1.1 provides for three superior courts: the Court of Appeal, the High Court and the Crown Court (which at present comprise the Supreme Court for England and Wales and are provided for by the Supreme Court Act 1981, c. 54). Authority is conferred upon Parliament to establish and provide for intermediate courts (e.g. the county courts – County Courts Act 1984, c. 28) and inferior courts (e.g. magistrates' courts – Magistrates' Courts Act 1980, c. 43; and coroners' courts – Coroner's Act 1988, c. 13). Similarly, Parliament is authorised to establish tribunals which it may designate as intermediate or inferior courts, thereby bringing tribunal members within the constitutional safeguards with respect to appointment and removal of judges of such courts.

Under Section 1.2 the Court of Appeal will comprise the Master of the Rolls as its president (who in present practice is the senior judge of the Civil Division of the Court) and a minimum of 20 other justices. At present, the Court of Appeal comprises a maximum of 18 Lords Justices of Appeals and a number of ex officio judges, including present and past Lord Chancellors, the Law Lords, the Lord Chief Justice, the President of the Family Division and Vice-Chancellor (the last three being members also of the High Court), in addition to the Master of the Rolls (Supreme Court Act 1981, c. 54, section 2). In addition it is common for Queen's Bench judges to be assigned to the Court to assist in the business of the Criminal Division (ibid., s. 9). For purposes such as that, dual membership of the Court of Appeal and the High Court may be required.

The Court of Appeal at present sits in two divisions: for criminal and for civil appeals (ibid., s. 3). Similar arrangements will continue to be needed, but they and the designation and title of the justices who will head either division will be for Parliament to prescribe. (The Lord Chief Justice at present heads the criminal division.)

Under Section 1.3 the High Court will comprise the Chief Justice as its president and a minimum of 50 justices. At present the High Court comprises a maximum 80 puisne judges, in addition to the Lord Chief Justice, the Lord Chancellor, the President of the Family Division, the Vice-Chancellor and the Presiding Judge, who are also members of the Court of Appeal (Supreme Court Act 1981, c. 54, section 4). Given the extensive use at present of deputy High Court judges for Queen's Bench business and the rapid growth in public proceedings, it is improbable that a lesser number of justices than at present will be required.

Judicial functions are also performed for the High Court by Masters of the Queen's Bench and the Chancery Division, the Taxing Masters and certain Registrars of the High Court and in family matters by district judges (formerly district registrars) (Courts and Legal Services

Act 1990, c. 41, section 76). For the purposes of the Constitution, these have the status of intermediate court judges.

The High Court at present sits in three divisions: the Chancery Division, in practice headed by the Vice-Chancellor; the Queen's Bench Division, over which the Lord Chief Justice presides; and the Family Division, whose head is the President of the Family Division (ibid., s. 5). In addition, there are a Patents Court (as part of the Chancery Division), an Admiralty Court and a Commercial Court (as part of the Queen's Bench Division), to which puisne judges may be assigned (ibid., s. 6).

Whilst similar arrangements will continue to be needed, a further Division of the High Court may be appropriate to deal with public proceedings (i.e. judicial review and constitutional issues, such as challenges to legislation enacted for England and Wales or by Regional Assemblies or under the Bill of Rights). In this case too, the arrangements and the designation and titles of justices to head the divisions will be a matter for Parliament to prescribe by legislation.

Under Section 1.4 Crown Courts will comprise all the justices of the High Court and such number of other judges as Parliament will determine. The latter, through performing functions of superior court judges, are to have the status of intermediate court judges for the purposes of constitutional safeguards with respect to appointment and removal (cf. below: Sections 2, 3 and Article 108).

At present the judges of the Crown Courts comprise the puisne judges, circuit judges and recorders (i.e. practitioners appointed to sit part-time) and, for certain appeals, any such judge sitting with a maximum of four justices of the peace (Supreme Court Act 1981, c. 54, section 8). There are some 500 circuit judges and 550 recorders. Considerable numbers of deputy circuit judges and assistant recorders are also appointed (Courts Act 1971, c. 23, sections 21 and 24). With the exception of justices of the peace, who do not have the required legal qualifications (Section 2), similar arrangements will be consistent with the Constitution.

The advantage of part-time or temporary appointment at this level, for example as recorders, is that those who may come under consideration for judicial appointment are able both to gain judicial experience and to give some indication of their suitability for appointment.

Although a unitary legal system is retained for England and Wales, Section 1.5 gives recognition to the special status of Wales by ensuring that at least two members of the Court of Appeal and four of the High Court are drawn from those who have experience as intermediate judges or in legal practice in Wales. A Welsh member of the Judicial Services Commission is also provided for (Schedule 5). Arrangements with respect to intermediate or inferior courts, and to tribunals designated as such, that operate exclusively in Wales are provided for in Section 3.

Under Section 1.6 the composition and titles of intermediate and inferior courts, and of any tribunals so designated, will be for Parliament to determine by legislation.

At present, the County Courts are staffed by circuit judges (although Court of Appeal and High Court judges and recorders are also capable of sitting) (County Courts Act 1984, c. 28, section 5). Judicial functions are also performed by district judges (formerly registrars of county courts) (Courts and Legal Services Act 1990, section 74).

The magistrates' courts are staffed by stipendiary magistrates (some 65) or by lay magistrates (about 27,500) appointed pursuant to the Justices of the Peace Act 1979, c. 55, Part I.

Similar arrangements would be appropriate in implementation of this clause.

JUDICIAL QUALIFICATIONS

The principal judicial offices in the superior and intermediate courts must, under Section 2 of Schedule 4, be held by persons who are legally qualified or who have exercised rights of audience before the superior courts or who have served in a judicial capacity at a lower level. Additional qualifications will be prescribed by Act of Parliament.

Not all those exercising judicial functions in the superior courts need to be legally qualified. Provision is made now which permits lay magistrates to sit in appeals to Crown Courts and for lay persons with specialist qualifications to be appointed in a judicial capacity to courts exercising a special jurisdiction (e.g. Restrictive Practices Court Act 1976, c. 33, section 33) and as members of tribunals (e.g. the Employment Appeal Tribunal under section 135 of the Employment Protection Act 1978, c. 44).

Additional requirements have in the recent past required superior court judges to have practised as barristers for at least 10 years, in the case of High Court judges, or to have been a High Court judge or to have so practised for at least 15 years in the case of the Court of Appeal (Supreme Court Act 1981, c. 54, section 10). In the case of a circuit judge, appointees must have practised as a barrister for at least 5 years. In practice they are appointed from among those who have been recorders for at least 3 years (Courts Act 1971, c. 23, section 16, as amended by the Administration of Justice Act 1977, c. 38, section 12), who must be either a barrister or solicitor of at least 10 years' standing (ibid., section 21).

The Courts and Legal Services Act 1990 (c. 41, section 71), however, has now paved the way for increases in the numbers of solicitors appointed to high judicial office. They will be eligible not only by reason of holding office as a circuit judge but also as a result of having practised under the terms of the Act (section 27) before the superior courts for 10 years. In theory, but probably rarely in practice, other categories of persons granted an appropriate right of audience in the Supreme Court may be appointed to judicial office (ibid., section 71).

A major innovation made possible by Section 4.1.3 is the power to appoint part-time superior court judges on full tenure. This will be of especial benefit to the many women practitioners of ability and experience who find themselves unable to accept appointments which, because of the itinerant nature of the work, are incompatible with their family commitments.

The Constitution leaves the matter of the qualifications of judges of inferior courts, and of those tribunals designated for the purpose as inferior courts, to be prescribed by Act of Parliament.

As present legal qualifications are required for stipendiary magistrates (barristers or solicitors of not less than 7 years' standing (Justices of the Peace Act 1979, c. 55, section 13) or any other person who has a right of audience before any court and that length of experience (Courts and Legal Services Act 1990, c. 41, Schedule 10)). No other qualification than a residential one is prescribed by law for justices of the peace, who, with relatively few exceptions, will not be legally qualified (ibid., sections 6 and 7).

APPOINTMENT OF JUDGES

Section 3 of Schedule 4 requires appointments of superior court judges to be made by the Minister of Justice from names provided by the Judicial Services Commission. Unless dissatisfied with those names, when the recommendations can be returned for reconsideration, the Minister must choose one of the two names that must be put forward for each appointment.

At present, appointments are made in law by the Queen (Supreme Court Act 1981, c. 54, section 10). In practice, they are made on the recommendation of the Lord Chancellor, as a result of consideration and consultations instituted by his Department. Although more is officially published today than in the past about this process, it has been the subject of frequent and justified criticism for its apparently closed nature and narrowly based selection.

District judges of the High Court, formerly district registrars, are appointed by the Lord Chancellor. They are persons who already hold office as district judges (formerly county court registrars) for county court districts (Supreme Court Act 1981, c. 54, section 100, as amended as by the Courts and Legal Services Act 1990, c. 41, Schedule 10).

The involvement of a Judicial Services Commission, which is to have a large non-judicial composition (Schedule 5), is designed to open the process of selection and broaden its base. This mechanism is increasingly found in other jurisdictions (a Judicial Services Commission is a standard feature of the Westminster model constitutions in the Commonwealth) and is generally thought to have been successful, especially in immunising the selection process from political considerations.

The Judicial Services Commission is required to adopt procedures in makings its recommendations that will ensure that appointments, as far as practicable, fairly reflect the community they serve, leading to a significant increase in the numbers among the judiciary of women and members of minority ethnic groups (Article 104.2). The Commission would be obliged to take positive action to bring about such increases.

Appointments to the lower courts are also placed in the hands of the Minister of Justice acting in the usual event on the recommendation of the Judicial Services Commission. It is intended that only one recommendation will be made by the Commission for each appointment.

It is recognised, however, that some diversification of effort will be necessary, particularly with respect of the large number of magisterial (and tribunal) appointments that are required. Accordingly, committees of the Commission are to be appointed for Wales and for each of the regions of England in respect of appointments to courts in districts within their areas (Schedule 5). Such committees will be subject to guidelines that govern the work of the Commission, but not to its direction on the choice of names.

At present, circuit judges are appointed by the Queen on the recommendation of the Lord Chancellor (Courts Act 1971, c. 23, section 16), who here too is assisted by the consideration and consultations instituted by his Department. District judges (and deputy and assistant district judges) for county court districts – as registrars, etc. of the county courts are now known (Courts and Legal Services Act 1990, c. 41, section 74) – are appointed by the Lord Chancellor (County Courts Act 1984, c. 28, sections 6 to 8). Magistrates are appointed in the name of the Queen on the recommendation of the Lord Chancellor (Justices of the Peace Act 1979, c. 55, sections 6 to 13).

Appointments by the Lord Chancellor of lay justices follow recommendations made to him by local Advisory Committees. In the past, membership of those committees has not been open knowledge and the process by which candidates are identified, and selected, has been largely confidential. Whilst there are signs that some of this secrecy is being removed (committee membership is in future to be made public), it is still evident that the Lord Chancellor's direction (as long ago as 1966) that names should be drawn for all sections of the community and should represent all shades of opinion is far from being fully realised. In particular, there appears to be disproportionately low membership from ethnic minority groups, even in areas where there are concentrations of such communities.

Again, it is intended that the Judicial Services Commission will follow procedures for selection, particularly of justices of the peace, that will ensure that a fair reflection of the communities they serve (Article 104.2).

SUPPLEMENTARY APPOINTMENTS

Temporary appointments or assignments between courts is invariably necessary to meet changing demands. Section 4 of Schedule 4 embodies principles underlying present practice (cf. Supreme Court Act 1981, c. 54, section 9). The proviso ensures that in any hearing by the Court of Appeal, at least half of the judges are full members of the Court.

Section 4.1.3 also authorises the appointment of qualified persons to be part-time judges. This covers not only those, such as recorders, who perform their functions for a prescribed number of days in the year, but also those who may be appointed to a substantive, tenured judicial office but are required to sit only for a limited number of days each week or month. This will open up the possibility of judicial appointments for some, including many well-qualified women, for whom a full time post is not practicable.

These appointments and assignments are the responsibility of the Judicial Services Commission, which may make general rules on the matter or delegate the power, for example to one of its committees or to the senior judge of a particular court.

Section 4.2 authorises the continuation of the present practice of appointing persons to perform judicial functions of a subsidiary nature, for example district judges in the High Court and the county courts. For the purposes of appointment and tenure, these offices are equated with those of a full judge of the next lower court. Thus a district judge of the High Court will be treated as an intermediate court judge for these purposes.

JURISDICTION OF THE COURT OF APPEAL

Unlike the present Court of Appeal, from which appeals to the House of Lords may be taken in civil and criminal matters, Section 5 of Schedule 4 provides that the new Court of Appeal will be the highest appeal court, subject only to the special circumstances in which appeals to the Supreme Court are allowed (Article 98.2). Jurisdiction may be conferred to hear appeals from any of the courts or tribunals of England and Wales, except from decisions invalidating Acts of Parliament (which go to the Supreme Court – Article 94) or where restrictions are imposed by Act of Parliament or rules of Court.

Acts of Parliament may, however, make arrangements for intermediate appeals. At present these exist, for example, in the case of magistrates' courts, to a Crown Court by persons convicted of a criminal offence or, in the form of a case stated on a question of law, to the Queen's Bench Divisional Court of the High Court (Magistrates' Courts Act 1980, c. 43, sections 108 and 111). Appeals on points of law from a Crown Court on such appeals are heard on a case stated by the Divisional Court (Courts Act 1971, c. 23, section 10). There is a limited appeal forward to the House of Lords (Administration of Justice Act 1960, c. 65, section 23). It will be open to Parliament to allow these Crown Court appeals to go directly to the Court of Appeal or to substitute the authority of the Court of Appeal over the divisional Court for that of the House of Lords.

The so-called leap-frog appeal from the High Court in civil proceedings to the House of Lords which by-passed the Court of Appeal (Administration of Justice Act 1969, c. 58, Part II) would no longer be applicable. It has not been frequently used.

JURISDICTION OF THE HIGH COURT IN PUBLIC PROCEEDINGS

Challenges to the validity of primary legislation that are made in an intermediate or inferior court cannot be heard there (Article 94).

Such matters must be referred to the High Court under Section 6 of Schedule 4.

The constitutional importance of decisions of the High Court declaring primary legislation to be wholly or partly void is emphasised by allowing appeals, in the case of Assembly Acts, to go as of right to the Court of Appeal, whose decisions will generally be final in such cases. In the case of Acts of Parliament appeals go direct to the Supreme Court (Article 94).

Section 6.3 and 6.4 make provision with respect to the High Court's jurisdiction to deal with certain constitutional issues. These matters, where arising in England and Wales, fall to be decided by the High Court, except those concerning the validity of legislation that are within the exclusive competence of the Supreme Court. The matters that may be heard by the High Court concern —

(a) the contravention of the Bill of Rights;
(b) the validity of Assembly Acts and of any subordinate legislation;
(c) The validity of executive decisions, whether at the centre or in Wales or the regions;
(d) the validity of executive decisions by a body exercising powers under the Constitution;
(e) substantial issues concerning the interpretation of the Constitution or constitutional documents relating to Wales or the regions.

There is a right of appeal to the Court of Appeal in these cases or where challenges to the validity of primary legislation have been dismissed, except where to appeal would be frivolous, vexatious or an abuse of process (cf. Supreme Court Act 1981, c. 54, section 42).

COURT SITTINGS

As the High Court will have jurisdiction to deal with issues peculiar to Wales or to particular regions, it is desirable that arrangements are possible for the court to have a presence and to sit regularly in those places and this is required by Section 7 of the Schedule.

At present, the predominant part of the work of the High Court is conducted in London, though Queen's Bench and Family Division matters are extensively dealt with in various first-tier centres in the country (where both civil and criminal business is transacted). Provision already exists for sittings to be held outside London in accordance with the directions of the Lord Chancellor (Supreme Court Act 1981, c. 54, section 71). Similarly the Lord Chancellor may direct where in England and Wales Crown Courts are to sit. These may be at first-tier centres or, for criminal business only, at second-tier (to which a High Court judge is assigned) or third-tier centres (served by circuit judges and recorders).

RULES COMMITTEES

Section 8 of the Schedule authorises the establishment of Rules Committees with the function of making rules with respect to practice and procedure of the courts in England and Wales.

There are at present several such committees, all of which are composed of judges of the courts concerned, who are in the majority, and legal practitioners. The Supreme Court Rule Committee acts with respect to the High Court and the civil division of the Court of Appeal (Supreme Court Act 1981, c. 54, section 85) and the Crown Court Rule Committee for the Crown Courts and criminal divisions of the Court of Appeal (ibid., section 86). See also the rule committee established by section 75 of the County Courts Act 1984, c. 28 and by section 144 of the Magistrates' Courts Act 1980, c. 43.

The ability of the judiciary to determine the rules for routine practice and procedure is an important element of the judicial power and in the protection of judicial independence.

COURTS IN SCOTLAND

Part 2 of Schedule 4 provides for the establishment of the courts and the legal system of Scotland, the judiciary attached to them and their jurisdictional competence. As in Part 1, the existing system is largely retained. No changes have been made in relation to the Scottish system the equivalents of which are not also found in relation to England and Wales.

COURTS IN NORTHERN IRELAND

Part 3 similarly provides for the establishment of the courts and the legal system of Northern Ireland, largely retaining the existing system. The Constitution, it should be noted, provides the framework of the court structure and not how those courts will operate.

In that context it is worth noting that Section 14.1.3 provides that there will be a Crown Court for criminal proceedings but not whether the court will sit with a jury nor how many judges will preside. It therefore neither enshrines the non-jury 'Diplock' courts which hear scheduled (terrorist) cases nor abolishes them. The constitutionality of these courts could, however, be challenged under other Articles of the Constitution, for instance Article 6 which guarantees 'a fair and public hearing . . . by an independent and impartial tribunal established by law'.

PART 2: THE SUPREME COURT AND OTHER UNITED KINGDOM COURTS

Part 2 provides for the Supreme Court of the United Kingdom. Although bearing the name at present used to refer to the Court of Appeal, High Court of Justice and Crown Court in England and Wales (Supreme Court Act 1981, c. 54, section 1), this is an entirely new judicial body. Its establishment arises from the need to provide a judicial authority to enforce the division of powers instituted by the Constitution between the United Kingdom and the parts of the Kingdom that are given their own governmental and legislative institutions, and generally to settle constitutional questions at the United Kingdom level, as well as to ensure consistency in the interpretation of the Constitution. Its functions are, therefore, in large measure those of a constitutional court. At the same time, the Constitution envisages the Court exercising an appellate jurisdiction with respect to a limited range of private law matters which are of importance for the United Kingdom.

This Part also authorises the establishment of other courts and tribunals with specialised jurisdictions that are to serve the whole of the United Kingdom.

ARTICLE 96: THE SUPREME COURT

As a United Kingdom court, the Supreme Court is composed of judges who collectively have experience and standing in the three legal systems. Of the 11 justices, at least 5 must have served as superior court judges in England and Wales, 2 as superior court judges in Scotland and 1 as such a judge in Northern Ireland. The other 3 (unless the maximum is set at a higher figure by Parliament) may be appointed directly from those of outstanding distinction in the practice or teaching of law, as well as from the superior courts, in any of the parts of the United Kingdom.

This is a development of the current composition of the House of Lords (which is abolished). The Lords of Appeal in Ordinary (maximum number of 11) must be drawn from those who have held judicial office for at least 2 years in one of the superior courts of the United Kingdom or who, for at least 15 years, have had a right of audience before the Supreme Court in England (this includes barristers, solicitors and any others to whom such a right may be granted under section 27 of the Courts and Legal Services Act 1990, c. 41) or have been in practice in Scotland as an advocate or a solicitor entitled to appear in the superior courts or as a barrister in Northern Ireland (Appellate Jurisdiction Act 1876, c. 59, section 6, as amended by the Courts and Legal Services Act 1990, Schedule 10).

By convention, but not as a matter of law, at least one, and commonly two, Law Lords are from Scotland and one from Northern Ireland. Appointments directly from the bar to the House of Lords are largely unknown. Academic distinction in law has not previously been prescribed as a qualification for judicial office and is rarely found in common law countries.

The Supreme Court will be presided over by a new judicial office-holder: the President. The office of Lord Chancellor, who presides in the House of Lords when present and is president of the Supreme Court of England and Wales (Supreme Court Act 1981, section 1(2)), is abolished.

Under 96.4, arrangements for the appointment of Supreme Court justices are designed to provide more clearly against government direction and to introduce a more representative element into the process of selection than is the case for the Law Lords. Such appointments rest with the Queen, who by convention acts on the recommendation of the Prime Minister, after, it may be presumed, due consultation with (among others) the Lord Chancellor or, in the case of Scotland, the Lord Advocate.

The President and justices too will be appointed by the Monarch on the advice of the Prime Minister. Judicial appointments are a proper function for the Executive, provided that political considerations do not dictate the selection. This latter possibility is countered by restricting the choice to one of two names submitted to the Prime Minister, although the Prime Minister is entitled to ask for reconsideration of the names if not content with them. This procedure is akin to that recently adopted for federal judicial appointments in Canada, and is similar to that currently used for appointments of the senior clergy of the Church of England.

96.5 provides that the functions of the President during a vacancy or temporary incapacity are to be undertaken by the senior justice (by date of appointment) who is willing to act. This set out as a constitutional rule what is commonly the practice in appellate courts.

ARTICLE 97: COMPOSITION

Article 97 envisages that the Court will sit as a single body of eleven in matters of exceptional importance. In lesser matters it may sit in divisions to deal with several cases at the same time. As in the case of the House of Lords (Appellate Jurisdiction Act 1876, c. 59, section 5), the jurisdiction of the Supreme Court (both original and appellate) must be exercised by a minimum of three Justices. It will be open to the Court to adopt the present practice of the House of Lords to sit as five (or some greater number) for appellate matters.

To relieve a hard-pressed court, it is common to provide that acting judges may be assigned temporarily to sit (e.g. Supreme Court Act 1981, c. 54, section 9). Provision of this kind is made by 97.2. Acting justices must either be retired justices or persons eligible for appointment to the Supreme Court. In the latter case, prior approval of the Judicial Appointments Commission is required. Temporary justices must always comprise a minority of those sitting to hear any matter.

ARTICLE 98: JURISDICTION

Unlike the House of Lords, the Supreme Court is vested in 98.1 with an original jurisdiction in addition to an appellate jurisdiction. This is commonly the case for federal constitutions (cf. the High Court of Australia under Chapter III of the Commonwealth of Australia Constitution Act).

This original jurisdiction is a necessary consequence of the division of legislative powers under the Constitution which gives rise to the possibility of disputes concerning the legislative competence of Parliament on the one hand and that of the Assemblies on the other. Where challenges to the exercise of such legislative powers are made by a government (perhaps at the instance of its legislature whose competence is alleged to have been impugned), the Supreme Court, as a United Kingdom court, is the most appropriate authority to determine conclusively the constitutional issues that will be involved.

Challenges to the validity of such legislation raised by persons other than the government concerned will be determined by the superior competent court in the legal system where the matter is raised, subject to a right of appeal without leave where the statute is an Act of Parliament. In the case of an Assembly statute, the matter will be normally be dealt with by the courts of the appropriate legal system, but appeals may be taken to the Supreme Court if the interpretation or effect of the Constitution is in issue or the matter involves an alleged contravention of the Bill of Rights (98.2).

Under 98.2 the appellate jurisdiction of the Supreme Court has little in common with that of the House of Lords. Under the present arrangement, the House of Lords is the final appellate body for England and Wales and Northern Ireland in both civil and criminal matters and for the Scottish courts in civil matters only. Under the Constitution, these functions will be discharged by the highest courts in the each of the three legal systems (i.e. the Court of Appeal for England and Wales, the Northern Ireland Court of Appeal and the Inner House of the Court of Session).

The Supreme Court may hear further appeals in civil and criminal matters in very restricted circumstances only. These will generally be where the proceedings give rise to a question of law in relation to which uniformity throughout the United Kingdom or in more than one jurisdiction is, in the opinion of the Supreme Court, desirable or where the interpretation of a United Kingdom statute is in issue. It follows that the development of law exclusive to any of the legal systems is the responsibility of the courts of that system. Appeals may also be provided for from courts or tribunals exercising a jurisdiction for the United Kingdom as a whole.

Uniformity in the application of laws of the European Community (or other treaties that may give rise to rights or obligations within the United Kingdom) for which the United Kingdom government has international responsibility necessitates conferment of jurisdiction on those issues and may have particular application in relation to private law matters. Community treaties have effect in United Kingdom law, and United Kingdom legislation must be construed subject to them (European Communities Act 1972, c. 68, section 2(2)). Regulations and, exceptionally, directives made by the Council of Ministers or the European Commission can also have direct effect.

The predominant part of the appellate jurisdiction, however, is concerned with matters that arise in the courts of the three legal systems in connection with the Constitution (in particular alleged contravention of the Bill of Rights), or as to the meaning of the Constitution or validity of Acts of Parliament or as a result of disputes between Assemblies or Regions or between the United Kingdom and Assemblies.

The public law dimension is reflected in the power to take appeals from decisions on the validity of executive action taken by the United Kingdom government or public bodies acting under the Constitution or United Kingdom legislation. (Such matters involving Assembly governments or public bodies acting under Assembly legislation can proceed to the Supreme Court only if they also involve any of the foregoing constitutional elements.)

To the Supreme Court, therefore, falls the ultimate responsibility for ensuring compliance with the written Constitution throughout the United Kingdom. To that end it has been vested with a jurisdiction and with powers to invalidate legislation that is inconsistent with the Constitution that hitherto have not been conferred on any United Kingdom court but are a usual feature of constitutions in Commonwealth and other common law countries.

A requirement of leave to appeal is commonly provided in relation to the last appellate body (e.g. Administration of Justice (Appeals) Act 1934, c. 40, with respect to appeals for the Court of Appeal to the House of Lords). 98.3 permits the use of a similar sifting process to be applied by law in respect of any category of appeal to the Supreme Court, except cases where an Act of Parliament has been held to be wholly or partly void, when a right to appeal is expressly granted.

ARTICLE 99: ADDITIONAL JURISDICTION

The Judicial Committee of the Privy Council at present hears appeals in a limited range of civil and criminal matters from dependent territories of the United Kingdom and from a small number of Commonwealth countries (mainly in the Caribbean). This jurisdiction has been gradually waning and, in volume of activity, may become of little significance after Hong Kong joins China in 1997 and if the projected Caribbean Court of Appeal is established.

The Judicial Committee is composed in the main of the Law Lords and Privy Councillors who hold or have held high judicial office in the United Kingdom. Certain senior Commonwealth judges from countries from which appeals still lie may also sit (Judicial Committee Acts 1833–1915).

The Judicial Committee is essentially a Commonwealth court. For some Commonwealth countries it still plays a constitutional role in safeguarding against the improper removal of their superior court judges. It is, therefore, not feasible, at least in the case of the independent Commonwealth countries, for the jurisdiction of the Judicial Committee to be effectively transferred to the Supreme Court by unilateral United Kingdom action. There is no legislative authority in the United Kingdom with respect to those countries. In consequence, such a change will require the agreement and appropriate legislative action in all the countries intending to retain appeals to a judicial body in the United Kingdom, before the Judicial Committee system can be replaced by the Supreme Court.

Accordingly, 99.1.1 permits such an appellate jurisdiction to be exercised by the Supreme Court only when it is invited to do so by a country from which appeals to the Judicial Committee could formerly be brought. In those cases, the President may invite a senior judge in that country to sit as a member of the court (99.1.2).

The Judicial Committee also has limited appellate functions in a mixed assortment of United Kingdom matters. For example, it hears certain appeals from higher ecclesiastical courts (Judicial Committee Act 1843, c. 38) and in wartime from Prize Courts (Naval Prize Act 1864, c. 25, sections 5 and 6). It may make declarations as to allegations of disqualification by members of the public against a member of the House of Commons (House of Commons Disqualification Act 1975, c. 24, section 7) and may give advisory opinions on a reference by the Crown (Judicial Committee Act 1833, c. 41, section 4).

These functions will disappear as no longer needed or be conferred upon other judicial authorities (for example in the case of Prizes on the Supreme Court under 99.2.1).

Under 99.2 additional jurisdiction may be conferred upon the Supreme Court by Act of Parliament, but to confirm its authority as the Supreme Court for the United Kingdom and all three legal systems, the consent of the Assemblies for Scotland and Northern Ireland is made a prerequisite.

ARTICLE 100: BINDING FORCE OF DECISIONS

Supreme Court decisions are final and conclusive, and in consequence a matter upon which a ruling has been given (including any relating to the question of the Court's jurisdiction) cannot be reopened.

As the Supreme Court is the final court in the United Kingdom, its decisions (as those of the House of Lords) are to be treated as normally binding on all other courts. Those inconsistent with a subsequent decision of the European Court of Justice in a matter of Community law, decisions of the European Court and the principles laid down by it must be applied by United Kingdom courts (European Communities Act 1972, c. 68, section 3(1)). It will not be necessary, therefore, to take such matters to the Supreme Court in order to reverse any such inconsistent decision.

Decisions of the House of Lords are regarded as normally binding on the Lords subject to their ability to depart from a previous decision if on reconsideration it appears right to do so (Practice Direction [1966] 1 WLR 1234). The Supreme Court is given full freedom to diverge from its earlier decisions – a power that may be needed if the interpretation and application of the Constitution is to respond to changing circumstances. The doctrine of *stare decisis* cannot be rigidly applied with respect to decisions on the Constitution, since Parliament cannot legislate to correct errors made by the Supreme Court. It may be expected, however, that in practice the Supreme Court will usually follow its own decisions if only to ensure the orderly development of constitutional rules. (Thus for example, the High Court of Australia, which has always asserted its right to review its own decisions on constitutional interpretation, will usually follow them, unless it considers them to be clearly wrong.)

ARTICLE 101: OTHER UNITED KINGDOM COURTS
AND TRIBUNALS

Authority is granted for the establishment by Act of Parliament of courts or tribunals of specialist jurisdiction for the whole of the United Kingdom or to exercise an extraterritorial jurisdiction. These may be created at the superior, intermediate or inferior court level.

There are at the moment two principal courts of this kind (other than the Judicial Committee of the Privy Council), both of which are likely to be continued. The Restrictive Practices Court (Restrictive Practices Act 1976, c. 33) is composed of judges from the High Courts of England and Wales and of Northern Ireland and of the Court of Session and of a number of non-judicial members. It has jurisdiction to examine agreements which restrict prices or the conditions attached to the supply of goods or services. Appeals lie to the civil appeal court of the appropriate legal system.

The other court is the Courts-Martial Appeals Courts (Courts-Martial (Appeals) Act 1968, c. 20). This too is composed, in the main, of superior court judges from the three systems. It hears appeals against convictions by courts-martial within or outside the United Kingdom. There is a further appeal to the House of Lords.

An example of a United Kingdom tribunal is the Foreign Compensation Commission (Foreign Compensation Acts 1950–1969), which adjudicates on individual claims in relation to compensation received by the British Government for loss of property by United Kingdom nationals, as a result, for example, of expropriations by a foreign government.

Responsibility for selecting the judges of these courts is vested in the Minister of Justice acting on the recommendations of the Judicial Appointments Commission. Their qualifications are to be prescribed by Parliament and will not be limited to those normally required for the judiciary.

ARTICLE 102: UNITED KINGDOM JUDICIAL APPOINTMENTS COMMISSION

The selection of names for appointment to the Supreme Court is the responsibility of a United Kingdom Judicial Appointments Commission (a device analogous to that found, for example, in Canada for appointments at the federal level, and in Israel). The membership of the Commission of sixteen is made up from representatives selected by and from the three Judicial Services Commissions established for the purposes of selecting for senior and intermediate judicial appointments in the three legal systems (see Schedule 5). The same ratio of 5:2:1 is used for State representation on the Commission as for the Supreme Court itself, although there is a guaranteed place among the representatives from the Commission for England and

Wales for the chair of the Welsh Appointments Committee of that Commission. In this way the claims of those from Wales for appointment to the Court may be advanced.

The membership of the latter Services Commission (Schedule 5) is such that the Appointments Commission must necessarily include at least five persons who are not judges and three who are lay persons.

PART 3: JUDICIAL SERVICES COMMISSIONS AND JUDICIAL COUNCILS

ARTICLE 103: JUDICIAL SERVICES COMMISSIONS AND JUDICIAL COUNCILS

Article 103 creates a Judicial Services Commission and a Judicial Council for each of the three legal systems. The membership of those bodies in England and Wales is set out in Schedule 5, the Assemblies of Scotland and Northern Ireland being required to make similar provision for the membership of the Judicial Services Commissions and Judicial Councils for Scotland and Northern Ireland respectively.

SCHEDULE 5: JUDICIAL SERVICES COMMISSION AND JUDICIAL COUNCIL FOR ENGLAND AND WALES

Schedule 5 adopts the device of the Judicial Services Commission generally incorporated into Westminster-model constitutions in Commonwealth countries, although the composition bears little resemblance to those established by such Constitutions. The Commission has a membership which has features similar to those proposed for the Advisory Committees of federal judicial appointments by the Canadian Bar Association (*The Appointment of Judges*, 1985).

The purpose of the Commission is to provide a mechanism for selection of candidates for judicial appointment that is independent of government and that can be representative of the community. Not only is this likely to ensure that political considerations are kept out of the appointment process, but it is intended to further the aim of providing a judiciary that more fairly reflects the community than is generally the case at present.

COMPOSITION AND APPOINTMENT OF MEMBERS

Under Section 1, the Commission, unlike those found in Commonwealth Constitutions, does not have a predominantly judicial or legal membership. Of the 15 members, 5 only may hold permanent judicial office and another 2 only may be lawyers. The remainder, including the President, must be persons who have never qualified as lawyers or served as paid judges. Given the information and results of consultations that will be available to the Commission, in addition to specialist knowledge and understanding of the judicial and legal members, there is no reason to believe that lay persons cannot be found to undertake the selection of persons as judges who will have the respect of the judiciary, the legal profession and the general public.

Precise qualifications for the members of the Commission are not appropriate for the Constitution. The requirement that they must be broadly representative of the community is intended to ensure that women members and members from ethnic groups, for example, are included, thereby meeting commonly expressed criticisms concerning the interests which seem to be underplayed in the present appointment process.

As with the appointments to the judiciary, appointments to the Commission are a proper function for the Executive, since the Commission is discharging a governmental function. Responsibility is conferred upon the Minister of Justice (who will discharge functions in this matter hitherto undertaken by the Lord Chancellor). The names of the lay members are to be selected by the Minister from a list of names submitted by the Public Services Commission (see Article 115). The principal senior judges, the Master of the Rolls and the Chief Justice (on behalf of the judiciary) have a right to be consulted on membership. Other consultations that will inevitably be required are not made a legal requirement. Rather than vest the senior judges with a power of veto, which might give an appearance of undue power in the judiciary, Section 1.2.3 requires the publication of any dissent by either judge which the Minister has disregarded. In practice, it is unlikely that a disagreement will reach that stage, as the Public Services Commission and the Minister of

Justice will be concerned to find members who will retain the confidence of the judiciary in the ability of the Judicial Services Commission to select suitable appointees.

TENURE OF OFFICE

Continuity of membership is an important consideration. Accordingly, appointments to the Commission are, under Section 1.3, for a minimum period of five years (which may be renewed). As for judges, the Constitution seeks to provide security of tenure for members by prescribing the precise circumstances in which it terminates. Under Section 1.5 these are: ceasing to have a qualification (e.g. appointment of a lawyer to a judicial post); reaching the retirement age of 70; resignation; in the case of a judge, removal from office in accordance with the Constitution, acceptance of an office stated to be inconsistent with membership (this is intended to include, for example, parliamentary membership); expiration of term of office. Provision is also made under Section 1.5.5 for the removal of non-judicial members through the Public Services Commission, for example for behaviour incompatible with the office. Members cannot be removed on other grounds.

WELSH AND REGIONAL APPOINTMENTS

Under Section 2 appointments to intermediate and inferior courts sitting exclusively in districts in Wales or in the regions are handled through committees of the Commission (Schedule 4, Section 3.3.1).

Recognition of the special status of Wales is found in the creation by the Constitution of the Welsh Appointments Committee with a chair who is a member of the Commission. The Committee has an overall structure patterned on the Commission. Again lay members (4) are a majority of the 7 members. The appointments will be made by the Minister of Justice, who must consult with the Chief Executive of Wales, who has a power to publish the fact of dissent with any appointment.

Regional Appointments Committees are to be established by Act of Parliament. It is intended that these will follow the pattern of the Welsh Committee.

In both cases, the requirements in respect of tenure of office will correspond to those for Commission members.

These Committees will not be subject to the direction of the

Commission on selection, although their administration and procedure will have to conform with its dictates. Reports as to their activities must be made periodically to the Commission.

CONDITIONS OF SERVICE OF COMMISSION MEMBERS

Under Section 3 the President of the Commission is to be a full-time appointment; other members and those of the Committees are part-time paid appointments.

ADMINISTRATION OF THE COMMISSION

Section 4 states that servicing of the work of the Commission and its committees will be provided by its own staff. It is intended that the functions and officials (some 50) of the Lord Chancellor's Department at present concerned with judicial appointments will be transferred to the Commission. This should ensure that the considerable experience already acquired by the Department is built upon, and that there is a sufficient degree of autonomy to enable necessary information about potential appointees to be gathered and evaluated.

ARTICLE 104: FUNCTIONS OF JUDICIAL SERVICES COMMISSIONS

The principal function of the Judicial Services Commissions is to appoint judges and to authorise them to sit in their respective courts, as required by Schedule 4.

104.2: this important provision is designed to ensure that the Commissions will seek out candidates for judicial appointment from a wider pool than in the past, leading to an increase in the numbers of, for example, women and black people, whilst at the same time maintaining the quality of those appointed in terms of legal ability and judicial capacity.

COMPLAINTS RELATING TO THE JUDICIARY

104.3: At present there is no formal procedure whereby complaints about judicial behaviour can be made by the public. It is, however, open to the Lord Chancellor to look into any complaint that may be made or referred to his Department, and this may result in the Lord Chancellor's displeasure being drawn to the attention of the judge concerned. Little publicity is given to these arrangements.

Other jurisdictions have introduced formal mechanisms for receiving and examining complaints which, in a serious case, may lead to proceedings for removal, or in a lesser case to findings being drawn to the attention of the judge. The judge is afforded a right to be heard, usually by a tribunal created for the purpose.

Such arrangements are found in Canada, where they are dealt with by the Canadian Judicial Council comprising the Chief Justice of Canada and provincial Chief Justices and Associate Chief Justices (Judge Act, c. J-1).

They are also found in Australia. In New South Wales, for example, complaints are dealt with by the Conduct Division (of 3 judicial members) of the Judicial Commission (composed in the main of senior judges). This may hold hearings, in public if necessary, at which the judge is entitled to be heard. A finding substantiating a serious complaint may result in proceedings for removal; a finding that a minor complaint has been proved will be brought to the attention of the judge concerned (Judicial Officers Act 1986, No. 100).

104.3 requires the Commission to establish a procedure to consider complaints and in a proper case for reference to a Judicial Conduct Tribunal with a view to removal (Article 109). Lesser cases are to be dealt with by informing the judge of the finding and, in appropriate cases, by compensation out of public funds.

The procedure established by the Commission may not permit judicial decisions to be complained against. Nor can complaints of maladministration against the judiciary be entertained by the Commission or by the Parliamentary Commissioner for Administration, although the latter may look into such complaints against the administrative staff of courts or tribunals (Courts and Legal Services Act 1990, c. 41, section 110).

OTHER FUNCTIONS OF THE COMMISSION

104.4: As is frequently the case with major public bodies, the Judicial Services Commission is required to make an annual report to Parliament. This, in principle, will enable Parliament to examine in committee and to debate how the Commission is performing its responsibilities and the policies that it is apparently pursuing. In particular, there will be an opportunity to bring out how the

Commission is endeavouring to achieve a judiciary which is a fair reflection of the community.

104.5: Additional functions may be conferred upon the Commission by Act of Parliament. For example, it may be appropriate to extend its powers to recommend appointments of, and to investigate complaints against, senior court officers of the High Court and Court of Appeal, for example those listed in Schedule 2 of the Supreme Court Act 1981 (as amended by the Courts and Legal Services Act 1990, section 77 and Schedule 10) to the extent that these are not already treated as judicial appointees. Appointments are made by the Lord Chancellor (with the concurrence of the Minister for the Civil Service as to numbers and salaries), who may also remove for misbehaviour (Supreme Court Act 1981, sections 89 and 92).

ARTICLE 105: FUNCTIONS OF THE JUDICIAL COUNCIL

Article 105 contains the central provisions concerning the Judicial Council established by Article 103. This is again an innovation, designed in part to support the independence of the judiciary.

The Council is to be a professional body, composed entirely of judges representative of the various levels of courts in the system. Under Section 5 it is left to Parliament to determine by legislation the exact numbers, the nature of selection and, thus, of representation (subject to a requirement of a Welsh presence) and the terms of appointment.

There is increasing recognition that executive control of the provision of resources and over judicial administration can weaken the capacity of the courts to carry out their functions. One eminent commentator on the international scene has written that: 'an important measuring stick in the assessment of collective judicial independence is the administrative independence of the judiciary. This includes, for instance, supervision and control over administrative personnel, preparation of court budget, maintenance of court buildings, and the like' (S. Shetreet, in S. Shetreet and J. Secchenes, *Judicial Independence*, p. 644).

Since the major changes following the Beeching Royal Commission in 1969 (implemented under the Courts Act 1971, c. 23), there have been major developments in England and Wales in judicial administration. In comparison with other major common law countries (such as the United States, Canada and to an extent Australia), in this country responsibility for court administration policy, resourcing and management is markedly that of the Executive, with the judiciary playing a largely day-to-day role. Administration is a function of the officials under the Lord Chancellor's Department, with the Lord Chancellor and, in some matters, the Home Secretary, carrying the responsibility for resourcing the system. It might be argued that the anomalous constitutional position of the Lord Chancellor as both head of the judiciary and a senior Minister of government ensures that the judiciary may make an input into policy-making in respect of administration, with a view, for example, to ensuring that the necessary resources are provided to enable the system to function properly.

The replacement of the Lord Chancellor by a Minister of Justice will remove altogether a formal judicial involvement in these matters (see 43.1.3.2). New arrangements are therefore needed. One approach would be to vest full responsibility for administration of the courts in the judiciary itself, assisted by a court service appointed by and answerable to the judiciary (see I. R. Scott, *Court Administration: The Case for a Judicial Council*, University of Birmingham, 1979). This would present serious difficulties of financial controls and of accountability for expenditure of national resources and in developing a budget in what must be considered to be an area of major governmental responsibility consistently with principles of ministerial responsibility and parliamentary supervision.

The approach adopted by the Constitution assumes the continuation of the responsibility for court administration in the Executive through a Minister of Justice, who will discharge the relevant functions at present undertaking by the Lord Chancellor and the Home Secretary. The judicial input is provided through a Judicial Council, representative of the judicial interest, which will be the formal channel for making that interest known to the Minister of Justice.

The Judicial Council is to be an advisory and consultative, rather than a decision-making, body; its prime responsibility will be to provide a judicial input into the development of the budget and on the allocation of resources for the court system, which the Minister will have to negotiate with the Treasury and pilot through Parliament. Its perception of the resource needs of the court service (for example, on such matters as computerisation) and upon the way in which existing resources are being deployed on the administration of the courts will be central to the input made by the Council. It may be expected that the Minister will involve the Council before any major policy changes are made, for example, in implementation of Treasury objectives (as where reduction in court staffing levels is sought) that will alter the ways in which the courts are run.

It would be open to the Council to tender its own advice on matters which it deems important, and it will not be dependent upon its advice being sought by the Minister of Justice. The Judicial Council would not be concerned with the prosecution service or with legal aid resources.

PART 4: JUDICIAL INDEPENDENCE AND CONDUCT

ARTICLE 106: APPLICATION OF PART 4

This Part makes specific provisions designed to contribute to the independence of the judiciary, and includes new arrangements for removal of judges in ways which balance the need for security of tenure with that of discontinuing the services of those who are no longer suited for judicial office. It applies with respect to all the courts in the United Kingdom and its three legal systems.

ARTICLE 107: PROTECTION OF JUDICIAL SALARIES

Article 107, which applies to the judiciary at all levels, replicates provisions found in a number of jurisdictions (cf. Constitution of India, art. 124(2), proviso). Under present law, salaries of the superior court judges, circuit judges and stipendiary magistrates may not be reduced (Courts Act 1971, c. 23, section 18; Administration of Justice Act 1973, c. 15, section 9, Supreme Court Act 1981, c. 54, section 12).

There is no precise provision under present law precluding adverse changes in relation to other conditions of service (e.g. in respect of pension entitlements which are provided for by the Judicial Pensions Act 1981, c. 20). Although many conditions of service are guaranteed by law, in principle, there is at present no legal constraint upon amendment to that law in ways which affect existing holders of judicial office. 107.1 precludes the enactment of such laws, as well as changes to other conditions of service that are not contained in legislation nor are regulated by subordinate laws.

As is commonly the case in Commonwealth Constitutions, 107.2 reproduces provisions in existing statute law for ensuring the payment of judicial salaries direct from the Consolidated Fund without providing an opportunity, during annual approval, for debate in Parliament concerning judicial conduct (Supreme Court Act 1981, c. 54, section 12(5); Courts Act 1971, c. 23, section 18(2); Administration of Justice Act 1973, c. 15, section 9). This again applies to all who hold judicial office and are paid salaries.

ARTICLE 108: TENURE OF JUDICIAL OFFICE

108.1: An important constitutional safeguard for judicial independence that is frequently provided is the prescribing of a comprehensive statement of circumstances in which members of the judiciary may be required to quit office. Four cases commonly set out in constitutional documents are included here: the attainment of a specified retiring age, established here at 70 (currently 75 in the case of the Law Lords); resignation; removal from office solely on the grounds and by the procedures set out in 108.2 and Article 112 (in contrast with the uncertain grounds and range of procedures that appear still to exist in English law); acceptance of an office stated in law to be inconsistent with judicial office.

108.1.2 is included to cover a commonly recurring issue of the entitlement of a judge to complete matters which were commenced before, but not concluded by, the date the retirement age is reached. There appears to be no comparable provision in existing law.

The standard retirement age of 70 is provided for all judicial appointments. Under present arrangements, normal retirement ages are 75 for superior court judges (Supreme Court Act 1981, c. 54, section 11), 72 in the case of circuit judges and recorders (Courts Act 1971, c. 23, sections 17 and 21) and of district judges (County Courts Act 1984, c. 28, section 11) and 70 in the case of stipendiary magistrates and for justices of the peace (Justices of the Peace Act 1979, c. 55, sections 8 and 14).

In order that a full pension period of 15 years may be met it will be necessary to make somewhat earlier appointments to the superior courts. This will have the desirable consequence of ensuring that the average age of the senior judiciary is lowered. This will be possible, however, only if improvements in judicial remuneration are made that will be attractive to those at the height of their earning powers.

108.1.1.5 relates to judges of inferior courts (and of tribunals so designated) who will cease to hold office on the termination of a fixed term of appointment that is not renewed. The position of those who perform judicial duties in the superior or intermediate courts on a fixed term is more fully protected under 108.4.

108.2: The present law on removal of judges lacks clarity. Under section 11(3) of the Supreme Court Act 1981, c. 54, superior court judges hold office during good behaviour. Want of good behaviour would be found in 'conviction for an offence involving moral turpitude, and persistent neglect of duties: it does not appear to cover mental infirmity' (S. de Smith and R. Brazier, *Constitutional and Administrative Law*, 6th ed. Harmondsworth: Penguin, 1990, p. 380) The latter question is now covered in the case of superior judges by statute under which the Lord Chancellor, with the concurrence of senior judges, may declare an office vacant for permanent incapacity (Supreme Court Act 1981, c. 54, sections 11(8) and 11(9)).

It is convincingly argued (S. de Smith and R. Brazier, op. cit., p. 380) that in strict law such judges may be removed by the Crown *either* for misbehaviour *or* on any other grounds on the basis of an address by both Houses of Parliament (Supreme Court Act 1981, c. 54, section 11(3)), and that a variety of procedures may be used in addition to the address process (such as by the writ of *scire facias* or by injunction in the High Court at the instance of the Attorney-General restraining the judge from acting). In fact, no English judge has been removed in the last three hundred years by any of these mechanisms.

Removal of circuit judges and recorders may be made by the Lord Chancellor on the grounds of incapacity and misbehaviour and, in the case of recorders, for failure to complete the agreed frequency of sittings (Courts Act 1971, c. 23, sections 17(4) and 21(6)). There is no statutory procedure entitling the judge to a hearing before removal although it is argued that this is implied (de Smith and Brazier, op. cit., p. 381).

District judges hold office during good behaviour and may be removed by the Lord Chancellor for misbehaviour (Supreme Court Act 1981, c. 54, sections 92(4), 92(5) and 100(4); County Courts Act 1984, c. 28, sections 11(4) and 11(5)).

Stipendiary magistrates may be removed on the recommendation of the Lord Chancellor. No grounds are laid down in law (Justices of the Peace Act 1979, c. 55, section 13(3)). Justices of the peace may be removed by the Lord Chancellor; again no grounds are statutorily specified (ibid., section 6(1)). In addition they may be placed on the supplementary list, and thus disqualified from sitting in court (ibid., sections 8 and 9). A small number are removed every year, usually for activities or behaviour inconsistent with judicial office.

In the great preponderance of cases where judicial behaviour is considered to be sufficiently unsatisfactory to require attention, the judge in question will be encouraged by senior judges to tender his resignation.

It is clearly unsatisfactory that there should be any question concerning the circumstances in which removal can occur or, indeed, that there should be any substantial difference between the different levels of judiciary. Further, the lack of clarity in the notion of 'misbehaviour' can usefully be reduced.

Accordingly, Article 108 applies to all who hold judicial office in the United Kingdom, whether full-time or part-time, and contains a definitive statement of the cases in which removal is permitted. The statement of grounds is modelled upon that in the Judges Act of Canada (c. J-1, section 65(2)).

108.3: As mentioned earlier, existing law makes little provision with respect to the procedure to be followed in relation to removal of judges. Although this may involve an address by Parliament in the case of superior judges, the theoretical possibility remains of removal at common law by other procedures, such as the writ of *scire facias*. In the case of intermediate and lower courts, statutory provisions appear to envisage a procedure that is essentially executive, although it is almost certain that a right at common law to be heard would be confirmed by judicial review.

In most of the newer Commonwealth Constitutions, a clear procedure, involving a hearing and finding by a judicial tribunal, is standard, at least for superior court judges. In some instances, a decision that removal is justified must then be referred to the Judicial Committee of the Privy Council, whose advice on the matter is binding (e.g. Constitution of Jamaica, section 100). Legislation of this kind is found in the older Commonwealth countries (e.g. Judges Act, c. J-1, of Canada; Judicial Officers Act 1986, No. 100 of New South Wales).

The essentials of such an approach have been adopted in Article 112. The only procedures that may be invoked for a judge of any of the courts in the United Kingdom are those found in Article 12. Other processes cease to have effect.

RENEWAL OF FIXED-TERM APPOINTMENTS

108.4 is necessitated by the practice of appointing persons to perform judicial functions for a fixed term. For example, recorders in England and Wales, who are practising lawyers, are appointed to sit for a prescribed number of days in each of a stipulated period of years (Supreme Court Act 1971, c. 23, section 21). It is also a common practice with respect to tribunal appointments.

As a rule there is an expectation of renewal if desired, so that refusal to renew is tantamount to removal. This Article requires a positive decision by the relevant Judicial Services Commission, which implies that it will be taken only for good cause. The Commission may be requested to state its reasons, opening the way for judicial review. It remains possible to remove such an appointee *during* tenure in the same way as other senior judges (108.1).

These arrangements would not apply with regard to such appointments as assistant recorderships, which are usually seen as providing a short trial period for those under consideration for a fixed-term appointment, or to judges of inferior courts or tribunals (108.1.1.5).

ARTICLE 109: JUDICIAL CONDUCT TRIBUNALS

Three Judicial Conduct Tribunals are to be established to have jurisdiction with respect to the judges in the relevant legal system. Legislation enacted by the appropriate legislature (Parliament for England and Wales; the Assemblies in the case of Scotland and Northern Ireland) will be needed, which must provide for a membership that meets the minimum requirements of this Article. Although these tribunals are to have judicial members, selected by the heads of the judiciary concerned (and these are intended to be the majority), there will also be a lay membership chosen by the appropriate Judicial Services Commission. In other respects the Tribunals are to be independent of the Commissions. Whilst cases will necessarily have a legal dimension, the broader questions that may arise (on the seriousness or incompatibility of conduct with the office) involve more than legal judgment.

ARTICLE 110: COMPLAINTS RELATING TO JUSTICES OF SUPREME COURT

The arrangements for dealing with complaints against judges of the three legal systems are not wholly appropriate for complaints against judges of a court that is a United Kingdom court. Accordingly, Article 110 requires such complaint to be made to the head of the Supreme Court, who may then determine which of the Commissions is best suited to discharge the preliminary examination process.

Further, if a Tribunal hearing is called for, a national body will be necessary. This special Tribunal is to be composed of the President and one judicial and one lay member from each of the ordinary Tribunals.

ARTICLE 111: FUNCTIONS OF JUDICIAL CONDUCT TRIBUNALS

The Judicial Conduct Tribunals can deal only with complaints against superior and intermediate court judges. These must be referred to them by the appropriate Judicial Services Commission, which is expected to have undertaken a preliminary examination to sift out those cases which do not merit the Tribunal's attention (Article 104.3.2).

The Tribunal must enquire into the matter and as a matter of law will be required to allow the judge to be heard. (Procedural details, for example, with respect to any public hearing or representation, will be dealt with by legislation.) The Tribunals are to make any recommendations as to removal to the Minister of Justice. But if a case of misconduct or failure in office appears to be proved which does not merit removal, the finding will be brought to the attention of the judge (and by implication reported to the Minister of Justice and any complainant). These powers run alongside those of the Judicial Services Commission, which is authorised to direct payments of compensation to complainants (104.3.3).

SUPERVISION OF JUDICIAL CONDUCT TRIBUNALS

111.3 puts beyond doubt the authority of the courts to exercise a supervisory jurisdiction over Judicial Conduct Tribunals by judicial

review. This will ensure that these bodies act within their competence and respect the common law or any statutory requirements as
to fair hearing. In the case of the special Tribunal for Supreme Court
Justices or judges of other UK courts, this jurisdiction is to be exercised by the Supreme Court.

SUSPENSION OF JUDGES

As is commonly found in legislation in countries with a similar
procedure (e.g. Judicial Officers Act 1986, No. 100, (NSW), section
40), authority is granted by 111.4 to allow a judge to be suspended
on pay until the complaint is finally dealt with either by dismissal by
the Judicial Services Commission or the Judicial Conduct Tribunal
or by a finding and recommendation of the latter. The decision to
suspend must be taken by the Judicial Services Commission. This
is unlikely to happen unless the complaint is one which could, if
proved, lead to removal or which involves substantial misconduct,
such as conviction of a serious crime.

ARTICLE 112: PROCEDURE FOR REMOVAL OF JUDGES

The requirement of an address of Parliament before removal of
a superior court judge takes place may be regarded in different
circumstances both as a safeguard for independence and as undue
political invasion of security of tenure. If it is the sole procedure
followed, it is not a satisfactory method of establishing facts and
ensuring that a balanced decision on the merits is obtained. If,
as in the Constitution, parliamentary involvement can arise only
when a Tribunal has recommended removal, this procedure
becomes a legitimate means of ensuring that a matter of significant
and serious public interest is openly discussed before a decision to
remove is finally taken. There have been few such addresses moved
in the United Kingdom and only one, in 1830, against an Irish judge,
was successful.

This procedure, however, *must* be pursued under the Constitution
in respect of Supreme Court and superior court judges, at the
instance of the Minister of Justice, wherever an adverse recommendation is made by a Tribunal.

112.2: Recommendations by the Judicial Conduct Tribunal for

the removal of an intermediate court judge must be implemented by the Minister of Justice, the formal appointing body. In effect, therefore, the decision is that of the Tribunal.

112.3: Removal of magistrates and other inferior court judges does not involve the Judicial Conduct Tribunal procedure. Complaints in these cases must be made directly to the Minister of Justice, who must cause an investigation of the matter to take place. It will be necessary for a procedure to be formalised, to enable representations to be heard and a fair process to be conducted.

Judicial supervision of the fairness of the hearing and legality of the decision, the reasons for which must be given (and which must be based on the grounds specified in Article 108), is possible by way of judicial review.

112.4: Authority to interfere with pension rights (which would otherwise not be permitted by reason of Article 107) is given where a judge is removed but, in the case of all judges except those of the inferior courts, this must be determined by the recommendation of the Judicial Conduct Tribunal involved.

ARTICLE 113: JUDICIAL CONTROL OF COURT BUSINESS

Article 113 provides another important safeguard from political interference in the administration of justice, directing that the allocation and listing of court cases shall be under the control of judges chosen by the Judicial Council.

It is envisaged that judicial control over practice, allocation of judges to try matters and the like will be the responsibility, as the case may be, of the Chief Justice or Master of the Rolls or the presiding or other designated senior judge of the court of the circuit or district. Under the Courts and Legal Services Act 1990 provision is made for two presiding judges (who must be High Court judges) for each of the six circuits of England and Wales.

CHAPTER 10

The Public Services

ARTICLE 114: THE PUBLIC SERVICES

Article 114 establishes public services for the UK, Assemblies and local authorities. They are to be politically neutral and appointed on merit, and the first duty of the public servant is to the Constitution (114.3 and 114.5). The express duty to the Constitution is designed to counteract the judgment in the Ponting case and the Armstrong memorandum to the effect that a civil servant's duty is to his Minister and to the public interest as defined by the policies of the government of the day. This provision is linked to Article 117 (Public Services Complaints Commission), which establishes a mechanism for dealing with cases where a Minister may be abusing the public service. This is to cope with the sort of problems raised by the Ponting and Westland affairs.

114.4 allows Ministers to appoint personal advisers, on terms approved by the Public Services Commission.

114.6 takes account of the development of executive agencies and their accountability to Parliament and requires an Act of Parliament to sort out the problems created by this important change in the structure of central government.

ARTICLE 115: PUBLIC SERVICES COMMISSION

Article 115 sets up the new version of the Civil Service Commission. As it is to have responsibility for certain aspects of the public service in national, regional and local government as well as central government it has been renamed the 'Public Services Commission'.

Responsibility for the operation of rules governing appointment and terms of service in national, regional and local government is given to the Public Services Commission in order to secure that the principles of a politically neutral public service appointed on merit are followed throughout the country. But management of public services in national and regional government and in local government will rest with those authorities.

The Public Services Commission will also have responsibility for making other appointments to public offices including members of Health Authorities, governors of the BBC and so forth. Parliament will prescribe by statute the full range of its responsibilities. It is expected that the PSC would invite nominations, from Ministers and others, and would then make appointments after consultation. The objective is to control the use of patronage for party political and partisan purposes, but Ministers will nevertheless have an important input in the making of many such appointments.

To insulate the Commission from ministerial interference the recommendations for its membership are the responsibility of the House of Commons, and it is anticipated that the function would be given to the new equivalent of the Treasury and Civil Service Committee. The Commission will be accountable to that Committee. But it will be insulated from accountability to the government of the day.

Under 115.5 Commissioners hold office for a 5-year term which is renewable, and may be removed from office on grounds of misconduct or incapacity by the Head of State following a resolution of the House of Commons. They may resign and must also cease to hold office on reaching the retiring age (65) or if a candidate for election to Parliament, the European Parliament, an Assembly or a local authority. These provisions are designed to insulate the Commission from ministerial interference and to ensure its political neutrality.

ARTICLE 116: FUNCTIONS OF PUBLIC SERVICES
COMMISSION

In accordance with the presumption in favour of openness Article 116 provides for the drawing up of a code of professional conduct and regulations which make explicit the 'rules of the game'. The intention is that these should be published, so that they can be exposed to public scrutiny, as can their operation in practice.

In addition to drawing up the Code of Professional Conduct the Commission is also required under 116.1.2 to prepare regulations governing methods of recruitment, terms and conditions of employment, principles and procedure for promotion and transfer, vetting, discipline, grievances and removal from office.

116.2 is intended to ensure that the Commission will seek out candidates for appointment from a wider pool than in the past, leading to an increase in the number of women and members of the ethnic minorities at all levels in the public service.

ARTICLE 117: PUBLIC SERVICES COMPLAINTS COMMISSION

Article 117 sets up an independent Public Services Complaints Commission whose membership and terms of appointment are to be determined by Act of Parliament. The Commission is to investigate complaints, including complaints from members of the public services, about breaches of the code or regulations, maladministration of a public service, and improper conduct towards an official by Ministers, executives of an Assembly or members of a local authority. The Commission will operate in a way similar to the present Parliamentary Commissioner for Administration and will report to the Public Services Commission and to Parliament. It is expected that a Select Committee will deal with these matters, probably the Treasury and Civil Service Committee. The objective is to set up a mechanism that will prevent the use of the public service for partisan purposes or to deceive Parliament or subvert the Constitution. Public servants will be protected from discrimination if they complain. This is in line with the concession made to the Treasury and Civil Service Committee by the government in 1990.

CHAPTER 11
Administrative Justice

ARTICLE 118: JUDICIAL REVIEW

It is essential to the rule of law that no body performing a public function should exceed or abuse its powers. Article 118 requires Parliament to legislate for this by way of judicial review. Any person will have standing to sue a public authority if he or she has 'a sufficient interest in the matter to which the application relates', the present test for an application for judicial review.

It is not considered necessary to specify in the Constitution the precise grounds for review, which may best be left to incremental elaboration under the common law, which has been so successful in recent years. Nothing however prevents Parliament from codifying the grounds for review as has been done in Australia, or legislating standards of good administration if it so wishes. Article 118 in fact requires Parliament to provide two such standards: a general duty upon public authorities to give reasons for their decisions (118.1.2) and the provision of effective remedies, including payment of compensation (118.1.3)

ARTICLE 119: COMMISSION FOR PUBLIC ADMINISTRATION

Article 119 establishes a Commission for Public Administration. This Commission combines the functions now performed by the various Ombudsmen (the Parliamentary Commissioner for Administration and local commissioners) and the Council on Tribunals. It will also act as a body to commission research into public administration generally, along the lines of the US or Australian Administrative Review Councils.

The investigative powers of the Commission are wider than those of the present ombudsmen in the following respects: first, it may investigate at the request of a person with sufficient interest in the matter to which the application relates, thus doing away with the filter through members of Parliament (119.31). Second, the Commission may investigate on its own initiative or at the request of a Minister or executive (119.3.2). Third, the Commission may investigate both maladministration, the present test, and also *unfair* administration. Fourth, the jurisdiction of the Commissioner extends to all public bodies except those specified by legislation (119.4). Fifth, the Commission will be able to order effective remedies, which it cannot now do, including the remedy of compensation (119.5.1).

119.1 leaves the composition and appointment of the Commission to be determined by Act of Parliament, and 119.2 in effect provides for Parliament to cause the Commission to act through existing commissioners or bodies, so that it can incorporate the ombudsmen and others under its new umbrella.

The Commission is to report its investigations to Parliament, Assemblies or local authorities as appropriate (119.6) and to make an annual report to Parliament and to the Assemblies, which may include recommendations for improvement in administrative justice.

ARTICLE 120: COMPLAINTS PROCEDURES

Article 120 requires every public authority having dealings with the public to establish a complaints procedure and to provide redress where a complaint is upheld. This reinforces the provision for judicial review under Article 118, and may prove a cheaper and more expeditious alternative.

CHAPTER 12

Protection of the United Kingdom

ARTICLE 121: THE ARMED FORCES

Article 121 is drafted in the form of enabling provisions, leaving the detail to Act of Parliament.

It affirms that a standing army (and air force) is dependent on statutory approval at least once every five years. Although it has been argued, in *State Research Bulletin* (1981), p. 149, that the five-yearly renewal of the mandate for the Armed Forces, in the quinquennial Armed Forces Acts, does not meet the prohibition in the Bill of Rights 1689 on a standing army in peacetime without the consent of Parliament, such a view is not thought to be persuasive. A constitutional provision would remove all ambiguity. The Royal Navy's existence also arguably remains subject to the Royal Prerogative. Again, doubts as to its legal status would be removed by a constitutional provision.

121.1 gives authority for the Promulgation of Queen's Regulations for the Armed Forces including the Royal Navy.

121.1.2 and .1.3 reflect the current practice in the UK.

121.2 in respect to the Defence Council slightly modifies the current position by leaving the composition of membership more flexible.

ARTICLE 122: DECLARATION OF WAR

One of the major areas of concern relating to the current legal framework for military deployment is the power of the Executive to declare war or peace without reference to Parliament. This legal power is currently a Royal Prerogative by the Executive in the name of the Crown. Although it is, properly, a political decision, prior parliamentary approval is not now required before a state of war is declared. In practical terms, Parliament can, of course, pass a motion of no confidence in the government which has thus declared war (the Monarch actually signs a Royal Proclamation, but constitutionally follows the advice of her Ministers). Parliament may also deny funding for the conduct of a war, although presumably the Armed Forces could conduct military activities for a lengthy period of time before the necessity to levy further taxation to fund hostilities would arise. Parliament could also enact legislation after the declaration of war to remove the prerogative power to declare war and to regulate the deployment of the Armed Forces.

In terms of a written constitution, however, the objective is to ensure that Parliament's *prior* approval to a declaration of war is granted. One rationale for past reliance on the prerogative power was the logistical problem in convening Parliament quickly and in enacting appropriate legislation with sufficient rapidity to meet a sudden crisis of war proportions. Transportation and communications problems of previous centuries are, however, hardly justifications for the continued retention of the prerogative power to declare war, a power whose 'democratic' legitimacy is significantly less than where Parliament gives its prior approval.

Article 122 therefore requires that both Houses of Parliament, by a two-thirds majority, approve an Order in Council issued by the Head of State which declares a state of war or peace. Any attempt by the Executive to circumvent the constitutional provision by referring to a 'conflict' or to 'hostilities' rather than to a state of war could be met by legal challenge.

ARTICLE 123: DEPLOYMENT OF ARMED FORCES

The deployment of the Armed Forces and the responsibility of the Secretary of State therefor are removed by Article 123 from the scope of the Royal Prerogative and by constitutional provision placed firmly within the scope of statute law whose detailed provisions can be enacted subsequently. Currently, prerogative deployment of the Armed Forces is not justiciable before the courts. There may be grounds for adhering to this 'hands off' approach during wartime, in as much as the courts should not be expected to second-guess the appropriate military strategies or tactics to be employed during conflicts. But it may be noted that 'military activities' can embrace a wide range of activities remote from, as well as directly connected with, actual troop deployments. Thus, while Lord Parker of Waddington in *The Zamora* [1916] 1 AC 77 at p. 107 stated that,

> Those who are responsible for the national security must be the sole judges of what the national security requires . . .

Lord Scarman, in *Council of Civil Service Unions v Minister for the Civil Service* [1985] AC 374 [the *GCHQ* case] added that,

> These words were no abdication of the judicial function, but were an indication of the evidence required by the court. In fact, the evidence adduced by the Crown [in *The Zamora*] was not sufficient and the court ruled that the Crown had no right to requisition [contraband].

In other words, the invocation of a plea of national security by the Crown should not preclude judicial review based on, for example, the 'no evidence' doctrine expounded in *Secretary of State for Education v Tameside MBC* [1977] AC 1014 or on the 'precedent fact' doctrine in *Khawaja v SSHD* [1984] AC 74.

Using the above as a springboard we propose, in 123.6, to permit judicial review of the deployment of troops both in wartime and in peacetime, though the standard of review should be mountainous in the former case. In both cases matters of opinion, as distinct from matters of fact, are unlikely to be challengeable.

That the Crown has claimed a prerogative right to deploy troops in peacetime is incontrovertible though the legal basis therefor may be more debatable. See, in particular, *Chandler v DPP* [1964] AC 763 for peacetime deployment. Indeed, according to Steve Peak in *Troops in Strikes* (London: Cobden Trust, 1984), the deployment of troops on 'urgent work of national importance' under section 2 of the Emergency Powers Act 1964, for which no Royal Proclamation of emergency is required before triggering the powers, merely reiterates the common law prerogative power. Such powers would, therefore, implicitly cover peacetime deployment as well as wartime deployment, or deployment during a 'precautionary period' or during *un état de siège*. Indeed, Lawrence LJ explicitly states in *China Navigation Co. Ltd v Attorney General* [1932] 2 KB 197,

> The powers which the Crown exercises as to the disposition and use of the standing Army in times of peace are powers vested in the Crown by prerogative right at common law and are not powers conferred upon the Crown by Statute.

This was in response to counsel for the plaintiffs' claim that such deployment was conferred by statute (see also [Public Record Office] WO 32/2533, 'Historical Memorandum on the position of the Crown in relation to the Land Forces by way of reply to the Memoranda furnished by the Treasury Solicitor', by Sir Leslie Scott, KC, counsel to the plaintiffs).

Whether or not a historical precedent exists for the statutory regulation of the deployment of the Armed Forces in peacetime, the argument in principle for such regulation is justified in broad democratic terms.

Peacetime deployment covers three broad areas: Military Aid to the Civil Power (MACP) (123.2), relating to the maintenance of public order where the civil forces are inadequate to meet the perceived threat to internal security; Military Aid to the Civil Ministries (MACM) (123.3), relating principally to the use of troops to ensure the maintenance of essential supplies and services, especially during industrial action; and Military Aid to the Civil Community (MACC) (123.4), involving the use of troops to alleviate civil distress such as that following natural disasters.

Historically, MACP has been exercised under the common law when magistrates called upon the troops to maintain public order in circumstances where the police appeared to be unable to do so. Whether the power was a prerogative power or not is not free from doubt although the *Northumbria Police Authority* case, [1988] All ER 556, claimed to identify a prerogative power on the part of the Executive to 'maintain the peace of the kingdom'. The authority for that proposition was, however, distinctly weak. The opportunity should now be taken formally to abolish by statute under 123.2 the common law powers of the magistrates (whether derived from the prerogative or not) and to replace them by the limited powers of the appropriate Minister, subject to the approval of Parliament and to the concurrence of the Defence Council (in 123.5).

According to the *Manual of Military Law* (Part 2, paras 2 and 3), at common law 'a soldier must come to the assistance of the civil authority where it is necessary for him to do so but not otherwise'. A statute made under 123.2 may well incorporate this requirement.

In respect to MACM and MACC, legal authority currently derives from the emergency powers legislation of 1920 and 1964. In the former, a Royal Proclamation may be issued declaring a state of emergency when events occur:

of such a nature as to be calculated by interfering with the supply and distribution of food, water, fuel or light, or with the means of locomotion, to deprive the community, or any substantial portion of the community, of the essentials of life . . .

Regulations may be issued by the Privy Council which may have severe effects on civil liberties, though certain regulations are subject to affirmative resolutions on both houses.

David Bonner, in *Emergency Powers in Peacetime* (London: Sweet & Maxwell, 1985, Chapter 2), has persuasively shown how inadequate are the safeguards against Executive abuse contained in the current legislation conferring emergency powers. The constitutional provisions in 123.3 to 123.6 are intended to offer a framework for emergency legislation which upholds the constitutional role of Parliament *vis-à-vis* the Executive by guaranteeing fundamental rights, by stressing the temporary nature of such powers, by ensuring parliamentary oversight of Executive decision-making, by requiring the assent of considerably more than two members of the Defence Council (the current position) before troop deployment might be authorised, and by emphasising the role of judicial review in regulating the Executive in this area. The meaning of phrases such as 'urgent work of extreme national importance', and 'for the maintenance of essential supplies and to preserve life and livelihood' should be aided by interpretation clauses in the relevant legislation.

ARTICLE 124: VISITING FORCES

Article 124 is based on Article 23 of the Commonwealth of Britain Bill presented in the House of Commons by Tony Benn MP in May 1991. Its object is to ensure that Parliament's prior consent is obtained before the armed forces of any foreign country, or their equipment, are based in the UK or used in its airspace or territorial waters. The terms on which the armed forces of another state may visit the UK, including the powers and responsibilities of those forces, must be set down in legislation. The Article is intended to ensure that US forces and their nuclear weapons, for instance, could be sited in the UK only with the consent of the majority of members of Parliament. In the absence of this constitutional requirement it was possible for the government to allow US forces to be based in the UK, and to use its air bases to launch air strikes on Libya, for instance, without reference to Parliament.

ARTICLE 125: POLICE

The object of Article 125 is to ensure that Parliament and the Scottish and Northern Ireland Assemblies legislate to provide for the establishment, organisation, management and financing of whatever number of police forces those bodies shall determine for England and Wales, Scotland and Northern Ireland respectively. The Article makes certain particular requirements intended to enhance equal opportunities within the service, strengthen the system of accountability, and ensure the independence of the complaints procedure and that effective redress is given to individuals adversely affected by the 'defective performance' of the police in carrying out their functions.

125.2 ensures that those responsible for appointing police officers will be charged with the same duty imposed on the Judicial Services Commission and Public Services Commission: that they must adopt procedures which will ensure that adequate numbers of candidates of both sexes and from diverse, racial, religious and social backgrounds are considered for appointment.

125.4 seeks to address the concern about the lack of accountability of the police to elected representatives. Under the 1964 Police Act, each police force in England and Wales is, for instance, under the 'direction and control' of its chief constable. Police authorities (committees of the County Council, or Joint Boards in the former metropolitan counties) include within their composition one-third non-elected magistrates and are charged only with ensuring the 'adequacy and efficiency' of the force. They are given few powers with which to fulfil this responsibility and in the exercise of most of these powers are subject to the Home Secretary's veto. The Constitution, in 125.4, does not attempt to lay down the institutional arrangements for accountability nor to determine the precise relationship between the police and locally and nationally elected representatives. But it does require that the legislation shall provide the means whereby each police force can be held accountable 'with respect to the performance of its functions' to a body of elected representatives at the local, Assembly or parliamentary level.

125.5 would ensure that the actions or omissions of individual police officers or of police authorities are investigated by an independent body which would have the power to carry out investigations on receipt of complaint or on its own initiative. 125.6 provides that those adversely affected by the defective performance of the police or police authorities could obtain effective redress.

ARTICLE 126: NATIONAL SECURITY

Article 126 defines the meaning of national security, provides that no security services shall be established except by Act of Parliament, requires the establishment of a National Security Committee of the Cabinet, and makes the Prime Minister directly responsible to Parliament for the performance of the security services.

The definition of national security, the statutory basis for all security operations and the accountability to Parliament or the Prime Minister alter, strengthen or formalise existing arrangements which are largely under prerogative powers.

126.1 defines national security as the protection of the territorial integrity of the United Kingdom and the safety of its citizens, and the maintenance of the Constitution *against* espionage, sabotage or subversion, or the use of violence for political ends or against groups defined by race or religious beliefs. The intention is to make clear first what is to be protected and second against what activities that protection shall be afforded. An illegal or unconstitutional attempt to secede by any part of the United Kingdom would qualify as a threat to national security, as would any attempt to deny the rights of individuals as guaranteed by the Constitution, either by subversion or by the use of violence. The definition also provides for protection against the use of deceptive or clandestine methods of undermining constitutional government. This would apply to covert attempts to influence domestic politics by outside bodies, whether governmental or corporate, through the dissemination of misinformation and so forth.

126.2 provides that no public authority shall be established for the purposes of national security except by Act of Parliament and that only those employed by such statutory agencies may undertake national security work. This provision is intended to prevent the proliferation of security agencies and the use of unauthorised agencies for security work.

126.3 brings the officers of any statutory security service within the general provisions of the Constitution for the public service, but allows the Public Services Commission to make special arrangements where necessary for the effective performance of their functions. This recognises that security work has peculiar features, but brings it within the ambit of Public Services Commission, so that there is some independent scrutiny of any special arrangements.

126.4 requires the Prime Minister to establish a National Security Committee of the Cabinet to exercise general direction over the activities of the security services and gives the Prime Minister rights of access to all information and all records relating to the activities of the security services and direct responsibility to Parliament for the *proper and lawful* performance of their functions. The Prime Minister must make an annual report to Parliament concerning the activities of all the Security Services, which may exclude matters which the Cabinet Committee (and the Inspector General for Security Services) considers may be prejudicial to their performance. Like 126.3, 126.5.2 recognises the peculiar position of security work.

ARTICLE 127: INSPECTOR-GENERAL OF SECURITY SERVICES

It is difficult to guess how far the fact of putting the security services on a constitutional and statutory footing will make any practical difference to the ways in which they operate. Public accountability is inherently difficult. Ministerial control is likely to be exercised intermittently and it is clear that what Prime Ministers may be entitled to know is different from what they may want to know.

For this reason, following Canadian and Australian precedents, Article 127 establishes an Inspector-General of Security Services, appointed by the Head of State on the advice of the Prime Minister from nominations made by the Public Services Commission (roughly the method adopted for the appointment of bishops in the Church of England). The Inspector-General's duties include: to monitor compliance by the security services with their operational policies; to review applications for and the use made of warrants (presently provided by the Security Services Act 1985); to receive and investigate individual complaints about their activities; to conduct formal investigations into activities inconsistent with their operational policies, or improper; and to make recommendations, including for compensation to persons adversely affected by their activities.

For those purposes 127.3 provides the Inspector-General with access to whatever information or personnel he considers necessary.

The Inspector-General is to report as circumstances require to the National Security Committee and to submit an annual report to a Select Committee of the House of Commons, subject again to the exclusion of matters prejudicial to the proper performance of the security services' functions.

ARTICLE 128: SUSPENSION OF THE CONSTITUTION

Article 128 provides for the suspension of parts of the Constitution in times of emergency, subject to parliamentary approval or confirmation.

Under 128.1 the Head of State, acting on the advice of the Prime Minister, may by order in Council suspend provisions of the Constitution in the event of a grave threat to national security or public order or a grave civil emergency. This power may only be used to 'the extent strictly required by the exigencies of the situation and reasonably justified in a democratic society'. 128.4 and 128.5 further provide that the Order in Council must be approved or confirmed by a two-thirds majority of those voting in each House of Parliament. Orders can only be made for a specified time but can be renewed (128.7).

The Articles of the Constitution which may be suspended include the Bill of Rights, with the exception of the Articles guaranteeing the right to life, freedom from torture, freedom from slavery, treatment of persons in detention, right to a fair hearing in criminal cases, prohibition of retrospective offences, freedom of thought, and the equal protection of the law.

Other Articles which may be suspended include those governing the expiry and dissolution of Parliament and the Assemblies (60.1 and 78.4) and the electoral cycle (Schedule 3, Part 3), and constitutional legislation made under Article 70 as it affects any provision of the Bill of Rights or the civic rights of non-nationals under Article 33.

The aim is to allow the limited suspension of certain civil rights, e.g. to freedom of speech or movement and the suspension of certain domestic activities, e.g. elections during an emergency, subject to time limits, parliamentary control, and challenge in the courts by application for judicial review under 128.6.

ARTICLE 129: DETENTION IN EMERGENCIES

Article 129 provides safeguards for anybody detained during an emergency by an Order in Council under Article 128.

These safeguards include: the right to a statement of the grounds for detention within seven days; the publication of the previous detention within seven days; the review of the detention by an independent tribunal, within three weeks of the detention and thereafter at intervals of not more than six months; and representation before the tribunal (129.1.1–4)

Under 129.2 the tribunal reviewing a detention may make recommendations about its continuance, which will be communicated to the detainee, but the authority which ordered the detention does not have to act on the recommendation, unless an Act of Parliament or the Order in Council obliges it to do so.

These are minimal procedural rights for detainees which if properly implemented may help to reduce the chances of mistakes or maltreatment and also the apprehension and anxieties of those detained, their families and friends.